GW00982991

ETERNALLY YOURS

ETERNALLY YOURS

(Alim LiTerufah)

The Collected Letters of Reb Noson of Breslov

Volume 4

translated by
Yaakov Gabel

edited by
Moshe Schorr

Published by
BRESLOV RESEARCH INSTITUTE
Jerusalem/New York

First Edition

For further information:
Breslov Research Institute
POB 5370
Jerusalem, Israel

or:
Breslov Research Institute
POB 587
Monsey, NY 10952-0587

With deepest gratitude to

Meyer and Roxanne Assoulin

May the merit of Reb Noson
always be available for them

Guide to the Book

Eternally yours is the collected letters of Reb Noson of Breslov (1780-1844). The letters provide a vivid and intimate portrayal of Reb Noson's life. They also give the reader a chance to see for himself how it is possible to truly *live* Rebbe Nachman's teachings.

History: The letters have been arranged chronologically. At the beginning of each year we have presented a short historical review of what was then taking place in Reb Noson's life. This Volume covers the years 5603-5605 (1842-1844) when Reb Noson passed away on 10 Tevet (December 20, 1844).

Additional letters found in the *Alim LiTerufah* — from Reb Naftali (Rebbe Nachman's disciple), Reb Yitzchak (Reb Noson's son to whom most of Reb Noson's letters are addressed) and Reb Nachman of Tulchin (Reb Noson's leading disciple) — are also presented in this volume.

Notes: Editor's notes by the compiler, Reb Nachman of Tcherin, and publisher's notes appear at several places within the text. These help to clarify certain incidents mentioned in the letters.

Sources: Woven into Reb Noson's poetic style are numerous quotes from Scripture, Talmud and Rebbe Nachman's teachings. However, referencing all these quotes would have interfered with the flow of the text and so only certain sources, particularly those from Breslov teachings, have been included. In addition, not all of Reb Noson's words could be translated. Honorary titles and the like, although beautiful in the Hebrew original, were deemed too redundant in the English.

Table of Contents

Table of Contents

Letters from 5603 (1842-3)

The year in review

This year saw the completion of the publication of the *Likutey Eitzot*. It was printed in Lemberg through the efforts of Reb Nachman Tulchiner. The letters refer to his efforts to raise funds for the printing of the first volume, as well as to "the project" or "our business" and to Reb Nachman as Reb Nachman "Socher" ("the merchant"). There were two reasons for this. Reb Noson feared his opponents who wanted to suppress the teachings of Breslov. In addition, the members of the "enlightenment" were instrumental in introducing a ban on the printing of chassidic works and assisted the government in enforcing that ban. This year too, there were several raids by the Cantonists and the forced conscription of young Jewish children into the Czar's army for a period of twenty-five years. See *Through Fire and Water*, Chapters 32, 45.

396

With thanks to God, between Yom Kippur and Sukkot, 5603.

My dear, beloved son.

If you have not yet sent the *lulav* and *hadas*, you should do so through the carrier of this letter. No excuses. I am anxiously waiting for them. Praise God, I have, through His kindness and wonders, a beautiful, fine *etrog*. May you enjoy the happiness of the coming holy festival. May we merit to receive every type of salvation through the holiness of the awesome command-ments of the month of *Eitanim*, the month of TiSHRei, about whose name we merited to hear such awesome teachings (*Likutey Moharan* II, 8:11) — until the verse is fulfilled, "Come and sing (*TaSHuRI*) from the heights of faith!"

The words of your father,

Noson of Breslov

397

With thanks to God, Sunday, Noach, 5603, Breslov.

Warm greetings to my dear, honored friend, the learned, distinguished and illustrious Reb Avraham Ber, may he live; along with all his precious children, may they live.

Thank God, I am alive and well. Praise God, the days of the festival passed in peace and joy, with God's help. Would that we might truly draw the holiness of Tishrei upon ourselves at all times and attain all the *tikkunim* (spiritual rectifications) in which Israel engages during the month of *Eitanim*, the month of Tishrei, especially those discussed in the Rebbe's lovely, honeysweet utterances. We merited to taste a little of the *tikkunim* which deal with the awesome holiness of Rosh Ha-Shanah, the holiness of the mitzvah of Shofar, the Ten Days of Repentance, Yom Kippur, Sukkot, Hoshana Rabba, Shemini Atzeret and Simchat Torah.

He showed us hints and awesome secrets in the word "Tishrei," particularly in the lesson "Blow the Shofar" (*Likutey Moharan* II, 8), regarding the prayer of the "powerful one" which is strongly connected to the parting of the Red Sea. For the word "Tishrei is concealed right there in a verse referring to both these concepts (Psalms 74:13), "With Your Might You shattered the *Sea, You Broke the Serpents' Heads* upon the water" — the initial letters [of the Hebrew verse] spell out "Tishrei"! His prayer results in the creation of the awesome, miraculous phenomena of *baalei teshuvah* and converts, about which it is said "Who can comprehend the thunder of His strength?" This too is hinted at and concealed in the most amazing way in the word "Tishrei." For the final letters of the words in the verse, "You know *the soul of the stranger* [convert], *because you* were strangers..." spells "Tishrei!"

Who has heard anything like this?! Who has seen such things?! It is good to thank God constantly with all our hearts every day that we merited to hear all this. As if from a trap, our souls have escaped from those who oppose an original, holy light such as this. May we only merit to engage all our lives in his holy words and to fulfill, "Study it over and over." May we merit to study the Rebbe's works with the intention of practicing and fulfilling his holy words and his deep, consummately pure advice, which are suited to every person in the world at any level — whether he is spiritually ascending or descending, God forbid, in good times or bad, God forbid. The key is to "turn the lessons into prayers" — to petition God every day and to express oneself before Him in accordance with a teaching that one studies in the Rebbe's holy books. A person can find himself in all of them every day. Oh, God! When will we merit this?

Our lives are flying by like a passing shadow, like a dissipating cloud, like a passing breeze, like a fleeting dream. And only through prayer and supplication can we hold on to them [the holy books] so that they will endure for us and so that through them we may live forever. The best method is to follow this holy path, which is at once old and very new, of making prayers out of Torah lessons. Each person feels that he is far indeed from being able to do this but, in truth, this is really not so. "The matter is very close to you — in your mouth and your heart to do it" (Deuteronomy 30:14). Even if a person is unable to begin speaking at all — well, this too I have already addressed a great deal with true, pure advice, which has already been tried and tested and has helped us tremendously. I refer, in particular, to what God helped me to say last Rosh HaShanah on the lesson "Where is the sheep for the offering?" (Likutey Moharan II, 12) — that even in the "filthy places," i.e. amidst very evil thoughts and indecent ruminations, a person can constantly search for God, until he turns a spiritual decline into a great ascent and merits a revelation of "Bereishit — 'In the Beginning' — the Hidden Utterance."

Praise God, I elaborated on this further in connection with Sukkot and I joined to it the awesome story of the Sixth Day (*Rabbi Nachman's Stories* #13, The Seven Beggars; see *Likutey Halakhot, Rosh HaShanah* 6). *Ashreinu*! Happy are we that we merited to hear all this and to engage in it a little! May we merit to truly fulfill the Rebbe's desire and to follow all his pathways, to be happy every day; to look and to search and to cry out to God; to make prayers from Torah lessons; and to start anew every day from whatever good point that we have begun — for everything depends on this, as I have already discussed. One must never succumb to old age, God forbid, as the Rebbe warned us emphatically in a loud, strong voice, with the words, "It is forbidden to get old!" (see *Rabbi Nachman's Wisdom* #51). It is impossible to elaborate further in writing. You will understand for yourself, and thereby remind yourself to guard your memory carefully and to attach your thoughts to the World to Come generally and with every detail of your life every day, as is written in (*Likutey Moharan* I) Lesson 54. See it there.

I would now like to urge you to be sure to collect the pledges which our comrades made to me for the "business," as recorded on the note that I gave you. Even though, for a number of reasons, I have not yet sent Reb Nachman there, I am preparing to do so any day. The expenses are high, as you can understand for yourself, but the value of the project is inestimable. Even for two pairs of large silver candlesticks, five or six *loit* of large pearls or the like, a person needs a large sum of money. How much more so is this true for us, who want to buy much more than this! You can understand the analogy for yourself, as I have explained enough for an intelligent person to comprehend. I am extremely busy, so it is impossible to write very much.

If, in addition to this, you can get money from some people for my livelihood — so much the better. I really could use it right now, particularly since I need to engage in a large project such as this. My heart is full of conflicting thoughts about this and the Searcher of Hearts knows how difficult and onerous this "business" is for me for a number of reasons. It is therefore appropriate that I at least be freed from worrying about my livelihood, and especially in the winter-time I have many expenses. Also, extend greetings to my friend, Reb Moshe, the son of Reb Yosef from here. Urge him to work for my benefit now too by sending me all that he can collect from our comrades, as he did last year. I need not go on about this, as I know that they will act swiftly on their own. "One only encourages those who are eager to act of their own accord." You too should send me some money for my living expenses, and it will be credited to your total account. To my friend Reb Abba, I will write directly. Beyond this, I am relying on you to do everything in the best possible way, both for the "business" and for my livelihood. Also send greetings with much love to my friend, your illustrious cousin, Reb Nachman, may his light shine, the grandson of our master, teacher and Rebbe, of blessed memory. I have already asked you and urged you to give him some really substantial help. God will reimburse you many times over. Write me a clear report about how he is doing.

The words of your true, eternal friend, awaiting your quick response.

Noson of Breslov

Greetings to my illustrious and influential friend, Reb Abele, may his light shine, along with all his children, may they live. I had intended to write you a separate letter, but there is not sufficient time. You understand for yourself that all that was said above was meant for you, and for all of you, as well. May God send salvation and may you merit to fulfill them [the advice of the Rebbe] quickly. Before you set out for home, you promised to send me money which would go toward your total. Be sure to send it to me immediately. God willing, I will inform you when Reb Nachman, may his light shine, leaves for his journey. He will be setting out soon and, God willing, he will have a safe journey. Right now, we are busy making all the necessary preparations. I am sure that you too will talk with all of our comrades about everything that I wrote above. Now my hands are stretched forth to Heaven, that He will act for the sake of His Name and the name of the true tzaddik, and will help us begin and complete our holy projects. You too, in addition to the money that you give to this holy project and your work in collecting from our comrades, should also "help from the city" (cf. 2 Samuel, 18:3) with prayer and supplications, that we should merit to finish what we have begun. For besides the extremely large expenses, we are still in need of salvation and tremendous compassion. I have cast my burden on God. He has begun and He will finish in fulfillment of the verse, "God will finish for me; Your kindness, God, is forever. Do not forsake the work of Your hands!"

The words of your true, eternal friend.

398

With thanks to God, Friday, Erev Shabbat, Lekh Lekha, 5603, Breslov.
My dear, beloved son.

I received your letter through R.Y, and I was really delighted. For I saw the great works of God, in that you remotely understood on your own the teaching *Azamra!* (Likutey Moharan I, 282). With this you see how the "messengers" are constantly going from one person to another for the sake of the eternal goal (see *Tzaddik* #317). All the errands and all the messengers, all the labors and all the activities in the world are all without exception only for the eternal goal. "In every place they burn incense and bring offerings to My Name" (Malachi 1:11) — "even idol worshippers...," as our Rabbis, of blessed memory, said. Even in "the concealment within the concealment" which is brought on by the committing of a large number of actual trangressions, God save us, there too God, Who is the Torah, is hidden. In fact, it is precisely *there* that the actual "Torah of God" is hidden, as is written (Likutey Moharan I, 56). Look it up there. And even if no-one is capable of understanding this, and certainly not we, nonetheless, *Ashreinu!* Happy are we that at least we believe in this! God is great and highly to be praised. His greatness is unfathomable!

You should know, my dear son, that our friend, Reb Nachman, may his light shine, left here yesterday on the holy "business." He set out from my house on foot late in the afternoon with great eagerness — for a long journey such as this! Praise God, he has a wondrous enthusiasm and desire for this project, and he did not want to wait until after Shabbat. Thank God,

Who has remembered us in our destitution and relieved us in our straits, that there exist people who volunteer their money and their selves for this project. In this I see the wonders of God in a way that is impossible to express. "You have done great things, Lord, my God; Your miracles and Your thoughts are for us. None can compare to You. It is impossible to express — they are too numerous to be told!" My eyes are to God. May He add to His kindness and mercy again and again, that we may merit to complete everything in accordance with His will and the will of those who fear Him. May God finish everything well for us. I am extremely rushed and it is impossible to continue.

> The words of your father who sees, comprehends and believes in God's salvation and miraculous kindnesses at all times and who is waiting expectantly for even greater salvations and kindnesses than these; until we all merit to truly be as God in His goodness wishes us to be, and to know Him in This World and the Next forever.
>
> *Noson of Breslov*

You will understand for yourself the pleasure that I had from this "messenger." For every person is obliged to say, "The world was created for me and everything that is happening in the world is all for me" (*Sanhedrin* 37a).

399

With God's help, Thursday, Chayey Sarah, 5603, Teplik.

Greetings to my beloved, learned son, Reb Yitzchak, may he live.

It is God Who establishes a man's steps, and in His compassion God caused me to travel to Teplik from my home on Monday. I very much wanted to travel by way of Tulchin in order to see you and our comrades, but God arranged it that a carriage suddenly came from Teplik and took me back here. There is a great deal to tell about this. How great are God's deeds and the wonders that He performs all the time! God willing, when we get together, we will talk about this, with God's salvation. You, my son, fortify yourself and be strong! Make yourself happy with all your might and with all kinds of stubbornness to be really joyful all the time and to thank God for the beauty of our portion!

> The words of your father, praying for you and
> waiting for your letter of joy and delight.
> > *Noson of Breslov*

Greetings to all my family and to all our comrades with a great love.

400

With God's help, Thursday, Chayey Sarah, Teplik.

Greetings to my modest wife, Dishel, may she live. Greetings to my eldest son, may he live, and to my other sons, may they live.

Praise God, I came here last Tuesday and I met the carriage with Reb Hirsh from Teplik that was coming for me. I ask each and every one of you to be sure to act peacefully, and that there be no fighting, no exaggerated demands nor jealousy among you, God forbid. Just be certain to strengthen yourselves every day to study Torah and to pray with concentration, and God will help me support you, with His salvation.

My beloved son, may he live. I ask you please, take pity on yourself. Do not become angry and do not quarrel with your brother, may he live. Do not cause any pain to your mother, may she live. Just apply yourself diligently to Torah study, concentrate when you pray, and say Psalms every day. Be sure to write me, and to be happy. Do not be angry that you do not have a hat. Have trust in God that soon, God willing, you will have everything. For the time being, though, you will have to wait a little. You gave me great pain when I went away. For God's sake, listen to me from now on! In the meantime, borrow a hat for Shabbat from my son-in-law, Reb Barukh, or from Reb Shimshon. Soon, with God's help, everything will be in order. Considering how very much I speak words of truth with you, you should already have thrown out all your nonsense and only be thinking about the ultimate goal.

My dear children! I ask all of you, for God's sake — think

carefully about the true purpose of This World! We, specifically, are poor, yet God helps us with what we really need. Do not set your sights too high on possessions. As for the real necessities, have trust in God that He will help me support you properly. Just fortify yourselves in Torah and prayer, and ask God every day to guard you from all evil and to help you to be good, *kosher*, Jews. For nothing remains of a person except his Judaism — whatever he succeeds in grabbing in This World. We have already discussed more than this at length. May God strengthen your hearts to fulfill my words, which emanate from those of our master, teacher and Rebbe, of blessed memory. Be well and happy.

The words of your father, waiting for salvation.

Noson of Breslov

401

With thanks to God, Vayeitzei, 5603, Uman.

Warm greetings to my honored, dear and beloved son, the learned Reb Yitzchak, may he live; along with all his children, may they live.

I arrived here today from Teplik, where I stayed on for last Shabbat, Parashat Toldot, as well. Thank God, by a miracle, I concluded matters there. Upon my arrival here at dawn I found your two letters, and, as you might expect, they inspired me tremendously. I was especially pleased by the information about Reb Nachman, may his light shine. Thank God, Who has helped me thus far. It would certainly be appropriate for you to reply to him immediately that you received his letter and that I am now here. I was already at the holy gravesite just now and I mentioned you there in my prayers for good. I then had to eat with Reb Naftali, may his light shine. You can understand for yourself that by now the post is about to leave and I am quickly writing this for your benefit. May God fortify your heart and bring you to joy at all times.

Know and believe that I and those like me have experienced to a much greater degree everything that has happened to you. The reason we were created was to go through whatever we suffer in This World. This is the whole greatness of the Fashioner of Creation, that He did not heed the accusation of the angels who said, "What is man that You should be mindful of him? Will he not sin before You and anger You?" But the Holy One, Blessed be He, said, "It is not for nothing that I am called 'Compassionate and Kind'." For every little step that a person takes to remove and separate himself from evil is extremely precious to God, no matter who the person is. As the Rebbe said explicitly, "While it is certainly true..." (that is, that we have already erred and strayed a great deal). But still, every motion in the direction of good is extremely precious. And, he said, "No matter what, the main thing is that a person hold on." In particular remember what he said there at the end, "God is great and we know nothing at all." This is the main point and it is above all else. I am extremely hurried and it is impossible to elaborate.

The words of your father who prays for you.

Noson of Breslov

402

With God's help, Monday, Vayishlach, 5603.

Greetings to my modest wife Dishel, may she live; to my learned son, Reb David Zvi, may he live, to my son, Nachman, may he live, and to my son, Yosef Yonah, may he live.

God is indeed directing the world, as you will hear about in the letter to my son, Reb Shachneh, may his light shine, and from the deliverer of this letter. It is God Who establishes a man's steps.

My beloved son, Reb David Zvi, may his light shine, I wrote to your brother Reb Yitzchak that he should buy a hat for you at my expense for three or four silver rubles, i.e. a hat made of *mardir* [a kind of cloth]. I ask of you — do not request for anything big, even this is extremely difficult and burdensome for me because I am spending other people's money. I am extremely hurried, and it is impossible to go on about this. I am certain that you will listen to me and that you will begin applying yourself diligently to studying, praying and to reciting Psalms with concentration and attention. Then you will enjoy good in This World and the Next, forever.

My beloved son Nachman, may he live, You certainly understand the pain that I have over your stubborn refusal to go to the study hall on Shabbat because of the hat. I therefore ask you to improve from now on. You should take a hat from my son-in-law Reb Barukh, may he live, and go to the study hall every Shabbat. For God's sake, do not continue with your foolish ways! Listen to me, because I am thinking about what is best for you. God willing, I trust that I will soon set up a *shiduch* for you. Then, with God's help, you will have a *shtreimel*, as well as a good hat. In the meantime, for God's sake, do not stay away from the study hall over such foolishness, and especially not on Shabbat. Be diligent in your studies. Pray and say Psalms with concentration and rise at least a little before dawn. For God's sake, guard yourself that I should not become angry with you. Listen to me and to our comrades. Then you will enjoy good in This World and the Next. I am extremely hurried and busy now and it is impossible to continue any longer.

The words of your father who prays for you.

Noson of Breslov

And to my son Yosef Yonah, may he live. Be diligent in your studies! Then you will enjoy good in This World and the Next.

Warm greetings to all our comrades with a great, bold love! At the moment there is absolutely no time to continue. Do not be angry with me, my brothers and friends, that I left you for Shabbat Chanukah. "This thing was from God and it is wondrous indeed," as you will hear and understand for yourselves. Please watch over my household, so that I will not need to go into debt, God forbid; especially not at a time like the present, when I am engaged in such meritorious work as this.

The words of your true friend forever.

Noson, the same

403

With thanks to God, Monday, Vayishlach, 5603, Uman.

My dear, beloved son.

Behold God's wonders! Yesterday I wrote you a letter which I sent with Reb Itzik Yoel from Breslov, to the effect that I intended to return home for this coming Shabbat Chanukah. Then suddenly in the evening the carrier of this letter, our friend Reb Nachman, may his light shine, came with my son's son-in-law, Reb Avraham Leib, may he live. They brought me a letter and a carriage with which to travel to Tcherin and they told me of the enormous desire and great yearning there to have me come. I was thus compelled to travel there, since I saw and understood that "this thing was from God and it is wondrous indeed." This was particularly so since the *Pidyon HaBen* [Redemption of the firstborn] of my great-grandson, the son of my son's son-in-law, the aforementioned Reb Avraham, is due to take place on Friday, Erev Shabbat. May God help me arrive there by Friday morning, so that I will merit with His compassion to be present at the *Pidyon HaBen* celebration of my great-grandson, may he live. What can I give back to God for all the kindness He has bestowed upon me?! I am extremely busy and rushed right now preparing to set out and it is impossible to continue at all. I only ask you, my dear son, not to be distressed about this at all. It is certainly for the good of all of us. Just strengthen yourself determinedly! I already wrote you some inspiring words in the letter that I sent with the post on Tuesday the week of Torah reading Vayeitzei; but judging from the letter

I received yesterday, you have not yet received it. I am sure that by now you have received it.

> The words of your father praying for you and waiting for salvation.
>
> *Noson of Breslov*

404

With thanks to God, Tuesday, Vayeishev, 5603, Tcherin.

Warm greetings to my dear, beloved son, the learned Reb Yitzchak, may he live; along with all his children, may they live.

You should know, my dear son, that God was with me and I arrived here in Tcherin last Friday, Erev Shabbat Vayishlach, in the morning before the Prayers. I came with tremendous hardship and effort, by amazing acts of salvation and great compassion from God. The roads were in extremely poor condition and we had numerous delays during the journey. But God's compassion is inexhaustible both at home *and* on the road. "This poor man cried out and God heard," and I arrived before the Morning Prayers, so that I was able to be present at the *Pidyon HaBen*. Praise God, we performed the mitzvah of *Pidyon HaBen* properly and on the correct day, and afterwards we welcomed the holy Shabbat.

Most of my discourse was about the concept of the *Pidyon HaBen* which I connected with the lesson "The one who has compassion on them will lead them" (*Likutey Moharan* II, 7; see *Likutey Halakhot, Pidyon Bekhor* 5) which speaks about Chanukah. I said some amazing new ideas on this which provide inspiration and new

life to all souls who desire the truth and who want to listen to
the truth and inspire and restore their souls forever. For it is no
small matter what our master, teacher and Rebbe, of blessed
memory, is still doing for us. How great are God's deeds! His
thoughts are very, very deep! The Rebbe's words are "alive,
enduring, faithful and lovely forever and for all eternity." They
constantly give life, in general and in particular, to each individual person, no matter where he is! And they also reach you
— yes, even now, whatever your situation and however confused and twisted your heart may be. Even now you need to
remind yourself anew that there was a Rebbe in the world; and
his light shines and radiates anew every day, even now, and it
will continue to do so for generations to come. He shines "the
illumination of son and student" into every person wherever
he is, to realize and to make known to every person at all times
that "God is still right there with you and next to you and by
your side, because 'the whole world is full of His glory'." "God
fills all the worlds and encompasses all the worlds and there is
no place from which He is absent." No matter what, you will
definitely attain *tikkun*.

I hope to God that our *tikkun* which God will effect will be
lovely and beautiful as is fitting for Him — not as our deeds
would dictate — so that we will not be ashamed even before the
truly righteous. God's kindness to us has been abundant and
great indeed, in that we merited not to oppose, God forbid, a
holy, awesome and pleasant light such as this! What is more,
we merited to know about him and to hail in his name; and this
is above all else! There is no darkness or infernal abyss that can

obscure a light such as the one that the Rebbe, through the pathways of his profound advice, radiates into each and every one of us at all times and in every place that "we really know nothing at all" (this refers to God's unfathomable greatness and how even a person's worst sins can be transformed into merits; see *Rabbi Nachman's Wisdom* p.106; *Tzaddik* #32). The Rebbe *has* finished and he *will* finish! God will not ignore us forever.

Just fortify yourself and be strong, my dear son! Rise and call to your God at all times! Marshal your strength to bring yourself to joy over every single good point — even the tiniest, most miniscule trace of a good point! Grab and eat! Grab and eat whatever Torah, prayer, charity and good deeds you can every day! For no matter what, the brief span of our lives will pass and be gone, like a fleeting shadow. And the fact that we merited to know about the true light that endures forever — this will surely stay with us eternally! It is impossible to elaborate on this any further in writing.

I have just written you most of the underlying mystical meaning of Chanukah and you need it very much. Now, "grow wise, my son, and rejoice my heart." Understand from a distance the hints to be found in the "sea of wisdom"; for "this sea is great and vast" indeed. And be careful not to be a *shlamazelnik*, a loser, God forbid. However *you* may feel about yourself, still, before God, every good motion and the slightest movement you make to remove yourself from bad in the direction of good is extremely precious. Gird your loins like a warrior — since, praise God, we have someone to rely on! With all this, you will always be able to begin to conquer the evil and bitter thoughts which constantly harass you, because the essence of their ability to overpower you derives from sadness and downheartedness. Just skip over them the best you can given the situation, and do not begin thinking them at all. Do not be intimidated or afraid of them.

Remember what the Rebbe related about the tzaddik who, before his soul left him, said, *"iber geshpringen* — I leaped through!"* (Tzaddik #522). Remember also what he said about how "a person in This World must pass over a narrow bridge — the main thing is not to be afraid" (Likutey Moharan II, 48). And if there are people who feel that they have already fallen off the bridge into the mud, mire and filthy places — then to the contrary! This person certainly does not need to be afraid any longer! "Because surely, even now, I know that it is necessary to hope and look to God, and to call to Him, even from falls such as these." Thus says the verse (Lamentations 3:55), "Water rose above my head; and I thought, 'I have been cut off.' I called Your Name, God, from the lowest pit." There are many similar verses in the Psalms such as (69:3), "I am sunk in the deep mire and there is no place to stand" and (88:7) "You placed me in the lowest pit." But the Rebbe, of blessed memory, already informed us that even from the deepest hell a cry is never lost and that a person must never despair of crying out (Likutey Moharan II, 12, 78). For "God is great and we know nothing at all" (see Rabbi Nachman's Wisdom #3; Advice p.96).

All these words of truth that I just wrote are the *real* bridge by which a person can pass over even the deepest abyss — provided that he does not become discouraged with himself and that he does not grow frightened in the least! He must trust and rely on the power of the elder of holiness who revealed all this and more; and he must fulfill what is written (Psalms 27:14), "Hope to God!," and despite what is happening, strengthen and fortify your heart and "Hope to God!" on the lines of Rashi's comment on this verse [i.e. "and if your prayer is not accepted, go back and 'hope' again"]. It is impossible to elaborate any further. I have already intimated to you that there are hints in "the sea of wisdom" which a person must understand for himself about how to be "knowledgeable in *halakhah*" to fulfill "if I ascend to heaven, You are there; if I go down to hell, here You are" (Psalms 139:8; see *Likutey Moharan* I, 6). For God's greatness is unfathomable.

There is no time to continue any longer. The light of the morning is rapidly approaching. "As with the light of the morning, the sun will shine." This is the light of truth and lovingkindness which radiates from the Infinite down to the endless depths, and this is the light of the Chanukah candles. May God allow us to receive the light of Chanukah, until we merit to have shine upon us the *makifim*, "the surrounding lights," of the true tzaddik — the "divisions of days and the divisions of years." May we merit a good livelihood and may an illumination of intense holy desire shine within our eating and our sustenance (see *Likutey Moharan* II, 7:7,10). *Ashreinu! Ashreinu!* Happy are we that we merited to know of these hints from such exalted lights, which give us inspiration even now! this we see with our own eyes that God is still with us! For had He wanted to do away with us, He would not have informed us of all this! God will finish for us. He has not abandoned and He does not abandon.

The words of your father, waiting for salvation.

Noson of Breslov

405

[*Publisher's note: This letter refers to the suffering caused by the Cantonist decrees, which ordained that young Jewish boys be drafted into the Czar's army.*]

With God's help, Wednesday, the third day of Chanukah, 5603, Tcherin.

Warm greetings to my dear, beloved son, the learned Reb Yitzchak, may he live; along with all his family.

I received your "good" letter last Sunday as I was having my morning meal, and you can understand for yourself my terrible pain. How my heart shuddered inside me. But "I considered my ways," and I have no plan or strategy about what to do, particularly since the roads are in extremely poor condition. Where am I to go running off to anyway? What could I do? For the time being I give praise and thanksgiving to God that you told me that they have already left there, etc. I assume that your son, as well, may he live, is not in his usual location. Now my eyes are looking, hoping and yearning all day long to hear some good report from you. Salvation is in God's hands.

Just last Sunday evening, after the lighting of the Chanukah candles, Reb Efraim with his mother-in-law arrived here from Kremenchug in a great panic, as they had received word previously from Reb Simchah Velvel from Breslov. When I showed them your letter, they did calm down a little, since his son at least is on his way, etc. On Monday, the first day of Chanukah, after midday, the two of them set out from here to meet them on the road to Terhovitza and Uman. I sent a short letter with them too. Now I am just waiting and hoping for some good report of salvation to arrive until Reb Efraim's return. At the moment, I have no idea what to do. My eyes are just raised to Heaven, until God opens my lips and I express myself before Him about all the troubles that are confronting us. For His sake and for the sake of His faithful one upon whom we rely, may He act in His compassion and may He speedily rescue us all; and may they not frighten us at all any more. I trust that God will do amazing kindnesses with us through the power of the elder of holiness and that He will quickly cause us to hear good tidings. We will be happy and rejoice in His salvation!

I am still waiting to receive your letter informing me if you received the somewhat long letter that I sent you last Wednesay to revive your weary soul. Most likely you have already received it and without a doubt it inspired you, even during this time of distress — may God save us quickly. At the moment, I have no idea what to write to you and your family, until the aforementioned Reb Efraim returns. Be certain to write to my family in Breslov. Tell them that you received my letter and encourage them to trust God and not to be afraid, because God is with us. Thus far has God's compassion helped us. Even when I am old and gray God will not abandon me; "until I declare Your strength to the generation and Your might to all who are to come." He has not abandoned and He does not abandon. No

matter what, it is still Chanukah and these are days of
thanksgiving — and we merited in these troubling times to hear
awesome teachings such as these on the holiness of Chanukah!
And in particular the lesson which teaches about "the illumination of the holy knowledge of son and student," which informs
all "those who dwell down below," that even if...even if...even
if...; nevertheless, "the whole world is full of His glory!" and
"God is still with us, do not be afraid!" (*Likutey Moharan* II, 7:3,8). The
post is leaving soon.

> The words of your father, sighing, broken, and
> waiting expectantly at all times for God's salvation.
>
> *Noson of Breslov*

406

With God's help.

Greetings to my dear, beloved son.

I wrote you already on Wednesday, the third day of
Chanukah, that I received your "good" letters and you can
understand for yourself how pained I am. Let God have mercy.
Now I am just constantly waiting and hoping every day to
receive a letter from you; perhaps you will inform me of some
sprouting of salvation. The post has not yet arrived today. Last
Sunday I received your short letter, but you did not tell me any
news at all. You uplifted me with it, though, because it is my
wish at present that you write me frequent letters.

As I am sure you already know, Reb Efraim from
Kremenchug travelled to Uman, and yesterday he came back

here with his son R.Y., may he live. He also brought with him
my son, N., may he live, which caused me both joy and pain, as
you can understand for yourself. I do not need to tell you that
you should inform my wife and family secretly that he is here,
alive and well, and that they should see to it that my younger
son [Yosef Yonah] not be at home either, as you already wrote.
Everything should be done prudently and in secret so that
nothing is discovered, God forbid. My eyes look in hope to God.
Thus far God's compassion has helped us, and He saved you
yourself from this terror several times in your youth, as you
know. So may He continue in His kindness and may He rescue
my sons and your son from this terror forever. May He act for
the honor of the elder of elders in whose power we trust, and
may He not put us to shame before our many enemies, God
forbid. May He redeem us from all trouble, in particular from
this one, and, as a father to his son, may He quickly pardon us,
uplift us and bring us to joy with His salvation. Amen. May it
be His will.

Praise God, "in suffering You gave me relief," and just at
such a time Reb Nachman is engaging there [in Iassi] in work for
the benefit of the greater community. Thank God, you already
sent him the sum that you mentioned, and you should now be
receiving a sum of fifty new rubles for the project. You will
understand for yourself when to send it to him, according to
what he will write to you from there. You are also receiving fifty
silver rubles which you should send to my home. As for your
own concerns regarding the money for the project, they are
really unfounded. Right now, I am sending you money for the

project and if I am forced to stay on the road longer, I will send you more, with God's help. I hope to God that you will not need to borrow, and that if you do need to borrow, that it should only be for a very short time, and then I will reimburse you immediately. I do not want to be a debtor. Salvation will come from God, so that all will be well. Be especially careful now not to get involved in a lot of worrying, sadness and ruminating.

On each occasion you write me that you are behaving in your accustomed manner and thinking a great deal all the time. This is not the way! To the contrary! Now that our troubles have so multiplied and have reached such abysmal depths, God save us — "one abyss calls to the next" — it is especially important *now* to make every effort not to think much at all! A person must simply cast his burden upon God and turn the sadness and sighing into happiness and joy! (*Likutey Moharan* II, 23). For nonetheless, nonetheless, we merited to escape the trap of opposing a light such as the Rebbe! His merit will certainly guard us and our descendants, and with God's great compassion it will save us and rescue us! I will not elaborate now. When I receive your letter, I will immediately give you an appropriate response.

You really uplifted me when you wrote that you were engaged this Chanukah in studying the lesson "Greetings to far and near" (*Likutey Moharan* I, 63) on which, with God's kindness, I composed a discourse on the laws of *Shiluach HaKen* (Discourse #5) which discusses the subject of Chanukah. Come and see God's wonders! I myself also spoke a great deal about this lesson here on the night of Shabbat Chanukah. I dealt with the subject of Chanukah and I talked about everything we are going through as a group and as individuals, all of which is included in what is said there on the verse (Genesis 22:4), "He saw the place from afar."

Pay careful attention, my son, to everything that is said there, and you will be able to encourage yourself tremendously at all times. It should all serve to bring you closer, though, and not to distance you, God forbid; to bring you to joy, and not the opposite, God forbid. Get into the habit of regularly studying the teachings that God has allowed me to develop based on the Rebbe's holy words. I hope to God that they will really inspire you. For we have nothing with which to encourage ourselves except the Rebbe's holy Torah lessons and conversations — and they warrant close study indeed. Praise God, with His kindness, I have developed from them amazing teachings which are enormously inspiring. Study them over and over. Fortify yourself, my son! Be strong and trust God, because He will not abandon us! And no matter what, no good desire is ever lost. Look! You merit at such a time like this to lend assistance and to work on our project! Blessed is the Good and Beneficent One Who supplied the cure in advance of the blow! This is always God's way, as our Rabbis, of blessed memory, said (Megillah 13a). There is a great deal to say about this, but it is impossible now, particularly in this context. I will write you more, God willing, when I receive your letter in this post. Salvation is in God's hands.

The words of your father, waiting for salvation.

Noson of Breslov

Just this moment Reb Abele, may his light shine, received

your letter in the post office. I hereby inform you that, praise God, I received it and that I was extremely pleased. May God send us salvation and may we hear more good news soon, that there will no longer be anything to fear. Salvation is in God's hands.

Noson, the same

407

With God's help, Tuesday, the 10th of Tevet, 5603.

Greetings to my beloved son, may he live.

You should know that I am preparing myself to travel tomorrow, God willing, to Kremenchug. I do not know what to write you until I receive your letter. May God bring you and all of us to joy. May we merit to truly return to Him and to purify our hearts to serve Him in truth, through His inexhaustible compassion and power of salvation.

Just now, right after prayers on Wednesday [morning, Parashat] Vayechi, the post arrived. Praise God, I received your letter and I was really delighted. I am pressured now to get into the carriage and to travel to Kremenchug; and, in addition, the post is leaving soon. It is therefore impossible to write much at all. Be certain to write me regularly. All your letters should only be sent here to Tcherin, since I will be back here, with God's help, by the time your response to this letter arrives. Then I will write you a proper letter. Also, God willing, when I return from Kremenchug, I will send you more money, with God's help, for the project and for my family's living expenses. Trust God that you will not need to lend money for the project, except perhaps for a very short time.

As regards the length of my stay on the road — *I* will not know either until I return here. Then "God's plan will emerge." In the meantime, fortify yourself determinedly and encourage yourself with my previous letters, with what you find to quench your thirst in the books of our master, teacher and Rebbe, of blessed memory, and with the teachings that I merited to develop and originate from those of the Rebbe. Study them over and over with close attention every day, whether little or much. They will certainly inspire you a great deal, with God's help. The drama which takes place under the sun with every person in his childhood, his youth, his adolescence, his middle years and in his old age — with him, with his wife and with his children — is all a matter of no small significance! And through them all we have nothing to lean on, in this generation, in these last days, except the power of the elder of elders of holiness. For he thought very, very deeply indeed about our final end. *Ashreinu!* Happy are we to have escaped from opposing him, God forbid! And we merited and still merit every day to draw and to imbibe from his well, his springs of salvation which are our very lives! Were his Torah teachings not our delight, we would have almost perished in our destitution. Thank God Who has helped us thus far! God is our hope — and salvation is in His hands — that He will begin from now on to grant us complete salvation in This World and the Next.

The words of your father,

Noson of Breslov

Greetings to our comrades.

408

Before dawn, Wednesday, Va'eira, 5603, Tcherin.

Greetings to my dear, beloved son, may his light shine, and to all his family.

I arrived here from Kremenchug yesterday near evening and I found all your letters; the letter from Thursday [the week of Parashat] Shmot also arrived yesterday. I read them all and I gave praise and thanksgiving to God that He has helped us thus far. As for the future, our eyes look expectantly for His lovingkindness whereby He will continue to perform great acts of kindness for us and rescue us from fears of all kinds. And in this matter in particular may we be totally secure! Salvation is in God's hands.

In the first letters that I received from you, in particular the one from my son, Reb Shachneh, may his light shine, it appears that they already arranged matters so that it will be as before, only more so [a reference to hiding the children from the Czar's army]. In the last letter, though, from Thursday [Parashat] Shmot you cry out exceedingly for me to hurry home. I understand that the essence of your cry derives from your good longing and desire to spend time with me in order to receive from me the words of the Living God which will give new life to your soul — and in this you were correct in saying what you did. But what you wrote about my coming home in order to further matters for the "business" in the future — this I do not understand so well. It is not clear to me that I need to rush home for this; especially since, judging from those first letters, it appears that everything has already been concluded quite favorably. In any case I had no intention of staying on here much longer. I only intended to spend this Shabbat here, the next Shabbat, which is Parashat Bo, in Medvedevka; then to travel for the next Shabbat to Terhovitza, and afterwards to Uman. I do not know how long I will stay there. For my whole direction, my whole desire and hope is just to be at the Rebbe's holy gravesite as often as possible. Maybe I will merit to express myself and to pour out my heart like water before God on my own behalf and on behalf of my children; to speak there about your terribly bitter lament, which is so very loud and harsh, and has persisted now for so very long. And all those who hold vigil in our shade have the same bitter cry.

With me here now is our friend, Reb Efraim, the son of Reb Naftali, may his light shine, who travelled with me in order to hear words of truth. Praise God, we spoke an enormous amount on the road, but nonetheless, he too is still crying out with enormous bitterness. The letter which I just now received from Reb Yosef, the son of Reb Lipa, is no different. Most likely you have read and heard about *his* bitter cry; and so it is for just about all of them. May He Who hears crying and sighs hear your cries and those of all of us. May He say "Enough!" to our suffering, and especially to the suffering of the soul which is the worst suffering of all. What consoles me in my destitution is that the rest of the world who are not with us, and even more so our opponents — they too ought to be crying out even more. But, not only do they not cry out as they should, they *even* oppose the tzaddik who has such great power to save! It is impossible to elaborate on this, though, in this context. If you want to, you can encourage yourself with this even now and at all times throughout your entire life! Do not let these words grow old for you, even though I have already spoken about this many times. This is no minor point for us. It is our life forever! With this alone we can turn all kinds of grief and sighing — even yours, even mine (because I have to bear bitter cries such as these from many, many souls) and the grief and sighing of all of us — to happiness and great joy!

Nonetheless, as a result of your aforementioned letter, I am now seriously considering travelling tomorrow, God willing, to Medvedevka, and afterwards for Shabbat Parashat Bo to Ter-hovitza. If God is with me and enables me to discern His will in this, you will be gaining a week, as I will be in Uman, God willing, a week earlier than expected, during the week of Parashat Beshalach. It is God Who establishes a man's steps, and I give over my every movement every day to Him, particularly in the matter of my travels. In His compassion, He will revive my soul and guide me on paths of righteousness for His Name's sake. I need not tell you that from now on you should send your letters to Uman, so that they will arrive there by the week of Parashat Beshalach or shortly thereafter. Still, when you receive this letter, you should write a short note here to Reb Avraham Ber, may he live, if you have some good news about the "business" in Nemirov, or particularly if you have some good report from Reb Nachman in Iassi that they have already begun, etc. May God allow us to hear good news soon, because here too all our comrades are waiting to hear good news about all of this.

Beyond this I have absolutely no time to continue. It is now close to the time for Shema and the Morning Prayers. After prayers I will have to hurry if this letter is to catch the post.

The words of your father, waiting for salvation.

Noson of Breslov

Greetings to all our comrades, in particular to my illustrious friend Reb Nachman, may his light shine, grandson of our master, teacher and Rebbe, of blessed memory. I received your letter when I returned from Kremenchug and, God willing, when I come home and we get together, I will tell you everything. At the moment there is absolutely no time. I understand your words, your cry and your lament very well, both over your livelihood and also over your essential livelihood, your *spiritual* livelihood — in particular that you should avoid becoming a debtor to God, God forbid. He is the Great Lender, "Whose store is always open and the shopkeeper gives credit," etc. (*Avot* 3:20).

You need to speak a great deal with me; and God is my hope that you will be able to draw forth words from my heart, words which emanate from your grandfather, the holy and awesome Rav, which will really inspire your soul forever. Also in the physical realm, in connection with your livelihood and all that you lack, his words will always help you. For they are alive and enduring and they are effective for every person, especially for his holy descendants. May God have compassion on you and on all your children. May you merit to gaze upon the rock from which you were hewn — to understand from afar his greatness and holiness, to accustom yourself to follow his holy pathways, and to constantly draw close to those who nurse from his holy teachings. Then you and all your children will enjoy good forever. May God grant salvation that you may merit this, in order that you may always enjoy good. It is impossible to continue any longer.

> The words of your true friend, who loves you heart
> and soul and who prays for you.
>
> *Noson*, the same

This letter missed the post and was not sent on Wednesday. You should know now that today, Thursday [of Parashat] Va'eira, I am ready to set out, God willing, to Medvedevka. It is agreed among those of us here that I must return here again for Shabbat Parashat Bo, and afterwards I will travel, with God's help, to Terhovitza. So you will understand for yourself how to proceed with your letters.

Do not be upset, my son, about my being delayed here for so long. It is all from God and for the best. You should also know, my son, that what I wrote about your having frightened me was simply the result of a mistake that I made in my reading of your letter. What you meant was that you cannot decide if you should write to Reb Nachman in Iassi about the project and the scare. At the time, I was extremely busy and I thought you were writing about these things. I subsequently read your letter again after the post left, and I understood what you meant. Then I was very pained about upsetting you for no reason, but at that point it was impossible to rectify. You can learn from this, though, that most of your many other fears are also over nothing. The world is a narrow bridge and we must cross it. The main thing is not to be afraid at all. There is an enormous amount to say about this. May God always bring you and me to joy. The time for the *Shema* and the Morning Prayers has arrived. May I merit to pray properly and in accordance with everything that I wrote you. For every person could certainly pray all his life with the teachings and hints that I wrote about.

Noson, the same

409

With God's help, Wednesday, Va'eira, 5603, Tcherin.

Greetings to my modest wife, Dishel, may she live, and to my learned son, Reb David Zvi, may he live. And greetings to my son-in-law and friend, the learned and distinguished Reb Barukh, may he live, along with his wife, my modest daughter, Chanah Tsirel, may she live, and to all their children, may they live.

You should know that I arrived here yesterday from Kremenchug and I intend to begin preparations for my journey to Uman, God willing. From there, God willing, I will be coming home. I have no news to write you. Praise God, He has helped so much; and I trust to Him that He will continue to do so and to help with all our needs both physical and spiritual. "For God alone my soul waits in silence." For God's sake, study and pray, and pour out your hearts before God every day! For we have no-one to lean on but our Father in Heaven. I am extremely busy and cannot continue.

The words of your father, waiting for salvation.

Noson of Breslov

My son, Nachman, may he live, also sends particularly warm greetings to his mother may she live. He is sitting and learning, with God's help, and most likely he will be coming home safely with me. I hope to God to arrange a marriage for him soon. It is all in God's hands.

Warm greetings to all our comrades, great and small alike. They all have my blessing. How very much I long to write you all many words of truth! Your souls are bound up with mine and our love is great and eternal. But there is just not enough time. I have already spoken with you extensively though, with God's help, and all the Rebbe's holy books are in front of you. May you study them always, and may you follow the Rebbe's holy pathways at all times, according to the person, according to the place and according to the time. For God contracts Himself from Absolute Infinity into the finest details of the finite world. He presents every person with thoughts, words and deeds according to the person, etc., as we mentioned, and sends him hints by which to draw closer to Him from wherever he may be on that particular day. Happy is the person who takes this to heart every day and who at the very least merits to fulfill the mitzvot of tzitzit, tefilin, reciting the *Shema*, praying, Torah study, and conducting his business with trustworthiness. For the performance of these commandments automatically effects all of the holy rectifications described there, as is written in the lesson "Lord, My God, You are very great" (*Likutey Moharan* I, 54:4).

We ought to be saying "*Ashreinu!* — Fortunate are we!" a thousand times for every single lesson and original teaching that we merited to receive from the Rebbe! "Were his Torah teachings not our delight," we could not survive now in this end of days, in these turbulent times, when the floodwaters are inundating each and every person, body, soul, possessions and livelihood. Praise God that in His great lovingkindness He so abundantly favored us by revealing Torah teachings such as these and profound advice such as this in the most amazing form, which relate to every single area of life, in general and in every particular! They are simple and direct as can be, and they are relevant for every single person! All the same, despite their simplicity, they are drawn from the wellsprings of salvation, from "deep waters — advice in a man's heart." So deep are the Rebbe's teachings and advice that even a person who has floundered into deep water — whom the floodwaters have washed over — can find God even there; and through crying out and sighing, through good desires and yearnings, and by cheering himself with every good point, he can draw close to Him from wherever he may be! For God's sake, for God's sake, do not, God forbid, God forbid, view these words of mine as old! They are renewed every day as in, "God's kindnesses never end, His compassion never ceases. They are new every morning, great is Your faithfulness" (Lamentations 3:22-3).

> Writing from the depths of my heart, for your good
> and success in This World and the Next, forever.
>
> *Noson*, the same

410

With thanks to God, Wednesday, Parashat Bo, 5603.

Greetings to my modest wife, Dishel, may she live, and to all my children, may they live. Greetings as well to my learned son, Reb David Zvi, may he live, and to his family, may they live; and to my son, Yosef Yonah, may he live, and my son-in-law and friend, the learned Reb Barukh, may he live.

You should know that I arrived today from Medvedevka and that I intend, God willing, to travel after Shabbat to Terhovitza for Shabbat Shirah and from there I intend to travel to Uman, and from there home, God willing.

I received your letter from Sunday, the week of Parashat Va'eira, and I was greatly pleased. May God continue to help us and all Israel. May we leave all troubles behind and may we no longer hear bitter cries such as these. Wherever we travel, wherever we go [we hear], "Save us, God; the waters are flooding us!" And we have nothing with which to encourage ourselves but our knowledge of a true Rebbe such as this, may his merit protect us. We rely on his power that we will never be ashamed.

411

With God's help, Tuesday, Yitro, 5603, Uman.

Greetings to my beloved son, may he live.

I arrived safely here in Uman today, about three hours before daylight. There I found that which my soul loves — one of your fine letters — and I was really delighted. It is impossible to describe in writing the tremendous hardship that I suffered on this journey, as road conditions have been unusually poor lately. My mouth is filled with praises of God for having brought me to this point! Now, both physically and spiritually, the verse has indeed been fulfilled (Psalms 40:3), "He has brought me up from the turbulent pit, from the deep mire, and He has set my feet upon a rock." What can I give back to God?

The post is to leave very soon and my mind is not lucid at all. Because of the terrible state of the roads, I suffered on the road enormous difficulties for two nights and the day in between during my journey from Terhovitza to here. I arrived here literally by a miracle. God willing, when I receive another letter from you, I will give you a proper response. At the moment, I plan to stay here until Erev Rosh Chodesh Adar I. "He restores my soul. He guides me on paths of righteousness for His Name's sake."

The words of your father who prays for you.

Noson of Breslov

412

With God's help, Tuesday, Yitro, 5603, Uman.

Greetings to my beloved friend, the learned Reb Avraham Ber, may he live, along with all his children, may they live; and to my friend, the learned Reb Abba, may his light shine, along with all his children, may they live.

I arrived here safely today before daylight after great toil and tremendous hardship due to the poor condition of the roads. Thank God Who has brought me thus far. I was already at the holy gravesite today, through God's kindness, and mentioned you all there for good. May the Master of Compassion take pity on me, and on all of you, and may He save us in all that we need to be saved, both physically and spiritually. I found a letter here from my son Reb Yitzchak, may he live, reporting that he received a letter from our friend, Reb Nachman, may his light shine, in Iassi. The "good work" has already begun and is progressing nicely — but he needs a great deal of money. My son, may he live, has already sent him all the money that he had [available] for the second time, along with a small sum that he received from Breslov. Now you will understand for yourselves how critical it is that you immediately send as much money as you possibly can for the project. The more one gives, the more Heaven gives one wealth, honor, life, peace and all good in This World and the Next, forever. I intend to stay here until Erev Rosh Chodesh Adar I. May God guide me on paths of righteousness for His Name's sake.

The words of your true friend forever.

Noson of Breslov

Greetings to all our comrades with a great, bold love!

413

With God's help, Sunday, Mishpatim, 5603, Uman.

Greetings to my beloved son, may he live.

I already sent you a letter through the post immediately upon my arrival here last Tuesday. At the moment, "there is nothing new under the sun" to tell you. "Above the sun" though, in the holy Torah, there is more than enough to innovate every day! Even someone who does not know and understand the awesome and original phenomena that are taking place in the world every moment of every day, as is written, "Who does new things...Who in His goodness constantly renews the Creation every day" — he must still have faith in this, as in "they are new every morning, great is Your faithfulness."

I have already spoken about this a great deal, but it is necessary to speak about it still more, so that these words "themselves" do not grow old for us. You should remind yourself anew, my son, that we merited to be from the seed of Israel. And by God's amazing kindness, as a bird from a trap, our souls escaped the concealment of the point of truth — the point of truth which radiates now in all the worlds, and especially in This World! But due to the tremendous darkness of our actions and the dullness of the intellect, this light is obscured and is deeply concealed (*Likutey Moharan* I, 17); until many people not only fail to enjoy his great light, but even attack and oppose him vehemently! What can we return to God for all the kindness He has bestowed upon us, that we have escaped from this?!

I warn you and urge you, my dear son, as a father favors his son, to remember this very, very well every single day in everything that you go through. For it is no minor point. It is impossible to convey the constant glimmer of knowledge that I have of this. Thank God Who has helped us thus far in His compassion, to be called in the Rebbe's great name! So may He continue in His kindness and allow us to be included with him in This World and the Next. May our souls be counted forever among all the souls who hail in his name! Praise God, this Shabbat I spoke a great deal about this based on the injunction of our Rabbis, of blessed memory, "A person should always complete the weekly Torah readings with the community" (see *Likutey Halakhot, Kriyat HaTorah* 6). God is my hope that we will merit this — not as our deeds would dictate, but by His amazing, infinite kindness. You are receiving enclosed here a letter to Reb Nachman. You may add to it as you wish. I am extremely pressured and I cannot continue any longer. Fulfill what our friend, Reb Efraim, may his light shine, wrote you — never to despair of crying out and of being joyful at all times. Send greetings to all my family in Breslov; there is no time to address each one individually. My son, Nachman, may he live, also sends loving greetings.

The words of your father who prays for you.

Noson of Breslov

414

With thanks to God, Monday, Terumah, 5603, Uman.

Greetings to my beloved son, the learned Reb Yitzchak, may he live; along with all his children, may they live.

I received your letters, specifically the letter with the two sample pages. How great are God's kindnesses! If my mouth were filled as the sea with song, [I still could not thank Him enough]! There is no time now to elaborate on this. Regarding your own situation, I have already written you a great deal and at the moment I have nothing at all to say about it. My sons, may they live, as well as our comrades, are eager to return home, and I hope to God that we will soon be getting together anyway. Then face to face we will speak the words that God sends us, and you will know anew that "God is great and highly to be praised! His greatness is unfathomable " and we know nothing at all! Look, we are now witnessing new wonders in connection with our "business." By this alone one ought to understand how great and beyond description are God's kindnesses and wonders. If, nonetheless, each person is still being relentlessly assailed — well, by this we can see the greatness of the Fashioner of Creation all the more in that He granted such power to free will! But we already know that the measure of good is greater and that "You are forever on high, God" [i.e. You always have the upper hand]. His kindness to us has been abundant!

The words of your father who prays for you.

Noson of Breslov

Greetings to all our comrades with a great love!

415

With thanks to God, Tuesday, Rosh Chodesh Adar I, 5603, Uman.

[*Publisher's note: This letter refers to Reb Noson's receipt of a few sample pages of the* Likutey Eitzot *from Reb Nachman Tulchiner. He sent them on to Reb Avraham Ber in Tcherin, to encourage the Breslover Chassidim there to fulfill their pledges of financial support.*]

Let happiness and joy take over! To my beloved and learned friend, the outstanding and illustrious "fruit of the tzaddik," Reb Avraham Ber, may he live; along with all his precious children, may they live. And to my learned friend, Reb Abele, may his light shine; along with all his children, may they live.

Come and look upon God's deeds! Come and see the might of your Master! Enclosed here for your perusal is a sample page from our project, which Reb Nachman sent me from his current abode by way of Brody. Let your eyes see and your hearts rejoice! Praise God, the work is of excellent quality and it is nice and neat and orderly, as it should be. Let my mouth be filled with God's praises that He has helped me thus far! So may He allow us to finish this project, and then to start and finish other books as well. May we always have a share in working for the eternal benefit of the wider community.

I received a letter from Reb Nachman in which he was shrieking like a crane to send him money at once. If he receives enough money, he will be able to complete the project very quickly. Therefore, my brothers and friends, I come now to inform you of all this and to rouse the ears and heart of each one of you to endeavor with all your might to send me money immediately — in particular, from those people who promised to send, whom I listed for you both in my previous letter and when I was there with you. For God's sake, act quickly and do not delay in the slightest — the workers are itching to finish the job! I intend to set out for home this morning and to stay in Teplik for Shabbat; and I hope to receive money from you before I arrive home. At the very least do not delay for long, God forbid. It is impossible to continue any longer. I am confident that you will act quickly and energetically for our project, so that we will be able to complete it properly. For according to what Reb Nachman, may his light shine, wrote me, I need still a great deal of money. So fortify yourselves mightily for this great project, which will benefit the wider community for generations to come. May God finish propitiously for you and for us, and may He cause merit to evolve through you. May God fulfill your hearts' requests for good and may you merit to engage in Torah, prayer and good deeds all your days. May you enjoy wealth, honor and good, long lives. May you flourish and be fruitful into ripe old age.

> The words of your true eternal friend, who prays for you.
>
> *Noson of Breslov*

Greetings to all our comrades, great and small — to each one of them as befits his own high level. You should also pass on this news to our friend Reb Efraim, son of Reb Naftali, may his light shine, in Kremenchug. He will rejoice over our salvation. Tell him also to work there with all his might for the good of the project and God will give him success.

> *Noson*, the same

416

With thanks to God, early Thursday night, Tetzaveh, 5603.

My dear, beloved son.

You should know that, praise God, I arrived here safely today. There is no news to tell you right now. The deliverer of this letter is in a hurry and I have to pray the Evening Prayers. But out of my love for you and your desire to know of my arrival home, I am informing you immediately. May God save us in all that we need to be saved. Let us be happy and rejoice in His salvation, especially since Purim is coming! May it come for good life and peace.

The words of your father,

Noson of Breslov

Warm greetings to all our comrades.

417

With thanks to God, Wednesday, Purim Katan, 5603, Breslov.

My dear, beloved son.

I received your letter along with the letters from Reb Nachman. At the moment I have nothing to tell you, other than you must be sure to come here for next Shabbat, i.e. the one that is coming up right now. You need to be here for our "business," so that I can take counsel with you face to face. That is beside the fact that both you and I want very much to get together soon.

Therefore, overcome the barriers and come here as quickly as you can, if possible tomorrow, God willing, at least by evening. There is much to talk about. May God allow us to discuss these matters in the proper way, so that we attain perfect counsel in all areas. Salvation is in God's hands. I am too rushed to continue any longer at all.

The words of your father waiting to see you in joy.

Noson of Breslov

Greetings to all our comrades with a great love! In particular to "the holy fruit," the illustrious Reb Nachman, may his light shine. I am hoping to see him too, alive and well. It is impossible to write anything at all in this context. We will speak face to face and God's counsel will emerge.

Noson, the same

418

With thanks to God, Monday night, Tzav, 5603, Breslov.

Greetings to my dear, beloved son, may he live.

I received your letter today along with the letter from Reb Nachman, may his light shine, and I was really delighted. I had wanted to send a man to your community. But when I saw that you wanted to wait until the information he referred to in his letter arrived, I cancelled my idea and agreed to wait until after Shabbat. If it were not so close to Purim, I would travel to your community today myself. The way it looks now I will come to you, with God's help, after next Shabbat, and perhaps in the interim the information will arrive. Right now though we must ask God to help us fast as we should on the Fast of Esther — to scream, to cry out and to pray as we should and to pour out our hearts like water before God, until we merit that He answers us, helps us and gives us complete and speedy salvation, until we merit to welcome Purim as we should amidst great joy. No matter what, praise God, we really have something to be happy about — more than enough, praise to the Living God, in that He separated us in every way from those who err! I will bless You for this every day, Compassionate One. The deliverer of this letter, Reb Asher, is in a great hurry and it is impossible to continue at all. May God bring you and me to joy with the happiness of Purim. Let us be happy and rejoice in His salvation!

The words of your father, writing hurriedly.

Noson of Breslov

419

With God's help, Wednesday, Taanit Esther, 5603, Breslov.

Let happiness and joy take over! To my dear, beloved son, the learned Reb Yitzchak, may he live — peace, life and all good.

How glorious is this day, on which I received the good news that, praise God, our project is completed! What can I give back to God for all the good He has bestowed upon me?! If our mouths were filled as the sea with song..., Praise God, the good news arrived at just the appropriate season — at a time of "happiness, joy, celebration and festivity for the Jews." So may it be with us, and may we merit to rejoice in His salvation this Purim and on all the coming Festivals! May He instill in us true knowledge of how to thank Him joyfully and bless Him for all that He has bestowed upon us in His compassion and abundant lovingkindness. Let my mouth be filled with His praises!

In light of the aforementioned letter which I received, I have decided that we cannot cause anguish to Reb Nachman like this, when he is expecting to receive money any day. As he wrote in his letter, he was expecting to receive money that very same day. I am therefore sending you the enclosed sum of money. The remainder — what is needed in the sum of ten half *proilen* [a certain coin], which is the equivalent of fifteen new rubles — you should lend from your own pocket. This is besides what I owe you for the merchandise. Be sure to send him this sum, along with the letters enclosed here, right away with tomorrow's post. You may add to the letter to Reb Nachman as you wish.

As you can understand for yourself, you will thus be doing a great mitzvah for him. The primary reason that I am moving so quickly with this is because of our work on the book *Likutey Eitzot* which I wish to begin immediately. It is a project for the benefit of the greater community, and "a mitzvah for the community takes precedence." God forbid then that we should be remiss in this matter and the faster we do it the better. If you want to, you may add another two half *proilen* and send him twelve; and I will send you ten new rubles this coming Friday or at least on Sunday, after Shabbat. I do not want to become involved with this now, as I am busy with preparations for Purim. The money is all ready, though, and it is as if it is already in my hand. I simply have to send for it. Write me a response immediately, as quickly as you possibly can, because I want you to send the aforementioned sum, along with the letters, with all possible speed.

You see that I am being extremely easy on you with this loan, since you have not yet lent even the thirty rubles that you promised. I trust God that you will not need to lend much after this because I hope to God that you will soon be receiving money from Tcherin and Kremenchug. I have borrowed here the money that I sent you. This is in addition to the money that I already gave the *sofer*, what I need to give him every week, and what I need for my own living expenses. My money as well is invested in this project, as you know, and I am going out of my way to borrow from others in order to alleviate your burden. But, my dear, beloved son, you are really being overly particular about lending money for such an important project, when you write in all your letters that your burden must be lightened. There is no time to discuss this now. As I said, I made it easier for you now and I will continue to do so in the future. It could even be that you will not need to lend any more at all, and you can rest assured that you will certainly be reimbursed soon for what you have lent.

Due to the preparations for Purim it is impossible to elaborate. I am confident that you will carry out my words quickly and exactly as I have asked. God Who is good will finish for us. May you and I enjoy the celebration of Purim, and may you merit to rejoice that on Purim you are engaging in bringing the Rebbe's holy Torah teachings into the world. This is the essential meaning of "they upheld and accepted" (Esther 9:27) in which the tzaddikim are involved in every generation, particularly on Purim. May God grant you and all of us to merit this Purim to accept upon ourselves anew to uphold the Torah, so as to fulfill, "they upheld what they had already accepted" (*Shabbat* 88a).

The crucial thing is that you and I should merit to constantly receive and understand the profound advice and hints, "the hands in the sea of wisdom" (*Likutey Moharan* II, 7:10) — which are the holy, original Torah teachings of our master, teacher and Rebbe, of holy, sainted memory. For these are hints of great profundity, and they are meant for you too, my dear son. They address the person "before the act and after," and deal with "depart from evil" as well as "do good"; for example, when a person needs to pray but is assailed and buffeted on every side by impediments and extraneous thoughts. Everyone is familiar with this phenomenon and it is referred to in the lesson "The depths covered them" (*Likutey Moharan* I, 9) which explains that when a person stands up to pray, the *kelipot*, the barriers, surround him, etc. The lesson also gives a sound piece of advice: that the person should endeavor at least to say the words of the prayers in truth according to who he is, as is written there on the verse "Make a window for the ark."

Happy are the ears which hear words such as these! But the essence of this advice in its totality must be understood through subtle indications made with the hands which cannot be articulated. The same thing applies to the advice the Rebbe wrote on how to shake off the heaviness and downheartedness which prevent a person from praying with concentration and enthusiasm. This is the lesson "*Azamra!* — I will sing to God with the little that I have left!" which teaches that a person must inspire himself with the tiniest of good points that still remain in him. This simply-stated advice is highly beneficial for everyone, "sweet to the soul and healing to the bone" and many souls have already been inspired by it. But there are many occasions when it is difficult for a person to inspire himself even with this, unless God helps him understand the hints through which He signals the truth to every single person no matter where he is, that "God's affection is still upon him" (*Shabbat* 88b).

We find the same thing in connection with the lesson about "the son and student" (*Likutey Moharan* II, 7) which informs all the lowly and inferior people in the world that God is still right there with them — for "the whole world is full of His glory!" The essence of this holy message, though, must be received in the form of hints, because "thought cannot grasp Him at all"; rather God "is known to each person according to his own estimation which is in the category of hints" (*Zohar* I, 103b). Therefore, each person must endeavor to understand these hints, until he draws Godliness upon himself in all places, and indeed comes to understand that "the whole world is full of His glory." This is why it is written, "And every creature will *understand* that You created him" (High Holy Days Liturgy).

It is impossible to elaborate on this any further. A hint is sufficient for the wise. Similarly, "after the act," i.e. after praying, if he still could not concentrate on his prayers and bad thoughts ravaged them, God forbid — then all the more so must a person

understand the countless hints which the Rebbe conveyed to us
with his holy hands, that it is absolutely forbidden to succumb for
any reason. Even in the matter of "avoiding evil," through these
hints it is possible to understand how very much a person must
strengthen himself not to begin thinking bad thoughts at all, not to
enter into debate with temptation (*The Aleph-Bet Book* p.152, #10), but to flee
from bad thoughts by "sitting and doing nothing" (i.e. not getting involved
with them at all). He will thus escape from all evil. But if, God forbid,
God forbid, his evil urge does overcome him, God save us, he must
fortify himself and not succumb any further, as the Rebbe cried out
(*Likutey Moharan* II, 78), "There is no such thing as despair!"

While the Rebbe revealed his paths of encouragement and
advice explicitly — and it is necessary to have faith in his words
and to fulfill them straightforwardly — the essence of his encouragement must be understood from a distance by means of
these hints, in particular the hints about the enormous greatness
and power of the elder of holiness, the elder of elders in whose
shade we take shelter. For it is from him that we understand the
greatness of the Fashioner of Creation and His enormous
lovingkindness which is absolutely without limit.

I have already spoken about all this extensively, but beyond
this a person must strive to understand these hints — and they are
without limit or end! So now you will understand anew that there
is no such thing as despair and that even I, you, and all of us must
strengthen ourselves with great, boundless joy every day — especially on days of joy, and even more so on Purim! *Ashreinu!*
Ashreinu! Happy are we that we merit to write words such as these,
which emanate from the hints within "the sea of wisdom," and

through which one merits "an illumination of yearning" during eating, provided that one is not a *shlamazelnik*, a loser! This is for me the whole underlying meaning of Purim. For the subjugation of Amalek, may his name be obliterated, was accomplished by "and when Moshe lifted his hands, Israel would win — i.e., when Israel looked upward toward Heaven" (Rosh HaShanah 29a). In other words, Moshe, our teacher, raised up his hands and hinted to Israel that they should look upward. Amalek is an extremely tough *kelipah*; it includes all the other *kelipot* and the entire Other Side. And when Amalek spreads himself out and makes war with Israel, it is impossible for the tzaddik to speak and to rebuke Israel directly. Rather he lifts up his hands and hints to them, "Look upward! God is still with you! The whole world is full of His glory!'"

The page is coming to an end and time is short, so it is impossible to continue. This will suffice for now. You also received this letter because of my desire to have you send money to Reb Nachman quickly. Were it not for this matter, I would not have dreamed of writing you a letter today. Therefore do not allow the celebration of Purim to prevent you from sending the money and the letter, as I requested above. To the contrary! Through this you can celebrate and rejoice with the song that Reb Nachman, may he live, is singing there — "Rose of Yaakov, merriment and joy!" — and merit to perform this mitzvah on Purim!

The words of your father,

Noson of Breslov

Really and truly be happy!

420

With God's help, Monday, Shemini, 5603, Breslov.

Greetings to my dear, beloved son.

I received a letter from you on Purim and then another one today as well. Thank God, Purim passed joyfully and, praise God, yesterday you did as I asked and sent Reb Nachman the sum of money you mentioned in your letter. Even though there *was* a delay and you did not send it on Purim day itself — the Torah exempts cases of duress. I did not know that my letter with the money would not reach you until the meal on Purim day. I expected rather that you would receive it on the Fast of Esther toward evening, since, at the time I wrote the letter, Reb Nachman, the son of Reb M. HaKohen, thought he would be leaving before Minchah. But God certainly arranged it all for the best. In any case, it was well worth the effort I expended, if only for the sake of the letter that I wrote then (above, #419). For while it is still difficult for you and me to clearly understand the hints, it is still necessary to speak about this a great deal. I already wrote on this subject in a slightly different form to Reb Efraim in Kremenchug. I intended to write you about it too in my letter prior to that one, but it did not work out.

Subsequently, in the middle of Selichot on the Fast of Esther, Reb Asher brought me your letter with the *mishloach manot* (Purim gifts) and, more important, he brought the letter from Reb Nachman, may he live. It was then that I began to feel joy, and the happiness of Purim was awakened in my heart and in the hearts of our comrades. For we saw God's eternal salvation and the hope that He holds out for coming generations, as Reb Nachman, may his light shine, wrote. Then, due to my enormous yearning and the yearning of Reb Nachman for this project, I was stirred to send him immediately whatever money I could. I thought the matter over carefully and I then wrote the aforementioned letters. In the process, God caused me to remember to write you about the hints and, praise God, my pen set down many amazing words of truth which I had really not thought about at all. How great are God's deeds! My dear son, every single activity, circumstance and movement that God brought about from the day I drew close to the light of our lives, as well as all that He effected after the Rebbe's passing in my work with all of you, both as individuals and as a group, can enable a person to understand and to see God's kindness and His absolutely infinite wonders! The mouth cannot utter them, nor the mind comprehend! "You have performed great deeds, Lord, my God! Your miracles and thoughts are for us!"

It is God Who determines a man's steps, and it seems no longer necessary for me to travel to Tulchin this week. The reason for this is that I do not want to send him any more money until I receive acknowledgement that he received the money and letter sent yesterday. Furthermore, I am waiting to receive letters from him which were already sent by way of Brody. I am surprised that they have not yet arrived, and I suppose that as soon as you receive them you will send them to me right away. In the meantime, I hope to God that money will arrive from Tcherin and other places. Salvation is in God's hands. May He complete the project in the best possible way, without any large loans, and may the money I borrowed up until today soon be completely paid off, with God's help. "Thus far has Your compassion helped me" and in His compassion He will never abandon us.

In my opinion, it would be a good idea to give my last letter, from Purim, to our friend Reb Yaakov, may his light shine, to read. Perhaps he will understand hints from my words which will be of benefit to him. The same thing applies to my illustrious friend, Reb Nachman, may his light shine, grandson of our master, teacher and Rebbe, of blessed memory. Send them both my loving greetings. If they really have a strong desire for me to come, they could *draw* me there after this coming Shabbat, God willing. Even for a short trip such as this to Tulchin I rely on God, because for me it is a difficult journey. May He Who determines a man's steps guide me on paths of righteousness for the sake of His Name.

Write me if you were happy on Purim as is fitting. No matter what, it is necessary now to pray to God that He accept our rejoicing on Purim along with all the other commandments of Purim, as if we fulfilled them correctly in all their details and fine points. May this enable us to attain the holiness and purity of the Red Heifer and to be purified from *tumat meit* (caused by contact with a corpse). Thus may we be pure for the Pesach sacrifice and thereby guard ourselves from even a trace of chametz both physical and spiritual (*Likutey Moharan* II, 74). May we exercise the utmost vigilance and not let our minds "ferment," God forbid, with evil and alien thoughts, God forbid, thus fulfilling "rebuke the beast of the weedgrass," until we return from chametz to matzah, from the letter *chet* to *hei* and from death to life (as in *Likutey Moharan* I, 5:4).

What can we return to God for all the good He has done for us?! For we merited to hear such awesome, amazing and exalted teachings about every single mitzvah, and in particular about the holy times of the year and the mitzvot which are connected to them! They give life to every soul in any place!

The Rebbe speaks a great deal, for example, about the holiness of Pesach as one of the three pilgrimage festivals in lessons such as "A field of knives" (*Likutey Moharan* I, 30), "Blow the Shofar I" (*Likutey Moharan* II, 1), and "I have commanded the ravens to feed you" (*Likutey Moharan* II, 4). Besides this, he speaks about Pesach alone in the lesson discussed above which begins "With the trumpets..." (*Likutey Moharan* I, 5) on the matter of guarding against "the fermentation of the mind"; and the lesson "Nine Rectifications" (*Likutey Moharan* I, 20:10) discusses the Haggadah reading, which serves to rectify the Covenant, as well as the Four Cups of wine on Seder night. There is also the lesson I mentioned above (*Likutey Moharan* II, 74) which teaches that Purim is a preparation for Pesach, and there are many other lessons as well.

The same thing applies to Sukkot, Shavuot, Rosh Ha-Shanah, Yom Kippur and so on, each of which the Rebbe discusses many times, both in a general way and in connection with their various details. So it is with the rest of the command-ments too, as anyone familiar with his holy books is aware. *Ashreinu!* Happy are we! How good is our portion! May we just merit to observe and to study each of these teachings at its appropriate time and season. May we "study the laws of Pesach before Pesach" — to express ourselves before God prior to Pesach that we will merit to draw close to Him through the holiness of Pesach and through the deep advice contained in these teachings which speak about Pesach. May we do the same for all the holy festivals!

There is no time to continue. What is more, I am suffering terribly right now over my grandson, Nachman, may he live, who is sick in bed. May God quickly heal him. I must go to visit him now. May God Who is full of compassion, the Creator of cures, quickly heal him and give him back his full strength right away. Salvation is in God's hands.

The words of your father, waiting for salvation.

Noson of Breslov

421

With thanks to God, Monday night, Tazria, 5603.

Warm greetings to my beloved son, may he live, along with all his family.

I received your letter today. In connection with what you wrote about your not having expressed yourself to me as you wished because you were occupied with your efforts to honor me — it is certainly true. I knew this, though, when I was at your house, and there *were* a number of occasions when you would have had time to speak with me as much as you wished. But there are a great many other barriers to this as well. It seems to me, however, that I did speak with you quite a bit through the many words of truth I spoke, with God's help, when I was there, and from them you will be able to understand a great many things both explicit and implied. We have also spoken extensively in the past and you have already seen a great deal in the Rebbe's holy books and in the original teachings I have developed from them.

The incitements of the Evil One, though, are beyond all estimation. Our entire hope rests upon the power of the elder of holiness, who surpasses all else! It is impossible to speak about this in this context. God willing, there will be other opportunities to speak face to face, when we meet again in the near future. For now, though, fortify yourself determinedly, and bring yourself to joy anew every day with the fact that God "created us for His honor and separated us from those who err" in every respect! For from the tremendous uproar and the barriers which prevent people from having contact with us, it is possible to understand how many exalted favors God has bestowed upon us in that we were saved from adopting their antagonism and their arrogant scoffing! Had we only been drawn close and escaped from being opponents of a light such as this, and not received a single new teaching from him — it would still have been enough! For every teaching, statement and conversation that we received from him we ought to be saying, "If we had come into the world only to hear *this* — it would have been reason enough!" How much more so when we have received all that we have!

The words of your father waiting for salvation.

Noson of Breslov

422

With thanks to God, Tuesday, Achrei, the 11th of Nisan, 5603, Breslov.

Warm greetings to my dear, beloved son, may he live.

I received all your letters this week and last. Thus far has God's compassion helped me and what I said came true — that I would owe you no more than 30 new rubles at Pesach. This is indeed a miracle and an amazing display of Divine Providence! It is good to thank God Whose compassion has helped me thus far! You, however, are too particular with me when it comes to lending me money. I hope to God, though, that I will not need to borrow from you anymore. Salvation is in God's hands. I have written you all this in the hope that, from now on, perhaps you will cease to ruminate so much over every slight matter. It certainly is true that a person must beware of dishonesty when dealing with other people's money, of going into debt, and of entering into enterprises which are beyond his means; and, thank God, you are careful about this. But it really is inappropriate to be so deliberating — especially in the matter of 30 or 40 new rubles, and, in particular, when it is for such an important project. I ask you, though, do not be downhearted or worried over the fact that I am writing about this, because I bear you no grudge whatsoever.

Starting now, my son, be careful to bring yourself to joy with what you yourself wrote in your letter, that you know that a light such as the Rebbe is shining in the world, a light which is so concealed and hidden from everyone; but for us, with God's kindness, his light is shining, and at least we do not oppose him, God forbid. The wondrous kindness that God has done and is still doing with us in this way, every single day, is a matter of no small significance! But the Rebbe already revealed to us that a person must inevitably experience bitterness in order to attain true peace. This is how the Rebbe explained the verse, "For the sake of peace I have great bitterness and You desired to save my soul from destruction" (*Likutey Moharan* I, 27:7). The essence of true peace — which is a cure for both body and soul eternally — is when people do not oppose the point of truth, the light of the true tzaddik in whom we take shelter forever. Outside of this there is no peace in the world. There is a great deal to say about this — more than the page could hold. But it is necessary to suffer bitterness for this peace. And if the bitterness does cut to the quick — the peace, the healing, the wondrous demonstrations of salvation and all the blessings which are elicited by such a "complete man," set everything right.

All this is embodied in the idea of the bitter herbs which have to be eaten with the Pesach sacrifice and matzah. These latter two represent extremely lofty and exalted levels of understanding which make peace between Israel and their Father in Heaven and in all the worlds. They connect "those who dwell on high spiritual levels" with "those who dwell down below on low spiritual levels" and they make His Godliness known and manifest in all the worlds. This revelation is accomplished primarily, however, through "those who dwell down below," by us lowly beings in This World, and particularly in this End of Days, in this long and bitter exile. It is precisely through *us*, through our eating of the bitter herbs and matzah as a remembrance of the Holy Temple and through our performance of the Pesach Seder, that God's Divinity is revealed in all the worlds! But we must include the bitter herbs which remind us of how the Egyptians "embittered our lives" (Exodus 1:14) and which must accompany this matzah, because only through bitterness is it possible to receive peace, as discussed above.

We are currently in the holy days about which it is said (Songs 2:8), "The voice of my friend is coming, skipping over the mountains, jumping over the hills." These mountains and hills are the barriers, impediments and conflicts which prevent us from drawing close to God. The evil impulse is likened to a mountain, and this is particularly true for a person who has already stumbled — may God protect us from now on. But the Holy One, Blessed be He, skips over them all, because "my friend is like a deer or a fawn. He is standing there behind our wall" (Songs 2:9). "Our wall" refers to the walls which block each person as a result of his great physicality. But in truth, even a wall of iron cannot divide Israel and their Father in Heaven (Pesachim 85b). For God "is standing there behind our wall. He is looking through the windows [CHALonot]..." about which it is said, "Petition [CHALu] before God," as is explained in the Tikkuney Zohar... "He peeks through the lattice. My friend spoke up and said to me, 'Rise, my lovely friend...'." (Songs 2:10). And if, all the same, the bitterness wants to prevail — well, we have already merited to draw close to a "complete man" who sweetens and rectifies everything!

There is also a hint in these words that we must cleave to

God's attributes and walk in His ways and "skip over the mountains and jump over the hills." For a person must skip and jump through This World, as I related to you in the Rebbe's holy name that he used to praise the tzaddik who said before his death, "*iber geshpringen* — I leaped through!" (*Tzaddik #522*). But we would not have merited to know about *this* either, much less to practice it, were it not for the Rebbe, of blessed memory! With his great power, at the very least we can skip and jump over everything! In the process we can also grab the mitzvah of eating matzah and observing all the other holy commandments, and thus there is hope for our final outcome! "There is a future for the man of peace." With this approach, a person can dance practically every day, and even more so on Shabbat and the Festivals! "The Kings of hosts, they flee, they flee!" (Psalms 68:13). No matter what, really and truly be happy! Just leap blithely through with no second thoughts! God is with us!

Remember well what the Rebbe said prior to his holy passing (*Tzaddik #88, 122*), "Seeing that I am going before you, what do you have to worry about?" Whenever downheartedness, grief and sighing want to take over, you can turn them all into happiness and joy through all the above! For even though I am so spoilt, I do not oppose this "whole man" even after such *machloket* (opposition), mockery and confusion! "Those on chariots and those on horses" — some in enormous wealth and others in great poverty. "But we will call in the Name of the Lord, our God!" My soul will rejoice in God! It will exult over His salvation! We will wonder all our lives over our souls' bitterness [and praise Him for saving us]! As birds from a trap, our souls have escaped a *machloket* such as this against the point of truth! Our help is in the Name of God, the Maker of Heaven and Earth! Let us be happy and rejoice in His salvation!

The words of your father,

Noson of Breslov

Greetings to all our comrades with a great love, in particular to my illustrious friend Reb Nachman, may his light shine, grandson of our master, teacher and Rebbe, of blessed memory! Let them read this letter, since I know that deep in their hearts they truly agree with all this. Perhaps they will realize their potential and rejoice in all this over the approaching holy festival, until they skip over the mountains and jump over the hills to get together with us often, especially on Shabbatot, the Festivals and on Rosh HaShanah. Thus they will merit to have their souls bound up with the Rebbe's forever.

Noson, the same

423

With God's help, Erev Pesach, 5603.

Peace, life and all good to my dear, beloved son, may he live. To him, his wife and his children — life, peace, health, and complete recovery, body and soul. Amen. May it be His will.

I received your letter just now and I was greatly pained as I began to read. I had hoped to receive good news. But I turned the tide and fortified myself to trust in God's kindness. He inflicts and He will heal. I trust that with His wondrous kindnesses He will quickly send your son, David Zvi, may he live, a full recovery, body and soul.

And you, my dear son, do not be distressed. Just summon your strength to turn this too into joy! I have already written you that a person must inevitably suffer a little bitterness. The reason for this is that it is impossible to receive peace, which is a cure for the soul and the body, except through bitterness (*Likutey Moharan* I, 27:7). But God is compassionate in the extreme and He casts all of a person's sins aside and only sends him a little bitterness, in a measure that he is able to endure. May God in His lovingkindness and miracles sweeten and nullify *this* bitterness too. May He send him [R. David Zvi, Reb Yitzchak's son] from Heaven a complete and speedy recovery and may he return to even greater vitality. For me, my eyes are raised up to God in prayer and supplication. May He send help from the Sanctuary and from Zion may He support him. May I soon merit to hear good news about him during the Intermediate Days of the Festival. Salvation is in God's hands.

It is good to thank God, Who has already supplied us with the cure for everything. For, as a result of your letter which I sent through Reb D., it turned out that God helped me and I transcribed in writing the ideas that God illuminated for me about Pesach. How great are God's deeds! In Him I trust, with the power and merit of our awesome master, teacher and Rebbe, of holy, sainted memory, that everything will turn into good. Just fortify yourself with the utmost determination to rejoice on this holy festival and particularly at the Seder! Drink the wine of the Four Cups of Salvation in gladness, because "with God there is lovingkindness and abundant redemption" and His ways are extremely exalted. But it is necessary to believe that everything is for the good and that God's goodness and kindness never cease. This is particularly so since, praise God, we have someone to rely on in This World and the Next!

Believe that you too are engraved on the Rebbe's heart, and that he knows your pain and is working for your cure and your eternal salvation. Trust God and pray to Him! Fortify yourself in the joy of the Festival! What you really need right now is to strengthen yourself all the more to be happy, because joy heals all wounds and illnesses! This applies all the more on *this* holy Festival about which it is said (Isaiah 30:29), "You will have a song, as on the night when the Festival begins" — this refers to "the night of watchfulness," "this night" of Pesach. For it is then that all the ten kinds of music and song which are the source of all cures, physical and spiritual, for you, for us and for all Israel, are awakened. Amen. May it be His will.

I am so busy with the preparations for Pesach and Shabbat that I cannot continue.

The words of your father, waiting for salvation.

Noson of Breslov

424

With thanks to God, Wednesday, the 11th day of the Counting of the Omer, 5603, Breslov.

Warm greetings, life and blessing to my friend whom I love as myself, the illustrious, learned and distinguished Reb Efraim, may his light shine. To him, his wife and his children — life, peace, wealth, honor and all good forever. Amen.

I received your letter, along with the twenty-five silver rubles, all in good order, during the Intermediate Days of the Festival. May God repay the deeds of those who helped and of those who enlisted the help of others in such a great mitzvah for the benefit of the wider community. May they receive full reward from God and may they enjoy success in all their endeavors, both worldly and spiritual. May they spend their days in true good and their years in pleasantness, until they merit to gaze upon the pleasantness of God forever. Amen. May it be His will.

Pesach has already passed peacefully and a little joyfully, and we have already crossed the Red Sea. Eleven days of the Counting of the Omer have already passed in the 603rd year in the sixth millennium since the creation of the world. The holy days of Shavuot are approaching. May we only merit from now on to count the Omer with the appropriate concentration and feeling, such that each one of us will merit to cleanse himself of his impurity and pollution and to attain the great fear and awe of the Giving of the Torah. May it be fulfilled that "the fear of God be upon us, so that we will sin no more at all."

I have nothing new to tell you right now and, besides, I am expecting you to come here, God willing, this coming Shavuot — no excuses. I wrote you already that our project has been completed, though I am deeply in debt, and I am hoping every day for Reb Nachman to return safely home. Nonetheless, I will not withhold the favor of sending you half a folio page as a sample. It is slightly smudged from having been handled so much, but it is fine, nice work, with God's help. I hope to God that you will soon receive the complete volumes. You will all need to give more money for them, though, as I must pay more than thirty silver rubles per hundred to bring them here and I have no-one left to borrow from. This is besides the fact that I still owe more than a hundred and twenty silver rubles. Salvation is in God's hands. I am confident that you will certainly do everything in your power to support me in this project, so that I will not be in debt, as well as to support me in my livelihood. I have a great many expenses and now in particular, since, praise God, I have arranged a marriage for my son, may he live. Therefore, be sure to bring me money, a little or a lot, both for the project and for my livelihood; and God will finish for you.

The words of your true eternal friend, who prays for you.

Noson of Breslov

425

[*Publisher's note: This letter refers to the final receipt of the printed copies of the* Likutey Eitzot. *Shipping was extremely difficult in those days and severely handicapped by the Czar's ban on printed Chassidic works. Thus, receiving the published copies took a very long time. In addition, at this time Reb Noson initiated the printing of his own writings, the* Likutey Halakhot, *which took place in Iassi, and references to "the project" refer to this work.]*

With thanks to God, Monday, Behar, the 30th day of the Omer, 5603, Uman.

Warm greetings and blessing to my honored, beloved friend whom I love as myself, the learned, distinguished and illustrious Reb Avraham Ber, may he live; and to my learned, illustrious friend, Reb Abele, along with all his family, may they live.

I do not have time to write very much. I arrived safely here in Uman on Tuesday of last week and I intend to stay on here until Lag b'Omer [the 33rd day of the Omer]. Then, God willing, I will travel to Teplik for Shabbat and from there — homeward. May God guide me on my way. I discovered upon my arrival here that the oil had run out and that the *ner tamid* [eternal light] was not burning at the Rebbe's holy gravesite. I am informing you of this, so that you will be sure to bring oil, if you come yourselves, or to send money for oil to my son Reb Yitzchak, may his light shine, in Tulchin, so that the eternal flame will not stand extinguished, God forbid. This flame effects a sweetening of harsh judgments for you, for us and for our entire group. In the meantime, I was forced to purchase oil on credit, until you come and pay off the debt. Be sure to do exactly as I say. Salvation is in God's hands.

As far as our work is concerned, I have already informed you several times that I am deeply in debt. I am waiting constantly for salvation and for your safe arrival here. You should be certain to bring me whatever money you can and God will do what is good. Reb Nachman, may his light shine, has not yet come and I do not know if he will be here for Shavuot. As a result of his delay, he might work there on the book *Likutey Eitzot*. The truth is that I yearn deeply for this book to be published. It is very difficult for me, though, to take on any more debts, God forbid, and I am really at a loss about what to do. God willing, when you come to Breslov for Shavuot, we will speak face to face and God's counsel will emerge. I am confident that you will certainly work for the good of the project with all your might, as well as for the requirements of my own livelihood, and in particular to cover the expenses of the approaching holiday of Shavuot which amount to a very large sum indeed. May God have compassion and may He abundantly bestow all good. May you be the agents through which a mitzvah is performed and may this merit devolve upon you. Your charity will stand you in good stead — because this work of mine will benefit the wider community on an absolutely enormous scale for generations to come. "Deep, deep. Who can fathom it?" But you must help and support me very, very much. Salvation is in God's hands.

The words of your true, eternal friend, waiting for salvation at all times.

Noson of Breslov

426

With thanks to God, Friday, Erev Shabbat, the 41st day of the Counting of the Children of Israel, 5603.

Greetings to my beloved son, may he live.

Mazal tov! My daughter, your sister, may she live, gave

birth to a boy last night! May it be God's will that he will bring
us all good *mazal*, happiness, joy, and complete salvation in all
that each one of us needs to be saved. Amen. May it be His will.

May God allow me, you and all of us, at least from now on,
to prepare ourselves as we should for the approaching holy
festival of Shavuot. May we merit to pour our hearts out like
water before God over how very far we are from the holiness
of Shavuot, which is a great, highly refined level of understanding and great, pure and abundant compassion (*Likutey
Moharan* I, 56:7). Perhaps we will be answered and merit, at least
from now on, to direct all our longing, yearning, desire and
hope toward truly drawing closer to God anew every day,
wherever we may be; and no matter what happens with a
person, wherever he may find himself, from *there* he should
search for God every day, because "no good desire is ever lost"
(*Zohar* II, 150). We will not be taken in by the foolishness of wealth,
God forbid, because all is vanity. And whether a person has
money or not, his days will pass all the same. The main thing is
good desire (*Rabbi Nachman's Wisdom* #51). May God grant us the joy of
Shavuot and "let us rejoice over the words of Your Torah and
Your commandments forever and ever." For they alone are our
life, etc.

The words of your father,

Noson of Breslov

427

With God's help, Wednesday, Naso, 5603.

My dear, beloved son.

I received your letter just now and I am standing and waiting here for God's salvation — for our friend to arrive soon. Our friend Reb Yisrael, may his light shine, cannot do anything right now, until our friend's safe arrival.

The messenger was paid one gold piece and may the Master of Salvation send salvation soon. Reb David found the two tzitzit, but he does not want to travel home until after Shabbat. He said that he will send them to you at the first opportunity. It is also very surprising to me that the man wants them for such a high price, but anyway he cannot do anything until the arrival of our aforementioned friend. But Reb Yisrael, may his light shine, asks you, and I too encourage you in this, for our sake to check into this matter whenever you come across merchants who deal in this. Maybe you will find them for less. It should also be a reliable person. But the deal cannot be closed until our friend arrives.

Reb David, may his light shine, just came into my room and told me that he gave over the two tzitzit to the deliverer of this letter. I am extremely busy and it is impossible to continue. May God bring you to joy and strengthen you so that you will neither worry nor think any unnecessary or extraneous thoughts at all. Just spend your day in Torah, prayer and good desires and yearnings to God. Conduct your business with faith and fortify yourself to be happy that we merited what we have — to grab some good and to know about the point of truth. Let us be happy and rejoice in His salvation!

The words of your father,

Noson of Breslov

428

With God's help, Friday, Erev Shabbat, Behaalotekha.

Warm greetings to my beloved friend whom I love as myself, the learned, illustrious and distinguished Reb Abba, may his light shine; along with all his children, may they live.

I received your letter and I saw your enormous yearning and your heart's burning for the truth. This caused me both joy and pain. It caused me joy, since I saw the goodness of your heart which longs for "God's courtyards"; and pain, over the many barriers which prevent you from fulfilling your good desire and which, for the most part, exist only in your mind and heart. But the desire and good yearnings are also very precious. May you feel this way all your life, to yearn and long for God and His holy Torah, until you merit at all times to fulfill your good desire and wish, and to truly do the will of your Creator —the purpose for which you were created. How terribly pained I was that you did not merit to be here together with us this past festival of Shavuot. God willing, when we get together, we will discuss this with God's lovingkindness and great salvation. For now, though, fortify yourself mightily each day to grab Torah study and prayer with concentration and feeling to whatever degree you can, and in particular to express yourself before God and to turn the Rebbe's Torah lessons into prayers. This means both to say the prayers which God has already helped me set down before you, which flow forth from the Rebbe's holy teachings and which are wondrous new creations the like of which have never existed; and also to make prayers for yourself from the Torah lessons according to what you are experiencing at any given time. The holiness of Shabbat is approaching and it is impossible to continue at all.

> The words of your true, eternal friend. You also
> have before you the letter that I wrote to my friend,
> Reb Avraham Ber, may he live. Be sure to read it.
> He should also read this letter of yours, as should
> the other young men, our comrades who desire to
> hear words of truth. All of them will hear and learn
> to do good.
>
> *Noson of Breslov*

429

With thanks to God, Monday, Shelach, 5603, Breslov.

To my dear, beloved son, may he live. Peace, life and all good to you, your wife and your children, may they live.

I received your letter last week. I read it carefully and, despite the pain and grief that it expressed, I managed to strengthen myself with happiness. For I saw that, amidst your enormous pain and your bitter plaint which have persisted now for so long, amidst the sweep of your distress, you nonetheless inspire yourself and give life to your soul with the "exquisite delights" which you received from afar from the holy words, "the consummately pure and refined utterances of God," which emanate from "the flowing stream, the source of wisdom." This is the way! This is my comfort in my destitution and this is your comfort and the comfort of all Israel.

For in all the generations preceding us as well, every single individual endured all that he did every single day of his life. It was about this that King Solomon, may he rest in peace, cried out (Ecclesiastes 2:17), "How evil is the drama which takes place under the sun!" There are many other similar statements in which he cries out bitterly over the drama which takes place under the sun. He laments in particular the pointless con-templation — the convoluted, negative thinking and ruminat-ing which repeatedly surround a person and which are described in the phrase "my heart is dizzy" (Psalms 38:11). We do not *know* about the past. We only remotely understand that certain things occurred then and that this is why the exile has continued for so long and we have not yet returned to our land. This certainly applies to this present generation, since now the responsibility lies with us.

As I have already spoken about extensively, everything that is said in the words of our Rabbis, of blessed memory, and in the other holy books about how all the worlds depend upon the person in This World, only applies to the people *alive* in This World during that particular generation. Thus, now, the rec-tification of all the worlds and the opposite, God forbid, depends entirely upon me and you and on every individual now living on the earth, for "the dead do not praise God" (Psalms

115:17) and "the dead are free" (Psalms 88:6). This is precisely the reason that the Evil One so vehemently assails every single person each and every day — and practically all the time. This is particularly true for those who desire and yearn to abandon their folly and "to come into the holy." It is at *them* that the Evil One directs all his attacks, as our Rabbis, of blessed memory, said in a number of places (*Sukkah* 52a; *Kidushin* 30b), "The Evil Urge ignores the entire world and only provokes Israel. And he ignores all of Israel and only provokes Torah scholars." These Torah scholars are the students and youths who come to draw close to the place where the point of truth shines. But the battle is very fierce and the souls are very weak.

Had God not helped us beforehand by shining all good upon us so abundantly so that we came to know about the light of the Rebbe's holy Torah teachings and about his holy hints, all of which are "pure utterances," "exquisite delights" — and above all, were it not for the Rebbe's great, never-flagging power which he explicitly told us to rely on saying, "Rely on my power!" (*Tzaddik* #88, 122) — we would already have perished in our destitution. Thus it is written (Psalms 119:92), "Had Your Torah not been my delight, I would have perished in my destitution"; and, similarly "This is my comfort in my destitution — Your Word has given me life" (Psalms 119:50).

Now, that we have already merited to bask in the true, pleasant light of the Rebbe's Torah teachings which revive the soul and enlighten a complete ignoramus, until, through God's compassion, I merit to see in your letter, in the midst of your bitter lament, that you speak about awesome wonders, the likes of which have never been heard! For there you wrote that you are encouraging yourself with the power of the elder who can retrieve all the arrows even after they have been shot and with the power of all the ten kinds of song (*Rabbi Nachman's Stories*; The Seven Beggars, pp.410ff.). And you wrote that you must bind all kinds of "exquisite delights" from the Rebbe's teachings to your thoughts in order to give life to your soul.

This is just what I want! This is precisely how the Rebbe rescues a person and it is exactly what *he* wanted — that his holy words should enter the heart like arrows shot from the hand of a warrior and that people should use them to encourage themselves amidst the thick darkness to turn grief and sighing into happiness and joy! Fortify yourself with the utmost determination, my son, and begin each day to prevail in all the holy ways that the Rebbe taught to rid yourself of your confused thoughts and bad ruminations! For, nonetheless, his words are still true and correct: it is impossible to think two thoughts at once and a person *can* direct his thoughts as he wishes. Even if sometimes the mind swerves and flies off into bad places, into the filthy places, God spare us, it *is* in a person's power to turn his thoughts at will in the opposite direction, just as one grabs a horse by the halter and brings it back to the straight path (*Likutey Moharan* II, 50). Know and believe that all this has already helped you immensely; it is only that the Evil One keeps on attacking. For he is extremely persistent and a person must therefore also be equally persistent to remain on the side of holiness. The main thing is to believe that, no matter how inferior a person may be, every time he conquers his thoughts in this way it is extremely precious to God (*Likutey Moharan* I, 233).

I have already spoken about this extensively, but the "old and foolish king" [i.e. the Evil Urge] does not hear all this. He keeps infiltrating and attacking so strongly. It is as if he is describing to us his old foolishness for the very first time. Therefore, a person must summon his strength and believe anew in all the holy advice and words of inspiration, and he must *sound them* into his mind as if for the very first time! Do not let them grow old for you because they are constantly renewing themselves, especially since God with His wonders has helped me develop many new teachings based upon them. Again and again I see new kindnesses — to the point that this year too, by God's kindness, we have completed all that we have through the agency of Reb Nachman, may his light shine. I yearn for him to come soon and I hope and trust to God that he will. I am now waiting every moment for him to arrive, through God's salvation, safely and unscathed, and that with God's kindness all will be as it should. We have no-one to lean on except our Father in Heaven.

The words of your father, waiting for salvation.

Noson of Breslov

Greetings to all our comrades with a great love; in particular to my friend, the illustrious Reb Nachman, may his light shine, grandson of our master, teacher and Rebbe, of blessed memory.

I also received the letter from Reb Mordekhai on Friday and you can be sure that I was simply "delighted." I nonetheless

trust in God's lovingkindness that He will also help him and
that He will certainly not abandon him. At the end of his letter,
in which he describes the bitter pain that he has over his
livelihood and the humiliation that he has been experiencing,
he mentions the bitterness caused him by his thoughts. One
trouble on top of another, God save us. But, quite to the contrary, precisely *because* of this, I said, we can turn everything
around to the good! For since we see that he is still being so
fiercely attacked, and that the battle is raging around him on
every front, we must therefore understand and believe that his
drawing close to the point of truth is a matter of no small import
and that through it he has indeed achieved a tremendous
amount.

This is the reason they are assailing him so! The power of
the elder of holiness surpasses all else, though, and "God is a
Man of War." Without a doubt He will also subjugate and put
down Reb Mordekhai's attackers, who exchange a world that
endures forever for a passing one, and who go on to brazenly
abuse his entire vitality and good point! He ought to be dancing
and rejoicing that he merited to be in our portion! It is already
known that all other idlers and money-changers are also constantly quarrelling; but him they are abusing for the most
honorable thing that he has — that which is his entire vitality!
He should trust God and rely on Him, that He will certainly not
abandon him and that everything will turn out for the best. He
too should read the above letter carefully and he should pay
close attention to these words. Let him constantly awaken anew
like a person waking up from his sleep. Most of all, he should

also "sit and do nothing" in his thoughts as well and he should flee from sadness with all his might. He should turn all kinds of grief and sighing into joy, particularly the very abuse that he is suffering, in that he merited to escape from being an opponent to the essence of his vitality forever.

430

With God's help, Monday, Masai, 5603, Teplik.

Peace and life to my dear, beloved son, the illustrious and distinguished Reb Yitzchak, may he live; along with all his children, may they live.

I received your letter here in Teplik today through the messenger who is the deliverer of this letter and I read it carefully. I was really not as shocked as you imagined I would be. Your whole story is nothing new for me at all and many righteous Jewish souls have gone through the same thing. I too endured even more than this, and now too many people are experiencing just the same sort of things. There are a great many people, however, who are much, much worse off than this, and *they* are not crying out about it at all. While the crying out is certainly of great value — for "crying out is good for a person" (Rosh HaShanah 16a) and "even if a sharp sword is being held to a person's throat, he should not despair of asking God for compassion" (Berakhot 10a). Our master, teacher and Rebbe, of blessed memory, the holy light, also stressed this point emphatically. But all the same, when the pain and crying out turn towards depression, sadness and grief, they are most harmful. Our master, teacher and Rebbe, of blessed memory, said that depression is extremely injurious when it added to those evil urges which fall into the category of "utter stupidity," as is written in *Likutey Moharan* (I, 72) and in many other places.

It is explained there that the more a person tries to push these thoughts away, the more they strengthen themselves. But he must simply "mentally" not look over his shoulder and not look at them at all. Even if they are raging furiously, he must not fear them in the least. And if they nonetheless keep on surrounding him — what can he do? The Torah exempts cases of duress. Yesterday someone else came to me and lamented to me that his wife has been sick for three years now, God spare us. There are many such cases. The truth is that your suffering is not insignificant and when you feel pain, so do I. We certainly do need a great deal of prayer and supplication to God, both on your part and mine. But it is crucial to do what the Rebbe, of blessed memory, instructed us: to designate an hour to express oneself before God and to tell Him everything in one's heart. If you are unable to speak, what can you do? Most of the time God will help a person to express himself later on that day or the next day. But in any case, a person must fortify himself determinedly to be happy the rest of the day and to spend it in a little prayer and Torah study and in taking care of his business.

Thank God, you have a number of matters to tend to and you can really pass the day in "Torah and worldly matters"; and "exerting himself in both of them makes a person forget sin" (*Avot* 2:2). The main thing is not to look back at all, not to look over your shoulder and not to be overly affected by the pain. For you have no idea what is taking place in the world to the righteous, the middling and the evildoers in every generation with every person every single day. "Everyone needs the possessors of wheat" (*Berakhot* 64a), that is, the truly compassionate leader. *Ashreinu!* How fortunate we are that we know about him and do not oppose him! We even work to follow his pathways and we gather together on Rosh HaShanah! God is my hope that you too will be counted among us during the coming holy days of Rosh HaShanah. So may it be every year of your life! This is our comfort in our destitution!

I had wanted to say more, but it is difficult and uncomfortable for me to write because of the pain in my ribs. God has already helped me tremendously, but the little pain that has not yet disappeared makes it very hard to write. Out of my love for you, though, I pushed myself to write these words and, God willing, I will write you more from Uman, with His kindness and compassion. Salvation is in God's hands. May everything quickly be rectified and turned to the good. Everything is for the purpose of spiritual rectification and a person must pass through all these kinds of places in order to be purified. This whole subject contains many hidden matters, but the most important thing is that a person should have a strong pillar to hold onto. How fortunate we are to have a firm foundation such as this tzaddik, the foundation of the world! He will certainly rectify us in This World and the Next.

The words of your father, waiting for salvation.

Noson of Breslov

Greetings to all our comrades with a great love!

431

With thanks to God, Thursday, Erev Rosh Chodesh Menachem Av, 5603, Uman.

Greetings to my dear, beloved son.

I sent you an answer from Teplik through the carrier and I arrived here safely on Tuesday, thank God. I have given twenty new rubles to Reb Shaul, may his light shine. You should take five new rubles from it for yourself. Mark it down as money received for the project and take it as repayment for money you lent. The scribe is to receive six new rubles, which were given to me in Teplik toward the Sefer Torah he is writing in Savran. Send these six new rubles to my daughter Chanah Tsirel, may she live. In addition to this, you should send her three new rubles from the people in Tcherin toward the Sefer Torah, which she should give to the scribe for parchment, should he need them for the Sefer Torah. I previously told Reb Nachman, may his light shine, to tell you that, if necessary, you should give money for parchment; and I am now sending three new rubles for this purpose to my daughter. If in due course the scribe needs more, you should give a small sum on my account. I do not think you will need to, though, as I will instruct my son, David Zvi, may he live. But, if my son does ask you to give some money for the scribe, do as he asks. In accordance with the salvation that God showers upon us, I will send you more money from Tcherin. Salvation is in God's hands. You should send the six new rubles remaining from the original sum to Reb

Shimshon or to Reb Shmelke, may they live, towards what they give my family for living expenses.

I am waiting every day for good news about the merchandise. I already said that if it does arrive there in time for it to reach Terhovitza by Monday the week of Parashat Va'etchanan — that would be wonderful. This seems highly unlikely though. As far as the Sefer Torah is concerned, they should proceed as God's counsel dictates and as I discussed with them.

In connection with your own situation, I already wrote you briefly and at the moment I am too busy and worn out to say anything. Fortify yourself determinedly, though, my son, and believe in everything that our master, teacher and Rebbe, of blessed memory, said, that every little step that a person takes to remove himself from evil in the direction of good is highly precious to God (*Likutey Moharan* II, 48)! Above all, accustom yourself in the midst of their fierce attacks to keep yourself happy any way you can. Do not be daunted in the slightest. Just turn your mind from them completely and get the habit of forgetting, i.e. forget at each moment whatever happened in the previous moment. No matter how serious it was — what's done is done and everything will turn out for the best. For we have an Ancient Father who is extremely powerful and He can turn sins into merits. Just fortify yourself with the utmost determination and remember that "a person in This World must pass over a very narrow bridge. The main thing is not to be afraid at all" (*Likutey Moharan* II, 48). The Rebbe spoke about this at length. A great deal has already been printed and written, but it is necessary to review it every day. God is great and highly to be praised! "God is great and we know absolutely nothing of it. Even when it comes to *you* people... For there is a phenomenon which transforms everything into good."

> The words of your father waiting to bring you to joy and to encourage you, until you merit complete salvation.

Remember too what is written in the Midrash (*Bereishit Rabbah 34:2*), "When the flax worker knows that his flax is good, he beats it more." This same idea is expressed several times in *Midrash Eikhah* as well. All this is stated there in the words of the Rebbe, of blessed memory, to teach that a person should be encouraged if he sees that his desires are pursuing him furiously. For from the fact that he is being refined and tested, he knows that there is a great deal for him to attain. It is impossible to explain this in all its facets, especially since all our strength and hope rest upon the power of the elder of holiness and, thank God, we have more than enough to lean on — no matter what! How very abundantly has God bestowed His kindness upon us that we merited to escape from opposing him, God forbid. May God finish well for us. Let us be happy and rejoice in His salvation!

Noson of Breslov

Give Reb Nachman two or three gold coins each week, as I discussed with you, and also give him five gold coins for his rent. He told me that you deducted from his weekly income the ten gold coins you gave him for rent. It is imperative that you return this to him. In the meantime, you should just give him the aforementioned five gold coins and I will write you further from Tcherin. [Silver rubles were the Russian currency. Gold coins were Polish ducats.]

Shabbat has just passed (the letter was delayed here) and I have a great deal to discuss with you. But it is Saturday night, and I am feeling weak. I only want to point something out to you in connection with what you are always writing, i.e. that your habit of thinking a lot about everything is causing you such suffering and confusion. I would just like to respond to you that the whole situation in which you find yourself does not make any sense. There is no obligation, God forbid, to think so much! To the contrary! Our master, teacher and Rebbe, of blessed memory, warned us many times against excessive thinking. He explicitly said that this practice, which is called *ibertrachten*, "dwelling on something," causes a person tremendous distress, God save us. If you are already accustomed to doing this, you must try to break the habit and prevail on each occasion to distract your mind and not to ruminate about anything. In particular, you must flee from bad thoughts and musings completely and not allow your thoughts to return to them at all. You must constantly forget whatever happened previously and trust in the Rebbe's great power that everything will be transformed into good. Just fortify yourself and be strong to carry out all this and "with the departure of the day of rest, may God provide you relief."

Noson, the same

432

With thanks to God, Thursday, Erev Rosh Chodesh Menachem Av, 5603.

Greetings to my beloved son, the learned Reb David Zvi, may his light shine.

I sent a letter to my son, your brother, Reb Yitzchak, may his light shine, in Tulchin, and he is going to send six new rubles to my daughter, your sister, Chanah Tsirel, may she live. I received these six new rubles in Teplik for the Sefer Torah of Savran. I am also sending my daughter three new rubles for the Sefer Torah for Tcherin, though the scribe may not need money for parchment. Understand, my son, how to proceed prudently with the scribe, so that he does not grab any money before writing either for the Sefer Torah for Reb Zvi from Tcherin or for the one of Savran. Tell the scribe that I am irritated with him. He told me that he had only received a deposit from Reb Shlomo of Savran, but Reb Shlomo told me that he gave him six new rubles, three for the deposit and three for parchment. He should therefore already have three new rubles' worth of parchment for the Sefer Torah of Savran. I am suffering over this lest there be, God forbid, a desecration of God's Name if he does not act correctly in this matter. Therefore, from now on, do not give him money for parchment unless you see that he takes the money to buy it right away. Most likely you will understand the proper way to deal with him, as I discussed with you at my home.

Now, my son, fortify yourself determinedly to start from

now on to engage every day in Torah study and prayer. Set fixed study sessions for Talmud, Codes, Chumash with the commentary of Rashi and NaCh. In particular, be certain to study every day the books of our master, teacher and Rebbe, of blessed memory. Study them with friends sometimes, and look at them carefully to understand how to practice what you learn. If you cannot study with others, study on your own. Guard yourself with the utmost care from anger, depression and fastidiousness with others, so as not to destroy your vitality over nothing. Fulfill, "Banish anger from your heart — remove evil from your flesh" (Ecclesiastes 11:10). For God's sake, take pity on yourself! For, "If not now, when?" since, now, you have no concerns or business to attend to, only Torah study, prayer and fulfilling commandments. Remember your Creator in the days of your youth. I have no time to continue any longer.

> The words of your father, encouraging you for your eternal good and praying for you.

> *Noson of Breslov*

433

With thanks to God, Tuesday, Devarim, 5603, Uman.

Greetings and salvation to my son, Reb Yitzchak, may he live; along with all his children, may they live.

I sent you a letter last Sunday with two of our comrades who were here at the Rebbe's holy gravesite, Reb Matil, the son of Reb Sh.A., and Reb Nisan, a relative of the rav. I am certain you received it. I informed you there that I gave twenty new rubles to Reb Shaul, and that you should give nine of them to my daughter, may she live, for the scribe. Five of them you were to take for yourself, marking them down as money for the project, and six of them you were to send to Reb Shimshon or Reb Shmelke for my family's expenses. I also wrote you a number of things which revive and encourage sighing, downcast souls like you, me, all our comrades and all the Jewish souls in distress and captivity. The physical exile continues and there is talk of "less than favorable" decrees. The Holy Temple is in ruins because of our sins. Above all, a spiritual exile reigns over our people as a whole and over every individual, and the strength to endure it is just about exhausted. For I too, poor man that I am, know explicitly the sufferings of a great many people, in addition to what I infer from near and from far.

May the Master of Compassion and Salvation rectify it all. May He send us "the compassionate leader" to fulfill, "The one who has compassion on them will lead them" (*Likutey Moharan* II, 7). The ultimate compassion is to take Israel out of sin, and the essence of this is to remove them from madness and folly and to instill them with knowledge, *daat*. Then they will understand his holy hints about how to flee from folly and divert the mind from it, and how to escape through "sitting and doing nothing."

Ask Reb Nachman, may his light shine, and he will tell you how very delighted one person was by what he saw in the new book — what I wrote on the verse, "And he [Yaakov] stole the heart of Lavan, the Aramite, and did not tell him he was fleeing" (see *Likutey Halakhot*, *Tefilin* 6:35). Listen carefully to this and pay close attention! Put what I wrote there into *practice* to divert your mind from these thoughts and it will serve you well, with God's help. Accustom yourself from now on to study diligently the books of discourses that God has granted me to innovate from the Rebbe's holy Torah lessons, i.e. in *Likutey Halakhot*. Study them every day and at all times, especially the discourses which I have written in more recent years. God is my hope that you will greatly benefit from them.

Now, my son, really fortify yourself to grab hold of your thoughts however you can! When you are transacting business, put your mind to that. Let it all be with joy and without anger, sadness, worries or depression. While praying, force your thoughts into what you are saying and bind them to the words with a tight, mighty bond. Even if you have to pray quickly — just keep your mind from extraneous thoughts. And even if your mind does suddenly steal away and flies off to wherever it does, forcefully grab it like a horse by its halter and return it to the holy words of the prayers. Even more so, when you are studying, keep your thoughts on your studies; and here it is easier, since after all you must understand what you are studying. Do not be concerned in the least over what else might happen to you. The main thing is to keep yourself from doing any evil. I have already spoken extensively about the power of the elder of holiness who himself said that, even if he were to commit the greatest possible sin, it would still not cause him to fall. After sinning, he would still be righteous, just as he was before. It is only that afterwards he would repent (*Tzaddik* #453).

I intend to travel tomorrow, God willing, to Terhovitza and from there in His kindness God will lead me to Tcherin for

Shabbat Nachamu. I will probably be receiving letters from you there. May the Master of Compassion send salvation and may He allow me to hear good news from you. May I also merit to hear good news about our merchandise. Thank God, the pain that I had is already much better, by His kindness, but I still need God's salvation for it to heal up completely. Most important, though, is the *spiritual* cure — and that is joy. For if we would just be happy, all the foolishness that we talked about above would automatically disappear. But how precious are Your kindnesses, God, that we heard the story about the one who has the power in his hands to cure the king's daughter and to remove all the arrows from her (Rabbi Nachman's Stories, The Seven Beggars, pp.410ff)! Her entire cure is joy which is generated by the ten kinds of song. *Ashreinu*! How fortunate we are! And how fortunate you are too that you are not an opponent of a marvel such as this!

The words of your father, waiting for salvation.

Noson of Breslov

Greetings to all our comrades with a great love!

434

With God's help, Tuesday, Ekev, 5603, Tcherin.

Greetings to my dear, beloved son, the learned Reb Yitzchak, may his light shine; along with all his children, may they live.

I received your letter last Shabbat and I already sent you another letter from Uman through Reb David. I had wanted to send it with the post, but it was delayed, as Reb David told you. It is now before the Morning Prayers, so I cannot write much at present. You are receiving twenty new rubles. Ten of them you should send to Breslov to Reb Shimshon and Reb Shmelke, may they live, for my family's expenses as I arranged with them; and the other ten you should retain in your possession. I intend to travel tomorrow, God willing, to Kremenchug for this coming Shabbat and from there to return here, God willing. I will remain here for Shabbat Parashat Shoftim which is Rosh Chodesh Elul and then travel from here to Medvedevka for the following Shabbat. Then I will go back to Uman. May God guide me on the straight path. May He grant me a safe journey in accordance with His will, which is good, and with the will of those who fear Him.

Regarding the books, it is certainly necessary to send for them. But do not make a large expenditure for only twenty of them. Rather consider the matter carefully, with God's counsel — perhaps you will be able to bring all the books which, as you know, were recently deposited there. I am confident that you will proceed in the best possible way, so that they will reach you soon and you will be able to bring many books for Rosh Ha-Shanah. It is worth spending money even for twenty, but not a large sum. You will understand all this for yourself and God's counsel will emerge.

I read your letter carefully and my comfort is that, thank God, you are following the Rebbe's pathways a little. May God strengthen your heart and mine and may He soon bring you to joy. Continue to accustom yourself more and more to studying the Rebbe's teachings every day. Endeavor to understand his hints clearly and to put them into practice as is fitting. You yourself already wrote that it is necessary to keep silent and that one knows nothing at all.

Praise God, last Shabbat, Shabbat Nachamu, I spoke some amazing new ideas about the holy lesson "The one who has compassion on them will lead them" in which the dictum "Silence is a fence for wisdom" is discussed (*Likutey Moharan* II, 7:8). I explained, with God's help, the three times that the word "*Eikhah*" (How?) is used, as well as the words "*Nachamu, Nachamu*" (Take comfort, take comfort!) (see *Likutey Halakhot, Netilat Yadayim LiSeudah* 6:80-82). The crucial point is that with the Rebbe's great power there is hope for us all, no matter what, and for all Israel.

Praise God, I really inspired the entire audience with my words which flowed forth from the fount of the Rebbe's holy wisdom. *Ashreinu!* Happy are we that we merited to be in his holy portion! It is impossible to explain what I said in this context, as the discourse was quite lengthy — and more than this remains in my heart. But a person — and you, you, in particular, my son — must constantly remember that one knows absolutely nothing and you do not even know what it is you do not know. However, it is crystal clear that, no matter what you are experiencing, whatever you are guilty of and whatever duress you are under; whatever your standard of observance of commandments and whatever good points you grab every day with God's amazing kindness and salvation amidst everything you are going through — with all this, God's kindness to you has been very great indeed that you merited to be in the Rebbe's portion, to hail in his holy name, and to be included in his holy gathering, and especially on Rosh Ha-Shanah, which is the essential time of the *kibutz* (gathering)!

This is the idea of the shofar which gathers in all the exiled of His People Israel, as we pray in the blessing "Sound a great shofar for our freedom and raise a banner to gather in our exiles" [*Amidah*]. This past Shabbat Nachamu I spoke extensively about the wondrous, awesome exaltedness of every gathering of ten Jews. For "the Divine Presence *Shekhinah* dwells upon every group of ten" (*Sanhedrin* 39a) and they may then pronounce those prayers which have a special degree of holiness. Then they awaken with greater potency all "those who dwell above" and all "those who dwell below" to publicly sanctify God's Name and to make known that "the whole world is full of His glory." Then *everyone* can be lifted up!

The key, though, is that they be bound to the true shepherd who is working to gather in his flock, as is written, "as a shepherd tends his flock, gathering in the sheep with his arm and carrying the lambs in his breast" (Isaiah 40:11). At the very least they must not oppose him, God forbid! For woe to the one who separates himself from a shepherd of Israel such as this! How very fortunate is the one who longs and yearns to be included in his holy gathering! With His kindness, we will never be ashamed, no matter what each of us may go through. The Rebbe's power is great, awesome and exalted in the extreme. It is beyond anything we can fathom! I recently heard from my illustrious friend, Reb Gershon, may his light shine, grandson of the Magid, of blessed memory, from Terhovitza, that he heard from the Rebbe's holy mouth that everyone receives *tikkun* from him on Rosh HaShanah. On Rosh HaShanah everything is rectified, even things that it is not possible to rectify at any other time (*Tzaddik #406*).

It is impossible to elaborate any further because the time for Prayers has arrived.

The words of your father, waiting for salvation.
Noson of Breslov

Greetings to all our comrades with a great love! Give Reb Nachman, may his light shine, two or three gold coins each week as you have been doing until now. Greetings to my friend, Reb Nachman, grandson of our master, teacher and Rebbe, of blessed memory. I do not have time now to write him anything — just that he should come in peace for Rosh HaShanah. Then all will be well, with God's help.

435

With God's help, Monday, the 2nd of Elul, 5603, Tcherin.

Warm greetings to my dear son, the illustrious, learned Reb Yitzchak, may his light shine; along with all his children, may they live — in particular, to my dear grandson, David Zvi, may he live.

I received your letter yesterday, Rosh Chodesh, before Prayers and I felt both pain and delight. At the moment I do not know what to write you. I have already written you a great deal and, besides, the days of Rosh HaShanah are approaching, when we will speak face to face, with God's help. Right now though, my son, fortify yourself mightily and begin to consider the blessing "Who kept us alive, sustained us, and allowed us to reach this time"! "This time" is holy Rosh HaShanah, when we will merit to gather together, with God's help. With this alone I inspire myself. You too ought to be inspiring yourself with the fact that another year has passed and the days of Rosh HaShanah have arrived, when we will gather at the Rebbe's holy gravesite!

The post is leaving soon and it is impossible to write much at all. You are receiving the sum of thirty new rubles. Six of them you should send to Reb Shimshon and Reb Shmelke for my family's expenses and four you should send to my daughter Chanah Tsirel, may she live, for the Sefer Torah of Reb Zvi from here, etc. The other fifteen new rubles you should take for yourself. [Also] mark down five of them for the project and the other ten are mine. You should write down that you received them from here, from Tcherin, and also indicate the day and the time, so that there will be a clear record. Bring me the record at Rosh HaShanah — that is, what you entered since the last accounting that I recently received from you — and also briefly list the total receipts and expenditures, both mine and the project's, from the date of the previous accounting.

Concerning the Sefer Torah, you should proceed in the best possible way and bring it to Uman, with God's help. Your letter to Kremenchug has not yet been sent. You do not, however, need to wait any longer for his letter, because I came from Kremenchug last Shabbat and Reb Efraim told me explicitly several times that he wanted to write you that you should bring *lulavim*.

Regarding our project, I am very pleased that you are working on this. May God soon allow you to come safe and well with the merchandise. All our comrades are eagerly awaiting it. I assume that you will write me soon about the salvation that God in His compassion is performing in this matter. Do not send your letters here any more, though, as I intend to travel to Medvedevka for next Shabbat and after Shabbat to make my way to Uman. I very much want to be there for Shabbat Parashat Ki Teitzei. God will send me salvation. Most likely, I will be receiving letters from you there in accordance with your good custom. Now, my son, fortify yourself determinedly with all the words you have already heard. Always remember the enormous greatness and awesome power of the elder of elders of holiness in whom we take shelter. By his enormous power, everything will be rectified, with God's help. We must give praise at all times to God that He set us apart from those who err and oppose him and be exultantly happy that we hail in the Rebbe's holy name. Rejoicing in God over this is our stronghold against everything that we endure all the time! His kindness to us has been abundant and the truth of God is forever!

> The words of your father, waiting to see you soon alive, well and happy. Let us be happy and rejoice in His salvation! May God in His compassion awaken your heart and the hearts of all of us to fortify ourselves from now on to prepare ourselves for holy Rosh HaShanah. May we be written and sealed for a good year, for good long lives and for peace.
>
> *Noson of Breslov*

Greetings to all our comrades with a great love and to my friend whom I love as myself, the learned, illustrious Reb Yaakov, may his light shine. "In the end, everything is heard." I urge you for your eternal good to come with joy for Rosh HaShanah. Do not look at what disadvantage it may possibly cause to your honey-trade during these days. God has many sources of profit and deliverance and He can send you profit many times greater from some other place. This is especially true on Rosh HaShanah when we are specifically engaged in "sweetening." This is precisely what one does with honey and it is the underlying, mystical meaning of shofar (*Pri Etz Chaim, Shaar HaShofar* 1; see also, *Likutey Halakhot, Netilat Yadayim LiSeudah* 6:89-104). We also eat honey then. Therefore you will certainly attain a much greater "sweetening" in This World and the Next by being counted among us this coming Rosh HaShanah. It is impossible to continue as the post is to leave soon. These few words will suffice for a wise man. For the one who heeds them it will be more pleasant and far sweeter than the finest honey.

Noson, the same

Greetings to my friend whom I cherish as myself, the illustrious, learned "holy fruit," Reb Nachman, may his light shine. I received your letter and I read it carefully. I also gave it to Reb Avraham Dov, may he live. I now need to get it back from him in order to give it to your uncle and brother-in-law, may they live, for them to read. At the moment, though, they are excusing themselves profusely because they have lost a great deal and they have no steady livelihood. All the same, I will make sure to speak to them again. Salvation is in God's hands. As for you, my dear friend, "throw your burden on God and He will sustain you." He will surely not abandon you. God willing, during the days of Rosh HaShanah which are approaching, we will speak face to face about everything in your heart. I also spoke to your in-law, Reb Leible, in Kremenchug. He said that he already has a gift prepared for your daughter, may she live, which he will send with Reb Efraim, may he live, this coming Rosh HaShanah.

> The words of your true friend who loves you heart and soul. Longing for your salvation with all his heart and looking forward to seeing you soon in Uman alive, well and happy.
>
> *Noson, the same*

436

With thanks to God, Sunday, Teitzei, 5603, Medvedevka.

May the Abundantly Kind and Beneficent One shower only good and kindness upon you and your family. May the amazing and awesome power of the lovingkindness of Rosh HaShanah elicited by the one who comprehends Rosh HaShanah in all its profundity, protect and help my dear, illustrious friend, the learned and distinguished man-of-standing, Reb Avraham Abba, may his light shine. Peace, life and all good to him and his family. May his branches spread forth, and may his splendor be like that of an olive tree. May his children and grandchildren sit like olive saplings around his table. Amen. May it be His will.

I received your letter, my dear friend, through our illustrious friend, Reb Avraham Ber, may his light shine. It was close to the start of Shabbat and I read it through carefully. How my heart goes out to you, because I know your pain! But what comforts me in my destitution is that you yourself applied the cure in advance of the blow by consoling yourself and bringing yourself to joy with the holy teachings of "the flowing spring, the source of wisdom" and especially with what I talked to all of you about prior to my journey on the teaching, "Were it not for the salt, the world could not endure the bitterness" (*Likutey Moharan* I, 23).

You wrote me that God had me speak these words just for you. I At the time, I imagined, though, that my words were primarily directed at Reb Yaakov, the son of Reb Z., may his light shine. So with this, my friend, you made me very happy indeed, because I saw the wonders of God and the enormous, amazing and awesome holiness of the Rebbe's holy teachings. In his great power, he is still with me, and again and again he supplies me with words of truth tailored to the point within each person's heart at that particular time. I indeed see myself as destitute, lowly and small in the extreme. But I trust in the great power of the elder of elders of holiness, until on each occasion I see by God's wondrous kindness that I am described in the verse (Isaiah 50:4), "God has given me a tongue of the learned that I can teach just what the hour demands to the person who wishes to hear it."

My dear, beloved friend. I have frequently discussed with you what I heard from the Rebbe's holy mouth. I have shown that many books are full of this and you have witnessed it with your own eyes time and time again. The world is full of suffering, troubles, pain and worries of all kinds, as is written in verse form in the holy *Shelah* [*Shnei Luchot HaBrit*] — "No day is without terror and fear. No moment is without affliction. No year...no *shmita* [seven-year period]...." Look it up there (see *Rabbi Nachman's Wisdom* p.420). But more than this, our master, teacher and Rebbe, of blessed memory, opened my eyes so that I see this constantly right before my eyes. There is no wisdom, no knowledge and no strategy that can save a person from all this except to flee to God and to His holy Torah, and in particular to express himself before God at all times — especially in a time of trouble and stress, when he feels his deficiencies most sharply.

Now, my son, see, understand and grow wise. Remember well everything I have said about how very much we ought to rejoice, take heart and trust God's kindness, and to remind ourselves many times over of the enormous kindness that God did for us in that we have escaped from opposing and dissenting against "the tzaddik, foundation of the world" who is "the eternal covenant of salt." All the sweetening of the world's bitterness is through him! So what would we do if, after all these afflictions, God spare us, we were henceforth to be at odds, God forbid, with our vitality, our root, and our hope? "Had God not been with us... Thank God, Who did not give us over as prey for their teeth." For God's sake, do not let these words grow old for you, even though I have spoken them many times! Fulfill (Proverbs 23:22), "Do not disdain your mother because she is old," as our Rabbis, of blessed memory, explained it (Berakhot 54a). You see that "the old and foolish king" [the evil urge] is constantly attacking as if for the first time. Though in reality his methods are old cliches, he is not ashamed to attack with them anew every time, as our Rabbis, of blessed memory, said. How very much more so, then, must *we* attend to and believe in the words of the Torah of Truth which really *are* new every day and to review daily the Rebbe's holy lessons, conversations and consummately awesome and profound advice!

The key is to look at them completely afresh every day, because they really are literally new every day, as in, "God's kindnesses are never-ending, His compassion never ceases. They are new every morning; great is Your faithfulness." For they flow forth from the elder of elders who said that he is very old and yet completely young (Tzaddik #272; Rabbi Nachman's Stories, #13, The Seven Beggars). Has anything like this ever been heard?! Praise

God, we have someone to lean on and plenty to spare! So fortify yourself determinedly now to pray with concentration and to bind your thoughts to the words of the prayers with a strong and mighty bond. Do not let the prayers be a burden on you, God forbid. Study every day, in particular the Codes and the Rebbe's holy books. Say Psalms and supplementary prayers with concentration and attention, and express yourself before God every day. Above all, summon your strength to be constantly happy, and fortify yourself in strong trust in God's kindness. He will not abandon you, "for with God there is lovingkindness and abundant redemption."

> The words of your true friend forever; praying for you, waiting for your speedy salvation and looking forward to seeing you soon alive, well and happy.
>
> *Noson of Breslov*

Warm greetings to my friend whom I love heart and soul, the illustrious man-of-standing, the "holy fruit," Reb Avraham Ber, may he live, along with all his children, may they live. May God strengthen your heart for Torah, prayer, charity and good deeds, and may you merit to walk in the ways of your ancestors. Begin anew every day, especially during these days when we need to be looking ahead to Rosh HaShanah, which is approaching, that we may merit a good new year, until we attain the long, good life with which the elders of holiness blessed the couple (see *Rabbi Nachman's Stories*, #13). Happy is he who waits for this! Happy is he who merits this! Happy the ear that hears all this! And happy are we who believe in and feel a little of the profundity and awesome holiness of these words, the like of which has never been heard! They all stretch up to the sublimest heavenly heights and beyond, and they reach down into the abyss to give life to each and every one of us in his own place. Who has heard anything like this?! Who has seen things such as these?! Thus far has Your compassion helped us not to completely forget, God forbid, all these awesome wonders and to engage in printing and distributing them. So may God add many times over to the kindness He has done with us, that we may merit to fulfill and to practice the Rebbe's holy words and to illumine the face of the globe with his great and awesome light. Words of truth will endure forever!

Noson, the same

437

With thanks to God, Sunday, Tavo, 5603, Uman.

May the Abundantly Kind and Beneficent One shower His kindness and good upon you by inclining your heart toward Him. May He strengthen you and imbue you with holy inner strength to have the good in you dominate the evil and may you incline to the side of life. May you be written and sealed amidst the holy gathering in the Book of Tzaddikim for a good, long life and for peace. To my dear, beloved son, the learned Reb Yitzchak, may he live; along with all his children, may they live.

I arrived here safely, with God's help, on Thursday of last week, Parashat Ki Teitzei. I had been waiting for good news about our friend Reb Nachman and, praise God, today between

Prayers and going to the holy gravesite, the carrier of good tidings, Reb Nachman, the son of Reb M. HaKohen, came and informed me of God's salvation. Reb Nachman had already safely arrived [from Iassi to Tulchin] with twenty silver [pieces] [a reference to the newly printed *Likutey Halakhot*]! What can I give back to God for all the good He has done for me thus far? How can I repay His compassion and lovingkindness?! If our mouths were filled with song as the sea, it would still not be enough! How deeply I yearned to hear good news about him, particularly since it is before Rosh HaShanah. "It is good to thank God," because, redoubling His kindness, He brought him safely with no anxious waiting at all! "His kindness to us has been abundant and the truth of God stands forever! Hallelu Yah!" Subsequently, I received your letter with this good news. Thank God Who has helped us thus far! Request from God and give your every movement over to Him. He will finish well for you. Amen. May it be His will.

Beyond this there is no time to go on. It is just necessary to believe that everything that happens to a person, no matter what it is, constitutes wondrous hints whereby he may understand God's actions and His unfathomable greatness. Before Rosh HaShanah in particular, it is necessary to give this extra attention. May we all merit to make an auspicious new start on doing this at Rosh HaShanah and may we completely throw off from ourselves all the mental confusion and the like that we have suffered thus far. For nonetheless, a person *can* direct his thoughts as he wishes. In particular, may we merit to put forth many prayers and requests and to speak frequently with our

Creator. May we begin to accustom ourselves to turn the Rebbe's Torah lessons into prayers every day, because this is the most basic foundation and it is above all else. Fortunate is the person who practices this! Praise God, I have an enormous amount to say about this, but the page is too short and the time does not allow.

> The words of your father, waiting to see you soon in joy.
>
> *Noson of Breslov*

Send greetings to my illustrious friend, Reb Nachman Socher [Tulchiner], may he live. If he has not yet set out from his home, be sure that he brings at least one or two pieces of "merchandise." For a number of reasons, I very much need to see them before everyone arrives here. If, for a minimal additional expense, he can come with all fifteen as you mentioned in your letter — so much the better. May God complete everything for the best.

I was surprised that you did not write me greetings from our friend, Reb Nachman, may his light shine, grandson of our master, teacher and Rebbe, of sainted memory, and likewise from Reb Y. Send me news about them through Reb Nachman or in your letter. I will constantly hope for God's salvation in all things, in general, in particular, and right down to the minutest detail — both for physical needs and for the essential healing and sustenance, the healing and sustenance of the soul — for me, for my family, for all those attached to me and for all Israel. Our needs are very, very plentiful indeed; they would be impossible to enumerate. But God can send abundant salvation and all our hopes rest on Him by the power of the elder who blessed the children with long, good lives. Let us be happy and rejoice in His salvation! Amen. May it be His will.

Greetings to all my family in Breslov and to all our comrades.

I received a letter in Tcherin from Reb Efraim, son of Reb Naftali, in which he asked me to write you that you should buy him valid, fine *lulavim* and *hadasim*. May God allow us all to be in the category of "a crying child," until we merit a beautiful *etrog* along with all the other three species (see *Rabbi Nachman's Wisdom* #87). May we merit to smell the good aroma of all the holy commandments, and particularly the holy commandments of this holy month, the coming month of Tishrei. Amen.

Letters from 5604 (1843-44)

The year in review

This year, a milestone in Reb Noson's life, saw the publication of his work, *Likutey Halakhot*. It was printed in Iassi (Modalvia) through the efforts of Reb Nachman Tulchiner. These letters also refer to Reb Noson's efforts to raise funds for the printing of the first volume, as well as to "the project" or "our business" and to Reb Nachman as Reb Nachman "Socher" ("the merchant"). In the summer, Reb Noson's son, Reb Nachman, was married.

Conversely, the year was also a very difficult one for Reb Noson. During the winter, his grandson, the son of Reb David Zvi, passed away. A few weeks later, Reb David Zvi's wife, Chanah, who was pregnant with their second child, also died, leaving Reb David Zvi a childless widower. Also during that same winter, severe storms damaged the *kloyz* (Breslov synagogue) in Uman, destroying the roof. It took until mid-summer to repair it.

438

With thanks to God, Sunday, Hoshana Rabba, 5604.

May you be sealed for good eternally. To my son, may he live, along with all his family, may they live.

I received your letter today before *Barukh Sheamar* (in the Morning Service). I read it immediately, though there was really no time, and you can understand how pained I was. This is especially so since your letter reached me at a time when I was suffering from my abdominal pain and nonetheless, on such a day as this, I was compelled to pray with the congregation. Thus, amidst my preoccupation, confusion and weakness, I received your "good" letter. I nonetheless believe that everything is for the good. I received the sum of three and a half silver rubles and I distributed it as you wished. May the merit of your charity stand by you to rescue you from all evil from now on.

I petitioned God *"Hosha Na!,"* "Save, please!" on your behalf and I asked that I should know how to answer you. But now as well you must encourage yourself with the fact that at least you are not an opponent of truth such as this! For the truth of the matter is that there are people who are far, far worse off than you and, in addition, they are vehement opponents — and they do more damage to themselves and to the world than they do by their many sins. Thank God that He has rescued you from one thing, that at least you are not an opponent! Believe me, there were times when I experienced exactly what you are going through now and even more. It was precisely *then* too that the Rebbe said to me, "'Blessed is our God Who created us for His honor and separated us from those who err.' And also, against *me* you would have fought!" (*Tzaddik* #176). I still encourage myself with this and it is the source of my entire vitality. I do not have time to write you any more about this. I hope to God that He will say "Enough!" to your suffering and to mine and that He will quickly save you. He will not stay at odds forever.

Right now you do not need to think at all about how you will fulfill your daily obligations. Just leap through the day! *Nur iber geshpringen!* Just leap through however you can! (*Tzaddik* #522). Do not think about the past, and certainly not about the future. There is nothing to do! Everything will fly past. We have someone to rely on! God is extremely great and we know nothing at all. He is constantly finishing. You *were* at Rosh HaShanah and you will be again, with God's help. Everything will turn into good through the song played on the 72 stringed instrument (*Likutey Moharan* II, 8:1) and the verse will be fulfilled, "On that day Israel's sin will be sought out" — i.e. they will search and look for the sins in order to turn them into merits — "and they will not be there" — for they will be included in Infinity. The descent is for the purpose of ascent (*Likutey Moharan* I, 22:11). Do not force matters in the slightest and do not start thinking at all.

As for what they are doing to you — do not look at this at all. "Just leap through!" Seize happiness and joy! Now too you need to turn the grief and sighing into happiness and great joy! The worse you think you are, the more you need to rejoice and turn the tremendous grief and sighing into happiness and joy — that a person such as this still merited to be at Rosh HaShanah [in Uman] and to prostrate himself upon a holy and awesome tomb such as this! He [the Rebbe] did not look at this world at all and for him the entire world does not amount to the wink of an eye! He can remove the ten kinds of arrows and he can cure everything (see *Rabbi Nachman's Stories* Story #13, The First Day and Sixth Day). This is the true explanation of "They shall obtain happiness and joy; grief and sighing will flee," which the Rebbe revealed (*Likutey Moharan* II, 23) — to turn all the grief and sighing into happiness and joy, as I just explained. Understand well how to really rejoice with it and do not start thinking at all. Just "leap over the mountains and skip over the hills" — these represent the measures of the song, etc. But *we* need only to "leap through" in the simplest sense. *Nur iber geshpringen!* Just leap through! Really and truly be happy!

> The words of your father,
>
> *Noson of Breslov*

439

With God's help, Wednesday, Noach, Rosh Chodesh Cheshvan, 5604, Breslov.

Greetings to my beloved friend whom I love as myself, the learned and illustrious man-of-standing, the "holy fruit," Reb Avraham Dov Ber, may he live. To him, his wife and all his children, may they live — peace, life and all good. Amen.

Praise God, the days of the Festival passed peacefully and a little joyfully. Your mother and sister, as well as your brother-in-law and his children, may they live, are all, thank God, alive and well. May God grant them life and well-being and sustain them honorably. May the verse soon be fulfilled for all of you (Isaiah 4:2), "The fruit of the earth will attain honor and splendor." Amen. May it be His will.

I have no news to tell you. But all the same I believe and see a little that wondrous new things are taking place every day. God in His goodness renews the Creation constantly every day. For the person who makes the effort to look at this, the changes are occurring every day, and they are all hints to remind us to draw close to God. So it is written in the lesson "At the end of two years — Remembrance" (*Likutey Moharan* I, 54), that a person must bind his thoughts to the Next World in a general way and in all the details of his life and focus his attention every day on the hints that God sends him. For God contracts Himself from Absolute Infinity into the minutest details of the finite world.

Pay very close attention to every lesson, every conversation and every hint contained in his holy teachings and stories. Happy is the person who holds onto them! Study them over and over. Study them every day and look at them carefully. For what God revealed to us in this generation through our holy, awesome Rebbe, of holy, sainted memory, is a matter of no small import. Do not let it grow old for you, God forbid! These teachings are original, new, wondrous and awesome in the extreme and they are constantly new every day all the time! They call out, proclaim and reveal God's Divinity in the world and that "the whole world is full of His glory," and they reveal a straight path and awesome advice to each and every person wherever he may be. I very much want to elaborate and continue talking about this, because it is necessary to speak only about this every moment of every hour, of every day. Other than this everything is worthless; vanity of vanities, totally without substance. [The rest of this letter is missing.]

440

With thanks to God, Thursday, Noach, 5604, Breslov.

Peace, life and all good to my illustrious and distinguished friend, Reb Efraim, may his light shine; along with all his family, may they live.

Praise God, the days of the Festival passed peacefully. Thank God Who has helped us thus far. I am writing now to remind you to be sure to work at collecting the money owed to me for the books, in particular from my illustrious friend, Reb Zvi Hirsh, the son of Reb Y.T., may his light shine, from Krakov. As far as I am concerned, his promise is tantamount to having the money in my pocket — I am only talking about giving him a little extra push. I need money right now, since, as I already mentioned to you briefly, I am deeply in debt as a result of this project.

At present I still have no information about the status of our project and not a single article of our merchandise has reached me yet. But salvation and hope rest with God and I hope that I will soon be receiving what I should. My mind is not at all clear right now because of this, since I cannot decide how to proceed until the arrival of our articles — you know which ones I mean. We have no one to lean on but our Father in Heaven. At present I am deeply in debt. My income is meager and my expenses high, may God have mercy. So it is incumbent upon you to do everything possible both for the good of the project and for the good of my livelihood, since the two of them are intertwined. You are obliged to do your part with all your might and to send me at once: the money from the aforementioned Reb Zvi, the money for the rest of the merchandise that I deposited with you, and whatever you can collect for my livelihood. You should send it all immediately because it is sorely needed right now.

May God finish well for you. May He sustain you honorably and may He send your wife, may she live, a complete recovery. May you merit to raise all your children, may they live, honorably and to good, long lives so that you will merit to truly walk in God's ways in the holy footsteps of our pride and strength, our master, teacher and Rebbe, of holy sainted memory. May you increase holiness and wisdom each day and may you literally be a new being every day, as truly is the case. For it is over this that we make the blessing [in the Morning Prayers] "Who gives strength to the weary," as our Rabbis, of blessed memory have said; and the subject is discussed extensively in the Rebbe's teachings as well.

You and I know well how very much we ought to be making the blessing "Who gives strength to the weary" practically all the time to the One Who gives weary men such as you, me and all our comrades the strength to suffer and bear what we do, for our ability to endure it is nearly exhausted. "If God had not helped us, we would have immediately dwelt in the grave." "Had Your Torah not been my delight, I would have perished in my destitution." It is therefore crucial that you accustom yourself to carrying out the Rebbe's words, which caution us in the strongest terms not to get "old," God forbid. Rather a person must make a new start every hour and certainly every day and he must deeply implant in himself the quality of forgetfulness.

For in this respect it is an excellent practice indeed to forget everything that has taken place up to the present time and not to consider the past at all. And if now too we are going through so many tribulations and we are unable to fulfill our daily obligations, we should nonetheless be happy and rejoice over God's salvation "that He did not make us gentiles" and "that He separated us from those who err" and the like. We must begin from now on to yearn with good, strong desires for God and His Torah and to pray that He do with us what He deems best. For the pursuits of This World and its desires, and the struggle for livelihood are all vanity of vanities. Vanity of vanities, it is all vanity. The food and clothing that God wants to give us, He will certainly give by His generosity, compassion and lovingkindness without excessive involvement and trouble on our part. He alone supports and sustains. Thus may we truly fulfill, "In Him will our hearts rejoice, for we have trusted in His Holy Name." Amen. May it be His will.

Let me know how all our comrades are doing and about you and your son, may he live. In particular, tell me about your son, my friend, Reb Yechiel, may his light shine, his wife, may she live, and about our illustrious friend, Reb Nachman, son of Chanah, grandson of our master, teacher and Rebbe, of blessed memory. Has Reb Nachman already left? What did he accomplish with his in-law and with you? If he is still there, send him loving greetings from me, from our comrades and in particular from his wife and children, may they live, from Tulchin. Reb Nachman from Tulchin is now at my house and he said that the aforementioned Reb Nachman's wife asked him to please send greetings to her husband. May God grant him success and may he return safely home. May he merit to engage in Torah and prayer all his days as befits his holy ancestry. There is no time to continue.

> The words of your true, eternal friend, waiting for your swift response and praying for you.
>
> *Noson of Breslov*

Extend loving greetings to my illustrious friend, the aforementioned Reb Zvi, along with all his household and children, may they live. And also to all our comrades; in particular to my friend, your father-in-law, may his light shine. You should receive from him what he owes — something like ten gold coins — and you should send them along with the other money that you collect. Also send me whatever money you can get for the *beidle*, the booth, but only without quarrelling and insults, God forbid, to fulfill (Psalms 69:7), "Let those who hope in You not be ashamed through me." Just life and peace. Amen.

441

With God's help, before dawn on Wednesday, Chayey Sarah, 5604, Breslov.

Let happiness and joy take over! To my dear, beloved son, the learned Reb Yitzchak, may he live, along with all his children, may they live; and in particular, to his son, my grandson, the distinguished young groom, David Zvi, may he live.

May the Lord of the Heavens and the Earth bless you with *mazal tov* and may the match be a good one in This World and the Next. May the blessing of the Patriarchs see fulfillment in them (Genesis 28:3), "May God Almighty bless you, multiply you and make you numerous." May their young ones go forth and may they be splendrous as olive trees.

You, my dear grandson, David Zvi, strengthen yourself determinedly from now on to be diligent in your studies. Put your head and all your thoughts into your studies and do not ruminate, God forbid; just think about other things. Strive every day to concentrate when you pray — evening, morning and afternoon — and accustom yourself to recite Psalms daily. If you are too busy going to school to study, at least recite a few chapters of Psalms; then when you have time you will say more. You will be fortunate indeed, my son, if you accustom yourself from your childhood and youth to walk in God's ways. Cast off the ways of your youth and guard yourself from doing any evil. Guard your mind vigilantly from thinking extraneous thoughts, God forbid. God willing, you will be here this coming Chanukah, with God's help, and I will speak with you face to face in accordance with your own good desire and initiative. I have related some further words for you to the deliverer of this letter, our friend, may his light shine. Be careful to always be joyful — but not through fighting and arguing with the other youths. Rather be happy and rejoice with the happiness of a Jew in This World and the Next forever. Amen. May it be His will.

My dear, beloved son. I received your letter. How overjoyed I was that God in His compassion, had He helped you! Here you see, my dear son, that God is still with you and with us, and that He is not abandoning you, God forbid. Therefore fortify your heart and take courage! Constantly hope to God, that He will continue to help you in whatever you need to be saved — physically, spiritually and financially. Everything will turn into good through the power of "the towering Eshel [tamarisk] tree" who is the source of our vitality and upon whom we rely. The Rebbe's power is extremely great and mighty in This World and the Next forever and in his great kindness he will neither abandon us nor neglect us. Your eyes will witness wonders, with God's help, as in "you will marvel...and so will I at the great and wondrous kindness that I will do for them."

In connection with the merchandise, you uplifted me tremendously with your last letter. May God encourage you and swiftly save you spiritually and materially. I am now relying on you that you will certainly exert yourself to the utmost in this matter and that you will handle everything in the best possible way, so that you will soon receive all the merchandise, with God's help. Request from God that He guide you with good counsel in this too. For, as we already know, the prayer "guide us with Your good counsel" is an awesome request indeed and a person requires it at all times and in all areas.

How very much you uplifted me when you wrote how you behaved correctly with respect to the project and that amidst your enormous, needless preoccupation over the marriage arrangements, you fortified yourself and took the time to write the letter to there. "You considered your ways; isn't this the main thing" (Psalms 119:59). Subsequently, it worked to your benefit, since you thereby shook off your preoccupation, and you then studied Talmud amidst the commotion of a busy time like this. This is the way! This is just what you should be doing, my dear son! May you always act in this way, to throw off all the things that distract you and to leap and skip out of all the ruminations and confusion into the activities which are really essential! There is never a moment when you cannot find something to engage in just then. On the study of the holy Torah alone a person could spend all the days and years that will ever be, particularly now that, thank God, many books are available such as Tanakh [Bible], Mishnah, Talmud, *Mussar* Literature, the Rebbe's holy books and the discourses that God has helped me to develop.

A person also needs to pray and to express himself before his Creator, or at least he can cry out, or rejoice in his heart that "He created us for His honor and separated us from those who err." It is also necessary to converse with others both about spiritual matters, about necessary business matters and sometimes also for the sake of peace. For this too is a mitzvah, as our Rabbis, of blessed memory, said (Berakhot 17a), "Never was a person first to greet Rabban Yochanan Ben Zakhai" [He always greeted others first]. What is more there are almost always new matters which crop up. Now, for example, you arranged this marriage and at the same time you needed to work for our project. You also have to engage now in all sorts of other business both for yourself and for me. So with all this a person can leap through and flee from what he must without looking back at all and fulfill, "Do not argue with the one who wishes to tempt you" (see *The Aleph-Bet Book Niuf* #10). And if he [the evil urge] comes upon you suddenly as if by compulsion, God forbid, what can you do? The Torah exempts cases of duress. You must simply fortify yourself in joy and flee with all your might by stealing off with your thoughts and diverting yourself in accordance with all the advice, hints and encouragement that the Rebbe taught us.

At present all of my thoughts are on the subject of joy in accordance with the teaching, "They will obtain happiness and joy," to turn all the grief and sighing into happiness and joy (*Likutey Moharan* II, 23); and also along the lines of the teaching "The middle of the world" in Chapter 24 [of *Likutey Moharan* I] which speaks about "the nine chambers which are not lights...." Last Shabbat and the one before, I spoke about this and, praise God, it inspired many souls. May we just merit to speak about this a great deal such that we may merit salvation and fulfill all that is written there, to perform every mitzvah in great joy until we attain everything discussed in these teachings. Happy is the person whose mind chases and strives to grasp these concepts in the way discussed there. There is not time to write any more, as the time for the Morning Prayers is approaching. May God command His kindness by day. Sate us in the morning with Your kindness. Let us rejoice and be happy all our days! Amen. May it be His will.

> The words of your father, praying for you and waiting for your salvation.
>
> *Noson of Breslov*

442

With praise to God, before dawn, Tuesday, Vayishlach, 5604, Breslov.

Greetings to my dear, beloved son, the learned Reb Yitzchak, may he live, and to his children, may they live.

I received your letters with the letter from Reb Shimshon. Regarding yourself, I have already written you a great deal and there is enough there for you to encourage yourself. Beyond this, you should look into the Rebbe's holy books and into what I merited to innovate and explain from them by God's salvation; because all that I write emanates from his words, from "the flowing spring, the source of wisdom." Study them over and over; grow old and gray with them, etc. All the same though, I had wanted to address you at length in accordance with your good desire. But God made everything good in its time and I needed now to send you a letter for Reb Shimson, may his light shine, and for Reb Efraim, may his light shine, in Kremenchug. So I thought that one letter would serve for all. You will understand for yourself that the words of that letter are also meant for you yourself and for all of you, to inspire you and all of us.

The morning light has arrived. God, hear our voice in the morning! May the "morning of Avraham" protect us. May God command his kindness and salvation in the morning to bring us to joy over His salvation at all times. Everything else I have conveyed to the deliverer of this letter and you will understand on your own how you should write to Reb Shimshon. Salvation is in God's hands.

> The words of your father, waiting for your speedy salvation.
>
> *Noson of Breslov*

Peace to all our comrades with great love.

443

With thanks to God, before dawn, the sun will rise, Tuesday, the 12th of Kislev, "And God saw that he [Moses] *went aside to look"* [This verse carries the acrostic of Kislev, the month in which this letter was written], 5604.

Peace, life and lovingkindness to my friend whom I love heart and soul, the illustrious and learned Reb Efraim, may his light shine. To him, his wife and his children — life, peace and all good in This World and the Next forever. Amen. May it be His will.

I received your letter last Friday along with the sum of thirty silver rubles. May God repay your deed and may you receive full reward for exerting yourself on my behalf and on behalf of a holy project like this which is for the eternal good of the wider community. So may you merit to work and to struggle more and more all the time with deeds, with words and, most of all, with intense desire and great longing for the general good, such that by God's salvation you will also have a large share in our project — to spread the Rebbe's teachings and to radiate the light of truth which is the light of truth of the pure menorah, the holy light of Chanukah, which is approaching to us and to all Israel.

Our eyes look to God. "Send Your light and Your truth, they will lead me." Those who hope to God will renew their strength. May the Possessor of Power and Rulership give strength to the weary and might to the weak, and may He allow us all of our days to start and to finish projects such as this to benefit the greater community for the sake of Heaven. God knows that my intentions are good and I am certainly not mistaken in the least, God forbid, in my desire for all of this. But my strength to bear the burden has run out. Old age is coming upon me and the truth is very hidden indeed. Our dear, beloved and fine comrades, the generous of God's People who respect the Rebbe's words and who do contribute as they should (may God give them their reward), even they still do not know what is in my heart about this, and certainly not to mention what I can sense from afar.

It is therefore incumbent now upon you, God's blessed, and upon each and every one of you who cherish a love for me and a love for the truth of our mighty master, teacher and Rebbe, may his merit protect us, to desire and to yearn at all times for all of the above and to express these desires in words and prayer. In the course of doing so you will also be able to express yourself about all of your other deficiencies — physical, spiritual and monetary. May God send you salvation. You must work at this with all your might; and salvation is in God's hands. It is impossible to elaborate any further in this context. I too longed very much to see you amidst joy, but there is a long way between us.

At present all of my work is centered around the lesson "Nine chambers which are not lights..." (*Likutey Moharan* I, 24). Most important is that I and all of us should merit to fulfill what is taught there, that the essential thing is the joy over the performance of commandments. For through this joy, the holiness is culled from the Chambers of Exchanges and it then moves upward triggering a flow of blessing to the intellect and to the organizing and limiting faculty of the mind. At the same time faith is drawn into the mind and into its organizing faculty, until the mind "strikes against the barrier" forming nine chambers. Happy is he whose mind pursues these levels of understanding!

Ashreinu! Fortunate are we! We can indeed say *"Ashreinu!"* thousands and tens of thousands of times every moment that we merited to hear and to see in a book, things such as these! How rapidly was the world declining... [text missing] ...after the destruction of the Temple, until through God's compassion "a holy angel came down from Heaven" to reveal these things in his holiness (cf. Daniel 4:6; see *Likutey Moharan* I, Prologue]. Granted we do not understand these teachings. But nonetheless, the mere revelation by the godly Tanna Rabbi Shimon bar Yokhai of things which had not been revealed since the days of our teacher Moses, as is revealed in the Holy Zohar, still constituted a sprouting of the seeds of salvation. Then how much further had the world declined until we merited in this generation to hear from the mouth of "the flowing spring, the source of wisdom" the holy, awesome advice which can enable a person to attain all this by performing commandments with joy! Praise God, by His wondrous kindness He has already helped me to write explanations of this amazing teaching and to develop original discourses from it through the power of the elder of holiness (see *Likutey Halakhot, Hodaah* 6).

But we still need salvation and abundant compassion if we are to actually *fulfill* this advice to perform the mitzvot with joy and attain all that is written in this lesson. But what comforts me in my destitution is that at least I know about this and I do not, God forbid, oppose awesome, amazing truth like this. What is more... [missing] ...in my heart I am extremely happy that so lowly a person as I merit the next moment to wrap himself in the tzitzit of the large and small talit, to put on tefilin, "the crown of the King" and to recite the entire prayer service — the Morning Blessings, the Sacrifices, *Pesukei d'zimra*, the *Shema Yisrael*, the *Amidah, Ashrei, u'Va l'Tzion* and so on. Perhaps I will even merit to really *mean* some of the words of the service when I say them, so that they will radiate light for me with the Rebbe's great power, to see the "openings in the darkness" to fulfill "make the Ark with three levels" (see *Likutey Moharan* I, 112). Come, let us shout out what God of the Heavens has done for us! Has anything like this ever been heard? Has such a thing ever been seen?

You are aware, my friend, that the wedding of my son, Reb

Nachman, may he live, is approaching. Therefore try to speak prudently with the appropriate people and to enlist their help in covering the wedding expenses. You should also speak with my *mechutenister* (in-law), the wife of the wealthy Reb Yaakov Yeravski and tell her to give appropriately. She should at least send a wedding present. Because just for this you must also make an effort to insure that there will at least be an appropriate wedding gift as is customary nowadays; particularly since you know what happened to my future in-law, may his light shine. May God quickly rescue him completely. In any case, he cannot help with the expenses as would otherwise have been fitting and as a result the burden rests more heavily on me. They must at least receive a sizable wedding gift. The basic wedding expenses are very great, plus there is my own livelihood — and I have young children to support. Our impoverished comrades come and go, God have mercy, [and I must have some provisions for them as well]. I will not go on about this, as you will act quickly on your own. Whenever you get money either for the project or for any of the aforementioned, send it on to me at once. God, Who is good, will quickly finish everything for the good.

The morning light is breaking forth and may your healing quickly sprout. Time for the Morning Prayers is approaching and it is impossible to continue. May God command His kindness by day. May He bring us joy according to our times of pain, and by His amazing kindness may the verse be fulfilled, "They are new every morning, great is Your faithfulness." Look up what is written in *Midrash Rabbah* in this week's Torah reading (see *Bereshit Rabbah* Parashat Vayishlach, 74:1) on the verse, "For the morning has come...." See how the verse "they are new every morning..." is used there, "By the fact that You revive us every morning and that You rejuvenate us during the 'morning' [the ascendancy] of the gentile kingdoms — [therefore we know that] 'great is Your faithfulness' to redeem us." There is an enormous amount to say and to rejoice about all the kindnesses that God has already bestowed upon us by bringing us close to the Rebbe, by allowing us to experience the lovely brilliance of Torah lessons like these, and by giving us confidence that His lovingkindness will never abandon us. As a father has compassion for his son, so will He have compassion on us and bring us to joy with His eternal salvation. God willing, there will be another opportunity to discuss this further.

> The words of your true, eternal friend, waiting for salvation.

> *Noson of Breslov*

Warm greetings to my illustrious and honored friend, Reb Shmuel, may his light shine, along with all his family. Please keep your word and remit the sum that you promised for the books immediately. Reb Efraim, your father-in-law, may he live, sent me money when your honorable person was not at home. Therefore pay this off now at once so that it reaches me quickly with God's help. Peace, life and success in your endeavors such that you will enjoy true... [missing].

> Your true friend,

> *Noson, the same*

Warm greetings to all our comrades, each one of them in accordance with the great honor that he deserves, and in particular to my friend, the illustrious man-of-standing, Reb Zvi Hirsh, may his light shine, to his children and to all his household, may they live. I received the sum that you gave to our friend, Reb Efraim, may his light shine. May God repay your deed. May He command all of His blessings to rest upon you and may He give you success in all of your endeavors. May you merit to perform many more similar acts of charity and may you always have an ever greater share in our work. This is your portion in life for all that you have labored. All of your toil is only for this, as you know. For our master, teacher and Rebbe explained that at the time when a person is transacting business, with every word that he says and with every step that he takes, he must be intending to make money in order to give charity (*Likutey Moharan* I, 29:9). The ultimate form of charity is to give to a righteous person or cause, and no charity is more important than that of supporting the printing. You understand this for yourself. There is no time to continue.

Your eternal friend,

Noson, the same

You should read this letter, because it was also meant for you.

Greetings to my illustrious friend, Reb Yehoshuah, may his light shine. For God's sake, do not depart from what I said when we spoke together and you assured me that you would give at least three new rubles towards the project! You will not receive a book for any less. I ask you now, is it right that the new book not be in your house? I am sure you will do as I say and may God give you success in This World and the Next.

Noson, the same

I too send greetings to my dear friend with a bold love and I thank you for your greetings to me. How good and pleasant is our mutual love. May God help us and may we merit to frequently get together at the home of my honored master, father, teacher and Rav, may his light shine, from whom the light of the true tzaddik radiates today, to receive deep advice from him on how to fulfill the Rebbe's holy words at all times and to bring ourselves to joy. Amen. May it be his will.

Our friend Reb Nachman, the printer, sends his loving greetings.

The words of your eternal friend.

Yitzchak Sternhartz

444

With thanks to God, Wednesday, Vayeishev, 5604, Breslov.

To my friend whom I love as myself, the illustrious Reb Efraim, may his light shine, and to all our comrades — greetings and abundant salvation!

Since the bearer of this letter, our friend, may his light shine, became available, I could not restrain myself from sending you greetings. This is despite the fact that I recently sent you a letter through the post along with a letter from your honored brother-in-law, may his light shine, and five new rubles. I have nothing new to tell you at the moment. You will, I am sure, work for my benefit as is fitting. The days of Chanukah are approaching and I just now wrote a letter to our friend, Reb Abele, may his light shine, and to our comrades. I reminded them about a few of the amazing, awesome teachings that we heard about Chanukah. *Ashreinu!* Happy are we! There is not time now to repeat them though. If you are in Tcherin, ask him to show you my letter. My whole desire and orientation right now in connection with holy Chanukah is how to attain joy. In His amazing kindness, God has already helped me to develop many new teachings on the subject. May we just merit to fulfill this and to always be happy, as the Rebbe so fortified us in so many ways and with so much deep, wondrous and awesome advice! Let us be happy and rejoice in His salvation!

The words of your true, eternal friend.

Noson of Breslov

I am extremely hurried and it is impossible to elaborate and to discuss this at length as I would have liked.

445

With thanks to God, Tuesday, the 2nd day of Chanukah, 5604, Breslov.

May the Master of Miracles perform miracles and wonders to save you in all that you need to be saved. To my dear, beloved son, the illustrious Reb Yitzchak, may his light shine, along with all your precious children, may they live; in particular to your son, the distinguished groom, Reb David Zvi, may he live.

"There is nothing new *under* the sun" to report. But since God had the deliverer of this letter, my brother-in-law Reb Barukh, may his light shine, come to my house, I decided not to withhold the favor you yearn for, and to put pen to paper in a letter to you. Perhaps God will send to my pen some new Torah ideas, which are "above the sun." For they spring forth anew everyday all the time, as in "Who in His goodness constantly renews the creation everyday" and "they are new every morning, great is Your faithfulness."

This is particularly so during the holy days of Chanukah which are days of thanksgiving; and thanksgiving is itself the delight of the World to Come (*Likutey Moharan* II, 2). For the truth is that God performs new acts of kindness everyday for every single person as is expressed in the verses, "they are new every morning, great is Your faithfulness," and "God's kindnesses never end, His compassion never ceases." An intelligent person will also understand this from Rashi's comment there that God's kindnesses are renewed every morning (see Lamentations 3:23). It is certainly necessary to thank God for these kindnesses every day; and this thanksgiving is the essential delight of the

World-to-Come which a person must draw upon himself each and every day. This is the purpose for which we were created — to constantly thank and praise His Great Name every day.

This is also the idea underlying all the blessings and expressions of gratitude which our Rabbis, of blessed memory, enacted that we say every day, in particular what we say in the blessing "We thank You" (in the *Amidah*), "We thank You...for Your miracles which are with us every day and for Your wonders and favors which are at all times — evening, morning and afternoon." To the degree that a person constantly thanks and praises God's Name at all times during his life, so will he be worthy of the World-to-Come and to engage in praise and thanksgiving then, which is the main delight in the World-to-Come. All this applies particularly during the days of Chanukah which were designated just for this purpose — "to thank and to praise Your Great Name," which is the delight of the World-to-Come. This is as is written in Lesson 2 of *Likutey Moharan* II in which our master, teacher and Rebbe, of holy, sainted memory, revealed awesome teachings about the holiness of Chanukah. What is more, many miracles, wonders and acts of salvation certainly take place every year; and while we know about some of them, many of them are also hidden, because "the person for whom a miracle is performed does not recognize the miracle" (*Niddah* 31a).

Now, my dear son, God has helped you and you arranged a good *shidduch* [marriage arrangement] for your son, my dear grandson, may he live. It is necessary to give thanks for the past and to petition over the future that the match will indeed turn out to be a good one and that the connection will be completed in the best possible way in all respects. There are also many other acts of salvation and miracles that God has done for us as a group and as individuals, particularly that we merited to publish the book, etc. You too have an inkling of how great this amazing and awesome salvation and miracle actually is. For in the midst of our deep exile in every respect — because no one in the world is as persecuted as we are and we are despised, wretched and oppressed among Israel itself, not to mention [among the gentiles] — God remembered us in our downcast state. For His kindness is infinite. "Had God not been with us...Had God not been with us when men rose up against us." What an unprecedented wonder it is that we were rescued from their teeth! They wanted to swallow us alive, God forbid! Thank God Who did not give us over as prey to their teeth!

And as if this was not enough for You, Merciful One, You allowed us this year to publish what You did! How great are Your deeds, God! Praise God, you have a large share in this by God's kindness. It is impossible to say much about this in writing though, especially in this context. Thousands of pages would not suffice. If our mouths were filled as the sea with song, etc.! The bottom line is that you too need to make yourself happy with these great acts of salvation which I just mentioned — especially since the list goes on and on. There are more of them than I could possibly relate! We must really and truly just be happy! May God allow you and me to rejoice in the holy joy of Chanukah. "May the Merciful One perform miracles for us now too, just as He performed miracles for us in the days of Matityahu."

> The words of your father, waiting to see you soon
> with your son, may he live, alive, happy and well.
> Be sure to come at least by Thursday night. Let us
> be happy and rejoice in His salvation!
>
> *Noson of Breslov*

Send greetings to all our comrades with a great love, in particular to my friend whom I love as myself, the learned Reb Yaakov, may his light shine. Tell him to come for this coming Shabbat, no excuses. He will certainly not regret it in This World or in the Next. The opposite is obvious, as an intelligent person will easily understand. May God let the light of truth shine forth, which is the light of the Chanukah candles, as is written in Chapter 2 which I mentioned above.

Noson, the same

446

With God's help, Thursday, Vayichi, 5604, Uman.

Warm greetings to my dear, beloved son, the learned Reb Yitzchak, may he live, along with all his family, may they live.

I arrived here last Tuesday, the 10th of Tevet, only to find that the roof of our study hall had been severely damaged. The previous Thursday the upper section of the roof over my upper room and over the whole ceiling of the study hall completely collapsed due to a storm and high winds. It was a miracle that no one was killed or even hurt. You can imagine the enormous pain, upset and fear that Reb Naftali and his family experienced when it fell — they nearly expired. Our opponents are gloating over us. The study hall is now standing with the upper part of the roof missing. Only the sides of the roof remain. You can understand for yourself the enormous pain and anguish I am feeling. But I hope to God, Who helped us this far to build this holy edifice by the great power of the elder of holiness, that He will finish for us and help us to fix the roof, as well as to make some other repairs; so that this incident may turn out for the good.

At the moment my mind is not at all clear and it is impossible in this context to express what I feel in my heart about all this. After a great deal of thinking about the course of my journey (and especially now with this new development), "God's counsel" has emerged and by His salvation I summoned my strength and hired a carriage today for Tcherin to leave immediately after Shabbat on Sunday. May God have compassion and may He give me a safe journey such that I may arrive there a day or two before Shabbat-Parshat Shemot. Salvation is in God's hands. May God fortify your heart and mine to make ourselves happy and to turn all the grief and sighing into happiness and joy that, after all that we must endure, we still merit to hail in the Rebbe's holy name and are not *happy* about the unfortunate collapse of the roof of a holy place like this. Rather we are grieved over the mishap and we trust God that He will soon repair everything. In truth, in this way and with everything we have said and written on this teaching, it really *is* possible to turn everything to joy! (see *Likutey Halakhot, Hodaah* 6:68).

This is an extremely amazing and awesome piece of advice indeed! But the evil one still attacks with downheartedness and sadness, and a person must be extremely persistent about reminding himself of the real truth every time. For the truth is that God really has helped us very much, beyond all calculation. The more [the evil one] causes me to feel sad and discouraged because of my many failings, mistakes and sins — while they certainly do exist — to the contrary, this is my greatest source of joy! For nonetheless I, yes, even I, merit to be counted among this holy gathering of people who hail in the name of "the flowing spring, the source of wisdom," whom "the holy angel [who has] come down from Heaven" also... (see *Likutey Moharan* I, Preface). The more I know the extent of my own wrongdoings, the more I need to turn them all into joy! To the contrary! Now I can be even happier that, all the same, I merited to be in the Rebbe's portion! Then through this — in conjunction with the Rebbe's other methods — God in His compassion saves the person until he merits to reach a state of great happiness. And the most basic method is through silliness and *acting* happy. Blessed be our God Who created us for His glory and separated us from those who err in so many ways! There is not time to elaborate any more.

> The words of your father, waiting to bring you, me and all of us to joy over God's great salvation, and waiting for salvation.
>
> *Noson of Breslov*

Greetings to your son, my dear grandson, whom I love as myself, the young, wise, Reb David Zvi, may he live. I was in the house of your distinguished future father-in-law, may his light shine and I spoke with him. His whole goal and desire is only that you be diligent in your studies and that you walk the path of a righteous man to pray and say Psalms with concentration and to distance yourself from scoffers and youthful frivolity. Just be happy with the joy of a Jew, draw close to us with a whole heart, and prepare yourself to hear words of truth from me to give life to your soul forever. Then you may give fulfillment to the verse (Proverbs 10:1), "A wise son will bring joy to his father." It is good for a man to take on the yoke in his youth — for childhood and youth are vanity. You already have free will. Happy are you if you choose life and the true, everlasting good which is Torah and prayer. Outside of this, all is worthless. Listen, my son, to the instruction of your father so that you will grow wise in the end.

The words of your grandfather,

Noson, the same

After I finished writing this letter, I received your letter from Tulchin through the post, as well as the letter from my son, Reb David Zvi, who is presently there. I was all ready to set out at once for Kremenchug, but I was forced to delay in order to answer you. My dear, beloved son, David Zvi, may he live. I wrote you already, before you informed me of the unhappy news about your son, of blessed memory, who has left us because of our many sins, and I admonished you not to be angry, irate or fastidious with others at all. Now I receive your letter about your difficult and heavy grief, and your pain is my pain. He was my son too — because "grandchildren are like children" (*Yevamot* 62b). What can I say to comfort you, my dear son. You, obviously, are not the first, God forbid. This is something that visits people all through the world; and, as King David said [when his son passed away], "Why should I cry? I am going to him, he will not return to me." (Shmuel II, 12:22). What is more, even this child who has passed on through our many sins is still your son in the World-to-Come. As our Rabbis, of blessed memory, said (*Sotah* 48b, see also Rashi), "[A young child who dies] takes a man, i.e. his father, out of Gehennom. For he [the child] claims 'If You were going to punish him anyway, was his anguish for nought?" The main thing though is that you be certain from now on to think very carefully about what you are doing in This World. What's done is done; God is gracious and compassionate and forgives abundantly.

But be sure to resolve from now on to cast aside the puerile, foolish behavior and the anger and fastidiousness. Even in cases where you are treated unfairly, just let things go; and all the more so when you are not in the right. Just "slip in and out smoothly" (*Sanhedrin* 88b). "Man was born to suffer," and this is especially so since you were not born into any wealth whatsoever. Still I hope to God that I will provide you with what you really need through His kindness. No luxuries though, just the necessities.

I hope in God's kindness that, God willing, your wife will soon give birth easily to healthy, surviving offspring. May God comfort you among the mourners of Zion and Jerusalem and may He bestow good upon you from now on. Just fortify yourself determinedly to fulfill my words and to walk in the pathways of our master, teacher and Rebbe, of blessed memory — to study much every day, to force yourself with all your might to pray with concentration, to say Psalms and supplementary prayers every day and to express yourself daily before God [in *hitbodedut*]. Hope to God and He will save and comfort you many times over.

I warn you and I ask you, my dear son — start heeding my words immediately. That is, if you are still at your brother Reb Yitzchak's house, return home at once and do not stay on in Tulchin any longer. Spend your days in Torah; this is our comfort in our destitution. Converse with our comrades, our friends, may they live, because most of their talk concerns the ultimate goal, the Rebbe's holy Torah teachings and how to be happy at all times. Heed my words, my son, that you may enjoy good in This World and the Next forever. I am too pained and pressured at the moment and it is impossible to continue. This will suffice for now. God willing, I will write you more upon my return here by His salvation, to comfort you and strengthen you. For God's kindnesses are never-ending.

> The words of your father, pained by your pain and waiting for your salvation.
>
> *Noson, the same*

Greetings to my learned son, Reb Shachnah, may his light shine.

Send greetings to my wife, may she live, and to all my family, may they live. Ask and warn your brother, my son, David Zvi, may he live, to be careful, for God's sake, and to take pity on himself, on me and on his whole family and not to get angry or irate and not to be demanding of other people in the slightest. To the contrary, since his nature is to be demanding and easily angered, God forbid, let him prevail to be just the opposite. "Amidst rage remember compassion" and turn anger into compassion. Then he will have good in This World and the Next. You too should fulfill all of this, because anger and resentment are extremely damaging, God spare us. Fortify yourselves in God's Torah and at least set fixed times for study. Trust in God and wait for His salvation at all times. Anger accomplishes nothing and does a great deal of harm, God spare us. "An angry person is left with nothing but his anger" (*Kiddushin* 41); and whatever *can* be accomplished is accomplished much more effectively through calm, moderated speech. "Words of the wise softly spoken are heeded." I am extremely hurried and it is impossible to continue any longer.

The words of your father with best wishes and waiting for salvation.

Noson of Breslov

447

With thanks to God, Monday night, the 2nd of Shevat, Bo, 5604, Kremenchug.

Greetings to my friend whom I love as myself, the learned, illustrious Reb Efraim, may his light shine.

I am presently at your house, after having arrived in Krakah last Thursday, [the week of Torah reading] Vaeira. But I did not find "the one that my soul loves," since you had already set out from here a second time for Nikolayev. You can understand for yourself how distressed I was, besides which I was pained by the great pain this will cause you. I hope in God though that He will rectify everything and that it will all turn out for the good — for God's thoughts are very deep indeed.

It is all included in what I heard from the Rebbe's holy mouth during my journey with him from Breslov to Uman, when he was travelling there for his ascent to the exalted heavenly heights [before he passed away]. You cannot imagine even the glimmer of understanding that I have in my heart about what took place at every single moment during that time, not to mention all that is beyond my ken. At that time he said the following words, "God is great and one knows nothing at all. Things are taking place in the world that people know absolutely nothing about" (cf. *Rabbi Nachman's Wisdom* pp.106-7, #3). While I have already discussed this extensively many times, and something of it is already in print in the book *Sipurey Maasiot*, we still need to understand, to know and to inform others every day that we really know nothing at all. Then precisely through this, you will fortify yourself in crying out and praying to God, as the Rebbe concluded there in that same conversation. Thus a person will experience great joy and come back to pure, straightforward simplicity. He will trust in God and His salvation and won't be hurried or flustered by anything. Rather he will think calmly at all times. There is a great deal to say about this, but there is neither time nor space on the page.

I will now express myself to you on a few matters. You already heard what happened in Uman — namely, that the top of the roof to our study hall caved in. I arrived in Uman on the 10th of Tevet still a bit unsure whether or not to undertake a journey here. Suddenly, when I arrived at the study hall, I saw the destruction and my heart left me. [Reb Naftali,] your father, my friend, may he live, at once told me about the terrific confusion and fear they experienced at the time when it fell amidst great panic and alarm, so that they nearly expired. Our many enemies and persecutors ran gleefully to their study hall to report what had happened and they said that, God forbid, our entire study hall had fallen. "All our enemies will mock us." "We do not know what we will do, but our eyes are upon You." In addition to this, just during the days when I was there, the order came out [from the authorities] to expel from Uman all non-registered residents. The police then made the stern proclamation, as they customarily do in such cases, that all such persons will soon need to leave. Persons without a dwelling shall not remain longer than two months and those with a dwelling may

stay until May. As you realize, your father, may his light shine,
is one of the people affected by this threat.

You know already that your father, may his light shine, has
longed and yearned for many years to travel to the Land of
Israel. He has now taken to the idea even more strongly and he
wanted to travel alone. His wife refused, though, saying that
she must go with him and they said that they would rely on
what I thought. All this is what our comrades told me, and on
Shabbat-day, Parshat Vayichi, I discussed the matter with him
at length. I explained to him that it is impossible for him to travel
alone for a number of reasons and I assured him that our
comrades would certainly support him honorably while he is
there. Those who presently give to him would commit themselves to sending him there whatever they give him here each year
along with some additional sum as well. Then you and I will
make sure that the money is collected. He has meanwhile
accepted and agreed to my proposal. But we already know that
your father, may his light shine, hardly has the strength to
undertake all that is involved in obtaining a passport and
making the other preparations and we said that I would talk to
you about this here. I thought that you could travel with me to
our region and that all three of us could discuss the matter
together in Uman. Perhaps you would need to travel with me
right away to Breslov and Nemirov to start working on obtaining the passport. I can not explain any further what remains to
be discussed in this matter.

It is also necessary to begin talking in these environs about
the *ma'amadot* [continual support for those who are studying Torah full-time]. I

already talked a little about this in connection with Tcherin. But now I came here and I did not find you, at a crucial time like this, when I need to confer with you about such an important matter! What's done is done. But now, as you will understand for yourself, it is essential that you hurry up and come to me so that I can talk this over with you. Especially since, I know that your heart is on fire with a burning love for me and that you yearn in any case to get together with me. Perhaps God will send words to my mouth to inspire you, to advise you and to encourage you in trust, joy and *hitbodedut*. Perhaps we can remind each other where we are in the world and what is taking place with us all the time, every hour of every day. You should therefore know that I intend to travel, God willing, to Tcherin for Shabbat. I will remain there until Thursday [the week of Parashat] Beshalach when I will travel with God's salvation to Medvedevka for Shabbat-Shira. From there I will try, with God's help, to return to Terhovitza, and I will most likely set out from there on Monday, God willing, which is Tu Beshevat.

Therefore, upon your safe arrival home, it would be excellent if you could quickly come to us for Shabbat-Shira in Medvedevka or at least by the following Monday. Just come by the morning, because I intend to move quickly, with God's help, and to set out immediately after the Morning Prayers on Monday. If we are able to get together there — very well. We will discuss matters together and perhaps you will travel with me from there to Uman, as I mentioned above. If however there is not sufficient time for you to come to Medvedevka, it goes without saying that you should be sure to come to our region soon. There we will speak face to face and God's counsel will emerge.

You should also, as you realize, speak about our study hall here, because at the moment I am unable to receive anything from them at all for this. Reb Hirsh from Krakah told me explicitly that it is necessary to wait for you. He wants to contribute some wood with nails and boards. I however am uncomfortable with the idea because I am afraid that it will end up costing us more and also, God forbid, that it will cause me delays if I need to wait for their wood. Money, on the other hand, will answer all of our needs. Reb Zvi said that he will speak about this with you when you come. In light of what I just said, you will understand how to proceed with this matter in the best possible way.

I will not continue any longer. An intelligent person such as yourself will understand how to act in all this, such that all will be concluded in accordance with God's will and the will of the tzaddikim whose souls are in Eden. May we merit to have a good share in work like this for the benefit of the greater community. Salvation is in God's hands.

> The words of your friend, teacher, comrade and brother who waits at all times for your salvation and for the salvation of our whole group and of all Israel. Amen. May it be His will. Signed at your holy home.
>
> *Noson of Breslov*

Our illustrious friend, Reb Nachman, may his light shine,

from Tulchin is also here with me in your house now. He remembered today, on Rosh Chodesh Shevat, that, God forbid, you would be angry at him for not dancing in your home. So he quickly did a little dance for you today in your home and he sends you greetings with a great, bold love. God willing, when we get together, I hope to God that we will dance and rejoice even more. Let us be happy and rejoice in His salvation! God's kindnesses never end and the truth of God is forever! Halleluya!

448

With thanks to God, Tuesday, Beshalach, 5604, Tcherin.

Greetings to my dear, learned son, Reb Yitzchak, may he live, along with all his children, may they live.

I arrived here from Kremenchug before last Shabbat, Parashat Bo. God willing, I will travel to Medvedevka this week and from there to Terhovitza. May God grant me a safe journey. I already sent you a letter from here [the week of] Parashat Vaeira and I subsequently received a letter from you this week. I am extremely busy right now, though I very much want to fulfill your wish and write you something to strengthen you to be happy. But I have already written you a tremendous amount and all of the holy books are in front of you. Study them over and over. At present I simply have no time. The post is leaving soon and I am writing now wrapped in my talit; I have not yet put on my *Rabbeinu Tam* tefilin. Fortify yourself determinedly, my dear son! Bring yourself to joy over His salvation that we merited to draw close to the one that we did! "He has done us good, He does us good and He will do us good." In His kindness God sent me some wonderful new ideas about these three "bestowals of good" and through His kindness they are already written down (*Likutey Halachot, Pidyon Bachor 5 and Matana 5*). It is impossible though to explain them in this context. Hope to God at all times and He will save you.

The words of your father waiting for salvation.

Noson of Breslov

449

With thanks to God, Sunday, Tisa, 5604.

Let happiness and joy take over! To my dear, beloved son, the learned Reb Yitzchak, may he live, along with all his children, may they live.

The deliverer of this letter came to my house and he brought the scarf. I was extremely pleased because I needed it badly, as the bearer of this letter will tell you. There is a great deal to write you, but it is time for the Afternoon Prayers and the deliverer of this letter is in a great rush. I have conveyed everything to him both regarding your travelling — that you should come for some Shabbat — and also concerning your coming to the wedding. In accordance with the custom the world over and particularly that of the holy people Israel, it is certainly necessary for you to be at the wedding. Many of our comrades who have no familial connection to me at all, only a spiritual one will undoubtedly be attending; so it certainly follows that *you*, my son, should be there. For who could be closer than you? Nonetheless, I do not wish to cause you aggravation if, God forbid, it is not possible — the Torah exempts cases of duress. It is however incumbent upon you to do everything in your power and to petition God that you merit to be at the wedding and to rejoice together with us.

Perhaps we will also merit, through our rejoicing together in the joy of the bride and groom, to have complete salvation sprout for you and for us in all that we need to be saved. It is all in God's hands. May He save you and give you success in all you undertake and, most importantly, in your spiritual endeavors. May you there, and we here rejoice in the joy of this coming Purim. Before that, though, may we cry out and pray as we should tomorrow, God willing, on the Fast of Esther until we witness the fulfillment of, "as You performed awesome deeds in those days, so may You work a wondrous eternal salvation with us" (from the *Selichot* of the Fast of Esther). I am extremely hurried and it is absolutely impossible to continue.

> The words of your father, waiting to see you in joy,
> along with your son, my grandson, David Zvi, may
> he live. Let us be happy and rejoice in His salvation!
> *Noson of Breslov*

450

With thanks to God, Sunday, Pikudey, the 19th of Adar, 5604, Breslov.

Warm greetings to my beloved friend, the learned, illustrious and distinguished Reb Efraim, may his light shine, along with his wife and children, may they live.

I arrived home safely on Thursday night [the week of

Parashat] Tetzaveh. I was [also] in Lipovec and I have fixed the date for the wedding of my son [Reb Nachman], may he live, for this coming Rosh Chodesh Nisan. Since then, the days of Purim came in their proper time, and by God's kindness we rejoiced over His salvation. I am extremely busy now preparing myself for the wedding, particularly as it is so close to Pesach. This is why I have told you all this and you will realize for yourself that you should exert yourself to the fullest for my benefit and send me whatever you can as quickly as possible. Be sure to let me know what you intend regarding your travelling to Uman for this coming Pesach and also about your being here as you discussed with me. May God lead you and guide you on paths of righteousness for His Name's sake.

My daughter-in-law is sick in bed now with a mouth infection and the suffering is hard to bear. May God soon cure her from Heaven. My wife, may she live, also took sick today — and at a time like this when we have so many preparations to make for the wedding and so close to Pesach! But "everything the Compassionate One does, He does for the best" (Berakhot 60b). Our eyes are lifted to Him until He favors us and fulfills the verse "May God Almighty give you compassion" and until He says "Enough!" to our troubles. May He quickly send them all complete recovery from Heaven and for the sake of His Name may He save us in all that we need to be saved.

Now too I have no vitality except from the fact that I merited to escape the trap of opposing the light of the point of truth which radiates throughout all the worlds. What can I give back to God for all the favors He has bestowed upon me?! Fortify yourself with the utmost determination, my brother! We too must fulfill what is written in the Introduction to the holy *Zohar* (p.4), "Happy is the person who stands in this world like a mighty pillar in everything." "All human bodies are pouches. Happy is He who is a pouch for Torah!" (*Sanhedrin 99b*). No matter where a person is or on what level, he still needs to be like a mighty pillar in everything, to never despair of crying out and praying and to be extremely adamant about every single word of our master, teacher and Rebbe, "the flowing spring, the source of wisdom." For what every person goes through every day of his life of vanity is no light matter! Who knows...? *Ashreinu!* Happy are we that in this passing shadow, in this Gehennom, in this bitterness, we know about a tzaddik such as this who brings life to the worlds and who can instill even us with joy and life! God is my hope that everything will be turned into good. Let us be happy and rejoice in His salvation! I am extremely pressured and busy and it is impossible to continue.

> The words of your true friend forever waiting for your swift response.
>
> *Noson of Breslov*

Greetings to your father-in-law, my friend, the learned Reb Shmuel, may his light shine, along with his honored family; and to my illustrious, learned friend, Reb Zvi Hirsh, may his light shine, from Krakovh, and to his honored family; and to my illustrious friend Reb Gedaliah Aharon, may his light shine, along with his honored family; and to all our comrades, each one of them according to his own level. I ask all of you to send

me wedding gifts. Each of them, as is customary, will be lovingly announced with the name of its giver at the wedding. It
would certainly be fitting and excellent for you to do so, because
I have no friends or benefactors besides our comrades. May God
grant you success in all your endeavors. I also extend most
amicable greetings to my brother-in-law, the learned, excellent
and honorable Reb Efraim, may his light shine, along with his
wife and children. And greetings as well to my in-law, the
learned and wise man-of-standing, the honorable Reb Shmuel,
may his light shine, and to his wife, the modest Pesiah.

451

With thanks to God, Tuesday, Pikudey, 5604, Breslov.

Greetings to my beloved son, may he live.

Yesterday morning I received your letter, which I had been
greatly looking forward to. Enclosed with it, however, was the
letter from Reb Avraham Ber, may he live, with its loud and
bitter cry that his daughter, Chanah Chayah, of blessed
memory, passed away from the infection that she had in her
mouth (they were using the doctor when I was there, as Reb
Nachman is aware). The anguish of his cry is just unbearable.
He just lost two children last year, a son and a daughter. May
God have compassion on him and may He say "Enough!" to his
suffering. May he merit from now on to raise his daughters, may
they live, and may God give him every kind of salvation.

Before your letter arrived yesterday I received a short letter
in the morning from our friend Reb Nachman of Heissen in

which he wrote that his wife and daughter are unwell and that his youngest daughter is quite ill. May God quickly cure them. The situation in my home you already know, that my daughter-in-law is in bed with terrible pain in her mouth and they do not know what it is. Her pain is absolutely indescribable. She has been like this for ten days now and eats nothing at all. Her entire sustenance is from plain water alone. My wife, may she live, has also been weak and today, praise God, she is up and around in the house. But she still has no strength. You can imagine the turmoil in everyone's hearts because I am not breaking down the doors of doctors, the heralds of destruction, God save us. Reb Efraim, the Rebbe's grandson, is the fourth case of fever in my house and he is still here. Again and again he laments to me about his poverty and straits, that he is forced to move from place to place and does not even have a coat to wear. And all this is happening now, when I am so busy preparing for the wedding and we are so close to Pesach. I am still short of a number of things and I do not know what to do. My grandson, the son of my daughter, Chanah Tsirel, may she live, is also weak and in great danger, God save us; and my daughter, your sister, cries to me every day. He has, praise God, recently taken a turn for the better, with God's help. May God soon complete his recovery.

As for the letters you are constantly sending me — I hear them, I understand them and I know your pain. In addition to this there are all the cries and sighs that I hear all the time from our comrades over their livelihoods, their children, domestic problems and what they are suffering because of the controversy. They [the *mitnagdim*] recently disgraced and attacked something in *The Aleph-Bet Book*. In the midst of all this, we must pray three times a day, study and remember the World-to-Come. In fact, though, this is what comforts me in my destitution. "Were Your Torah not my delight, I would have perished in my destitution." But how great are God's deeds that He informed us of what He did in advance through "the flowing spring, the source of wisdom" whose words are profound in the extreme and give life to all of us through everything that we endure! May God take pity from now on. But I in my poverty find many favors even amidst all these sufferings. I give thanks for the past and request that, in the future, God will rescue us in His compassion from every trouble and hardship, and I wait for salvation at all times. For "He has rescued me from every trouble." Blessed is our God Who created us for His honor and separated us from those who err, so that *we* do not disgrace his holy books. To the contrary! We look forward to them circulating and illuminating the face of the globe!

I could not restrain myself from relating a bit of my pain to you, though I have not yet told you half my heart's sufferings. But you should know, my dear son, that I have also not told you about the joy in my heart that, through His kindness, all the grief and sighing will be turned into joy! For the measure of good is greater and God is my hope that He will quickly save us for the sake of His Name and turn everything into good! Right now I, and all of us, need enormous compassion and great salvation. Our eyes are lifted to Him that He will soon take pity on us for the sake of His Name and for the sake of our holy and awesome master, teacher and Rebbe, the elder of elders. God will not abandon us. Beyond this I do not have time to continue, as I have not yet put on my *Rabbeinu Tam* tefilin.

It will be impossible to call the groom, may he live, to the Torah this coming Shabbat since, as you have already heard from Reb David, there is also a delay from my in-law's side [i.e. the bride's father]. At the moment this is a favor, though. I hope to God that the following Shabbat, which is Parashat Vayikra, he will be called to the Torah by God's kindness and salvation. I do not yet know where the wedding will be, here or in Lipovec. God's plan will emerge.

I have written you all this in order that you will understand how very much a person must prevail at all times to grab good from amidst the grief and suffering of this world. He must then rejoice over this good and turn all the grief and sighing into joy, that in this world replete with grief and suffering we merit [all that we do]! For such things happen all over the world. All the books talk about the bitterness of this world and as the Rebbe, of blessed memory, said, "It appears that Gehennom is *here*" (*Likutey Moharan* II, 119). Nonetheless, every day we grab *"Shema Yisrael!"* to declare the Unity of His Name twice a day and we put on talit and tefilin. This is our share of all our toil! We must boldly prevail and rejoice amidst everything that comes upon us, so as to fulfill, "We will rejoice in the words of Your Torah and in Your Commandments forever and ever. For they are our life..." (from the Evening Prayers). All this is in accordance with "the deep waters," the advice of "the flowing spring, the source of wisdom." With his great power, his profound, perfect words and his enormous wonders, he brings even us to joy until we soon merit to leave all our troubles behind. Let us be happy and rejoice in His salvation!

The words of your father,

Noson of Breslov

Greetings to your entire family, may they live, and to all our comrades, may they live; in particular to Reb Nachman, the grandson of our master, teacher and Rebbe, of blessed memory.

452

With God's help, Sunday, Vayikra, 5604, Breslov.

May the Master of Salvation and Comfort save and comfort my dear friend, the learned, illustrious, distinguished and generous Reb Avraham Ber, may he live; along with all his children, may they live long. May he raise them amidst joy and satisfaction to good, long lives and may he merit to have more sons and daughters who will live, flourish and truly do God's will. May they live to a ripe old age and may they fulfill the verse (Isaiah 4:2), *"The fruit of the land will attain greatness and splendor." Amen. May it be His will.*

You should know, my beloved friend, that last Monday, Parashat Pikudey, I received your letter, which had been delayed in Uman and Tulchin until that day. While I was in Uman, until Erev Rosh Chodesh Adar, it did not reach me. You can understand for yourself what great "pleasure" I had from your letter. May God allow us to rejoice as much as He has brought us sorrow. Shortly before I arrived here from my journey I sent you a letter. I addressed it to our friend Reb Abele, may his light shine, as I was terribly grieved over the weakness of his daughter, of blessed memory. I knew that she was closer to death than to life, though I did not know the situation exactly. Thus I addressed Reb Abele, may his light shine, as I wrote there and also hinted to you, that it is forbidden to question [the rightness of] God's ways. God is righteous and His judgments are correct; everything He does is with lovingkindness and mercy. But we pray to God that He will add further compassion and great kindness to fulfill, "May God Almighty give *you* compassion" and give the compassion over to *us* [i.e. give us what *we* consider compassion](see *Likutey Moharan* II, 62). May you and all of us thereby merit to raise our sons and daughters to adulthood, to live in wealth and honor and to truly do God's will.

I will now relate to you the troubles and hardship that have recently taken place in my home — may God have mercy from now on. You have already heard that the beautiful little son of my son, David Zvi, may he live, passed away, as I told you in Tcherin. This was a great tragedy for him. He is already sickly and a hunchback, and he is poor and destitute. He did not have even a *perutah* [small coin] of dowry money. All he has is what I in my own poverty have given to support him these last nine years. His whole vitality and consolation was this beautiful son of his. But this winter his heart's joy was taken; may God comfort him.

I was recently in Lipovec and I set the date for the wedding of my son, Nachman, may he live, for Rosh Chodesh Nisan. I came home for Shabbat Parashat Zekhor all ready to prepare myself for the wedding. It was then that my daughter-in-law, the wife of my son, Reb David Zvi, may he live, became very weak. She was in her eighth month of pregnancy and we were all hoping that she would give birth to a healthy baby and that this would comfort us all — especially my son, may he live. She then became extremely weak from the infection that she had in her mouth. Subsequently, on Wednesday, [the week of] Parashat Pikudey, she passed away, leaving this life, and the child was born after her death as is the custom among Israel. My wife and children, especially my son, David Zvi, may he live, are now mourning in my house and you can understand for yourself the enormous bitterness that has overtaken us. Who can we lean on but our Father in Heaven? May the Master of Kindness, Comfort and Salvation comfort and save my son, David Zvi, may he live. May He comfort all the mourners in my house and turn their mourning into joy. May the Compassionate One make up our losses, your losses and the losses of all Israel and may He comfort all of them among the mourners of Zion and Jerusalem.

I would now like to turn our discussion, my friend whom I love heart and soul, to the great and anguished lament which you wrote me. You indeed did well [to write me about this], because all of us are obligated to listen to our fellow's sorrow. May God grant salvation so that grief and crying will no longer be heard in our streets. Especially since you are from the holy stock, the offspring of the tzaddik, our glorious master, teacher and Rebbe, who is the light of our lives forever, it is certainly incumbent upon me to listen to your cries and to roll in the dust in supplication before God, praying for your salvation.

But, my beloved son and student, "fruit of the tzaddik," the tree of life, out of your enormous grief, God spare us, you seriously erred in a number of things that you wrote me. It hit me like a tempest when you wrote that I could not care less about you. Furthermore, there were things in your letter directed against God, Who conducts His World with lovingkindness, which you really ought not to have written. You spoke very foolishly indeed when you wrote that "a person is born into this world just to be tormented." May God forgive you; because in your deep dejection and anguish you wrote some things which were not appropriate. God knows the enormous pain that I have from the troubles of every single one of our comrades, even the lowly and the poor among them; not to mention those who are from the Rebbe's holy stock. All of them are engraved in my heart more than my own children and offspring. They are my whole life. This is all the more true for you yourself when, praise God, through His salvation, you have helped me so much, particularly in our [printing] projects. May God grant you salvation and may you go on to do the same many more times. Your eternal reward will not be withheld and your charity will endure forever. For this alone remains of a person. Is it conceivable to say or to write that I could not care less about you?! God forbid that you should write something like this. It is simply absurd.

And as for your writing, as if in praise of me, that if I had wanted, these things would not happen to you — well this is even more ridiculous. If our father Yaakov, said, "Am I in place of God?" (Genesis 30:2), what shall we who are the orphans of orphans say? It *is* true that even I in my destitution am obliged to pray for our comrades, and in particular for you and for all the Rebbe's descendants; and I also do have the Rebbe's great power behind me. Nonetheless, it is forbidden and impossible to stubbornly demand *anything* [of God]. We must only request with many petitions and supplications and God will do what is good. God hears the prayer of every mouth but, as it says in the holy Zohar, "there are times that He does not listen," God forbid.

It is time for the Afternoon Prayers and the post leaves soon, so it is impossible to continue. "The final word is, 'Fear God and keep His commandments'"; and it is forbidden to question God's ways. Hope to God and He will save you. May you merit to raise your daughters to *chuppah* and good deeds and may they live good, long lives. May you have and raise up more healthy sons and daughters to the service of God. May you attain great ascendancy and honor and may you begin from now on to add more good deeds and charity. May you express yourself before God every day and may you increase your daily study of the holy Torah, especially your study of the Rebbe's books. God is our hope that everything will turn into good. May you there and we here merit to receive the coming holy festival of Pesach in joy, and may God save us in all that we need to be saved. I am extrememly pressured and preoccupied now and it is impossible to continue. Please acknowledge receipt of this letter immediately. Also send me [the money] that you promised me for Pesach and try to collect all that you can from our comrades. My situation now is extremely tight and I have a great many expenses. I'm sure that you will act swiftly in this matter on your own initiative.

> The words of your true friend forever who loves you heart and soul, writing amidst bitter pain, hoping and waiting for salvation. But now too I try to turn the grief and sighing into happiness and joy. Salvation is in God's hands.
>
> *Noson of Breslov*

Greetings to my illustrious friend, Reb Abele, may his light shine. I have not yet received a response to my first letter, which I mentioned above, and at the moment I have no time at all. God willing, when I receive your letter with the money that you promised, I will give you a proper response, with God's help, including words of truth and righteousness emanating from "the flowing spring, the source of wisdom." Greetings to my friend, Reb Moshe Melamed, may his light shine — let him be sure to keep his promise. You will understand for yourselves that the wedding has been postponed until after Pesach and I am extremely upset about it. This will also add to the expense. The expenses for my daughter-in-law, of blessed memory, who passed away also amounted to a sizeable sum. May God have compassion and save us and turn everything into good. You do your part and God will finish for you for the best.

Greetings to all our comrades with a great love, to each one of them according to his own high level! It is impossible right

now to address everyone individually. Save us, God! Our eyes
are lifted to You! Nonetheless, *Ashreinu! Ashreinu!* Happy are
we that we are not opponents of a light such as the Rebbe! This
is particularly true for me, poor man that I am. God knows that
this is my entire comfort in my destitution. Blessed be our God
Who created us for His glory and separated us from those who
err in so many ways and gave us His Torah of Truth! "Had Your
Torah not been my delight, I would have perished in my destitution." "This is my comfort in my destitution; Your Torah has
given me life."

Noson, the same

453

*With thanks to God, Sunday, Shemini, the 11th of Nisan, 5604,
Breslov.*

Life, peace, happiness and joy to my honorable friend,
brother and dear comrade, the learned and illustrious "fruit of
the tzaddik," tree of life; to the praiseworthy man-of-standing,
Reb Avraham Ber, may he live, along with his wife, may she
live, and all their children, may they live. May God give them
long lives spent in goodness and pleasantness. May he merit to
raise his children to *chuppah* and good deeds. Amen. May it be
His will. Greetings as well to my friend, the illustrious man-of-
standing, Reb Abele, may he live, along with his wife, may she
live, and their children, may they live. May they all live to a ripe
old age and may they flourish as a watered garden. Amen. May
it be His will.

I returned home shortly before Purim. Immediately after Purim I sent you a letter and I have yet to receive any response. No word and no money. I anxiously await your letter's arrival every day along with the money which several people promised to send me for Pesach. Reb Moshe of Breslov obligated himself to take care of this matter and it is incumbent upon you as well to oversee it; but I have not yet seen a single word from you. Perhaps it is already on its way from there, but as yet I have received nothing. I sent another letter two weeks ago and we have not received any reply. I have nothing new to report at the moment. I just ask you, if the money has not yet left your possession or if part of it has, but not all of it, for the sake of the mitzvah and for the sake of the strong bond of love which exists between us, try with all your might to send it immediately — even on the Intermediate Days of the Festival. Do not delay at all! My expenses at home, and in particular the Pesach expenses, are extremely high.

I already informed you of the great tragedy that took place in my home, God spare us, that my daughter-in-law, the wife of my son, Reb David Zvi, may he live, passed away. May her soul enjoy eternal life. Now my son is left a widower and I have to marry him off again. He has a handicap, though, and you know what a "high" status *I* enjoy in the world. It is impossible to express all that is in my heart about all these various matters which surround me on every side. My eyes are constantly lifted to God until He takes pity on us for His Name's sake. Besides all this, the expenses incurred by her illness and burial also amount to a considerable sum. May God comfort my son in everything and may He soon save us in all that we need to be saved.

I also, as you know, need to think about repairing our study hall. The majority of people in your community have given nothing, though they promised to send their contributions before Pesach or immediately after the festival. Therefore, for God's sake, endeavor with all your might to collect from each person what he already pledged or what he needs to give now and send it at once, so that I will receive it immediately after Pesach. For just a few days after Pesach I must travel to Uman to tend to the aforementioned roof repairs. I only have on hand a small amount of money, though, and I am waiting to receive from our comrades the money they promised. Please act quickly and send what you have for the study hall, both from yourselves and from our other righteous comrades, the generous of God's People. May God bless them and grant them success in all their endeavors. The faster the better!

At the end of my letter that I sent you, I informed you that there had been a great quarrel in the home of your brother-in-law, Reb Simchah Barukh, may he live. Your mother, may she live, left and went to the house of the Rav [Reb Aharon, the Rav of Breslov] and subsequently your sister, may she live, also moved from her husband's house to the house of the Rav, may his light shine. The pain and grief I suffered from this cannot be described. At present, after much trouble, effort and talking on my part, praise God, your mother [Adil] and sister, Miriam Rivkah, may they live, returned to their home last Thursday, Parashat Tzav. But your mother, may she live, and Reb Simchah

Barukh, may his light shine, have still not completely reconciled their differences. What is more, I succeeded in persuading her to return home only on the understanding that your mother, may she live, will travel to the Land of Israel this summer.

As far as you are concerned, this is a great favor in all respects, as I discussed with you. Therefore, in my opinion, you should be certain to do as I wrote in the previous letter and to come to this area right after Pesach. This would be an excellent thing for you for a number of reasons. If you are not free to come immediately after Pesach, then come a few days later. I assume that you will come to Uman first and it is quite likely that you will find me there. Then we will delight in our mutual love for a few days. We will go out together "to pray in the field" of holiness, i.e. at the Rebbe's holy gravesite, and we will express ourselves there in prayer. We will also speak with each other — perhaps each of us will illuminate the other with his own "holy point" (see *Likutey Moharan* I, 34).

From there, you will travel to Breslov to honor your mother, may she live — by which you will be performing a number of important commandments, as you will understand for yourself — and most likely you will stay here until after this coming Shavuot. If our friend Reb Abele also comes with you, so much the better, provided that he first move out of his father's house with his wife to eat at his own table, as I discussed with him in Medvedevka. It is possible that my son's son-in-law, Reb Avraham Leib, may he live, will also travel with you, as he too wishes to spend a few days in Uman during the Counting of the Omer before Shavuot. May God guide you and your companions on the true and straight path in accordance with His good will, so that we may merit from now on to start being as He truly wishes us to be. We have no consolation for troubles we have endured in the past, nor any way of escaping them in the future through God's compassion, except by the merit, power and holy Torah teachings and conversations of our holy and awesome master, teacher and Rebbe, of holy sainted memory. He is your holy grandfather. May his merit stand you, me, all his holy descendants and all our comrades in good stead. "This will console us for our deeds and our toil."

There is much to say, but I am extremely busy now before Pesach. May God grant you and us a *kosher* Pesach and may we meticulously avoid any trace of *chametz* on the simplest level. May we also be particular about the *chametz* of the mind — since this is the key to holiness — and may we guard our thoughts from evil ruminations and from all kinds of bad, convoluted thinking. May we thereby straighten out the crookedness of the heart and not, God forbid, question God's ways. Rather, we should just know and believe that everything that happens to a person is for his good and we will return to the Lord our God every time — for He will forgive abundantly.

May we merit to be happy, to celebrate and to rejoice on this approaching holy festival of Pesach, since "in every generation a person is obligated to see himself as if *he* went out of Egypt." How great are the acts that God has done for us in this generation, that we merited to be in the Rebbe's holy portion and not, God forbid, God forbid, to oppose him! Especially you, who, thank God, are one of his holy descendants. God forbid that we should forget the faithful kindnesses that God did for us by revealing to us such "laws" such awesome, deep advice, such a revelation of Torah teachings and of Godliness! Come and look upon the might of your Master! What shall I say? What shall I say? Each person according to his own heart's perception is obligated to say, "I have witnessed marvels. How wondrous are Your works! My soul knows it well indeed" (cf. Psalms 139:14). Then he must bring joy into his heart every day over the enormous kindnesses and miracles that God has done with us in this way. This is especially true on Pesach when "it is a mitzvah to relate at length the tale of the Exodus from Egypt," the essence of which is what is taking place in each and every generation. May God allow us to fulfill, "Speak about all His wonders!" Let us be happy and rejoice in His salvation!

> The words of your true friend forever, waiting for your speedy response. Also, if the letter with the money has already gone out, quickly answer this letter, so that I will know how to proceed in connection with my journey to Uman after Pesach, God willing, to work on fixing our study hall. Salvation is in God's hands.
>
> *Noson of Breslov*

Warm greetings to all our beloved, fine comrades, to each one of them according to his own high level. Greetings in particular to my venerable friend, the illustrious man-of-standing, Reb Dov Ber, may his light shine, and to his precious sons

and offspring, as befits each one of them. May they attain
ascendancy and honor.

Greetings as well to my learned friend, the illustrious man-
of-standing, Reb Zvi Hirsh, may his light shine, and to his
precious sons and offspring as befits each one of them, may they
live; in particular to his son Yechiel, may his light shine, along
with his wife and children, may they live. Regarding the Sefer
Torah, you should know that it has already been completed,
thank God. There only remain thirty more columns to be written, for which he [the scribe] needs to receive six new rubles; and
these six new rubles remain with your honorable person. For I
only received fifty-four new rubles from your honor, besides
the five new rubles for the proofreader. Your honor also owes
one new ruble for candles which I gave you this winter, besides
the wages for writing. Out of these six new rubles, I was forced
to lend him one new ruble for Pesach. I therefore have coming
to me two new rubles from you, and [the remaining] five new
rubles you should give directly to the scribe when he comes
home, God willing, to finish the Sefer Torah at the beginning of
this summer. Thus your honor should send me two new rubles
immediately. You should give them to Reb Avraham Ber and
he will send them to me right away. If you also want to send me
some further sum for Pesach expenses, so much the better. You
will receive a double reward from Heaven. Please do as I ask at
once. God willing, you will reap great satisfaction from the Sefer
Torah and your charity will stand you in good stead, forever.

Greetings as well to my in-law, the illustrious Reb Peretz,
may his light shine; and to Reb Avraham Leib, may his light

shine, along with all of his children, may they live, to his granddaughter, may she live, and to his son-in-law, may he live. And warm greetings to the illustrious man-of-standing, my friend, Reb Yaakov, son of Reb Zvi, may his light shine, and to all his family, may they live. It would be right to address him directly, but time does not allow. He should be sure to send [money] for the the study hall and also to me for my expenses for the festival. May God send him His blessing in double the amount. Amen. May it be His will.

Greetings to my learned friend, Reb Moshe Melamed, may his light shine. Your father, your mother and your own family, praise God, are alive and well and send their greetings. I am confident that you are working to help me with all your might, but I just wanted to give you some extra encouragement. Most likely, some money for me is already on its way from you; but there is certainly more which could be collected with some effort. Therefore, do not be remiss in the least about this matter, because my situation is extremely tight, now in particular. May God have mercy and send salvation soon. Be happy and rejoice in the joy of the holy Festival and relate God's praises and wonders. "The more one elaborates on them, the more one is blessed" — with kindnesses!

Send greetings to all our comrades with a great love!

Noson, the same

454

With God's help, Monday, the 12th of Nisan, 5604, Breslov.

Greetings to my dear, learned son, the illustrious Reb Yitzchak, may he live; along with all his children, may they live.

The bearer of this letter just now came to my house with your good letter which I had been awaiting anxiously and the wine for Pesach. I thank you — in particular for acting quickly and sending it with a special courier. May God repay your deed and may He give you full reward. May you merit to welcome the holy Pesach in holiness and purity and to make a new start from now on at accustoming yourself to completely forgetting what has happened up to that time. Just be like a person who knows nothing at all! A person *can* direct his thoughts as he wishes. Summon all your might to keep a hold on your thoughts, and to steal away from evil thoughts by "sitting and not doing anything" [i.e. by ignoring them completely]. But if, God forbid, they do overtake you, fulfill "rebuke the beast of the grass" and drive them off. The main thing is to guard oneself from *chametz* [leaven] and at least not to allow one's mind to "ferment" with these thoughts, God forbid, as is written in the lesson "With the trumpets" (*Likutey Moharan* I, 5).

This is particularly true now when all Israel, and we among them, are working with all their might to remove all *chametz* from their possession and property. By the same token, we must all the more zealously eliminate from ourselves "the fermentation of the mind" right down to the minutest trace through the power of the true tzaddikim, who are represented by *matzah* because of the "*matzah*, the strife, which they create within the Other Side so that it will not draw close to the holy sanctuary" [the word *matzah* in Hebrew has two meanings: unleavened bread and strife]. Then, through this, we may merit to straighten out the twistedness of our hearts until we attain straightness of heart and true joy!

Ashreinu! Happy are we that we merited to hear all this! And so much the better that we merited to fulfill a miniscule fraction of it! My eyes are lifted to God that we will merit to completely fulfill this entire teaching. Let us be happy and rejoice in His salvation! Your letter really uplifted me, for I saw that my words are indeed entering your heart and by this I am fulfilling "Tell them to your children and to your children's children." My hope is that your son, my grandson David Zvi, may he live, should also come to me regularly to hear and receive the words of the Living God which flow forth from the "flowing spring, the source of wisdom." If he can come for the final days of Pesach, that would be excellent — because from what I hear it seems very likely that there will be guests for the final days of Pesach and he will be counted among them. May I just be worthy of relating all God's wonders! "You have done many things, Lord, my God; Your miracles and Your thoughts are for us!"

I wrote yesterday to Tcherin that every one of us should really take to heart and understand that it is a matter of no small significance that we merited in this generation to know about a light such as this! Each person according to his own heart's perception ought to be saying for himself, "I have witnessed marvels. How wondrous are Your works! My soul knows it well indeed" (cf. Psalms 139:14). It is time for the Afternoon Prayers and I must also write the letter enclosed here for Tcherin. It is therefore impossible to elaborate any further. Enjoy the happiness of the coming holy festival.

The words of your father, waiting for salvation.

Noson of Breslov

455

With thanks to God, Monday, Kedoshim, the 18th day of the Counting of the Children of Israel, 5604, Breslov.

May He Who gives valor and strength to His People strengthen and fortify your heart. To my beloved, dear son, the learned and illustrious Reb Yitzchak, may his light shine, along with all his children, may they live; and in particular to his dear son, my excellent grandson, Reb David Zvi, may his light shine.

I received your letter today before the Morning Prayers from Reb Nachman, may his light shine. At first, you cheered me with what you said, that you merited to be at the Rebbe's holy gravesite and to pour out your soul there. May He Who hears prayers and sighs hear your prayer and your sigh and may He quickly and speedily help you and save you in all that you need to be saved. Amen. May it be His will. But subsequently you cried out so harshly! I have heard these cries of yours frequently in previous letters and for some time now, but this time you went on to really express the bitterness in your heart. May God have pity and save you. What can I do for you, my dear son? We are required to believe that God is righteous in all of His ways. And if precisely *this* is what you are crying out about — namely, that God is righteous and *you* are the guilty one, God save us — well, He already informed us in advance of His abundant compassion and mercy which are absolutely unfathomable. As for this, I personally guarantee you that His compassion includes you too and that God will certainly not abandon you. For we have a father, the elder of elders, the grandfather of grandfathers! We have someone to rely on in This World and the Next forever and for all eternity — and with plenty to spare!

You should know and believe that everything you are experiencing has already happened to many great tzaddikim and righteous people. I heard some awesome stories on this subject from the Rebbe's holy mouth, but it is impossible to relate them in this context. Now too many, many people, falling into a number of categories, are going through much more than this. There are the great tzaddikim and wicked, great people and small, and the middling. The ones who suffer most of the bitterness are those who, compared with everyone else, are in the middle. These are the people such as me and you. For no matter what, you are certainly not one of the wicked, God forbid, nor are you one of the tzaddikim. Rather, you are one of those people in between among whom there are also incalculable thousands and tens of thousands of gradations.

It is impossible to imagine or to describe what is taking place with every single one of them every single day. Large numbers of them have sunk, God spare us, because they did not have someone who could truly encourage them. It is impossible to clarify and to know, however, what is actually happening with each person in this regard. This is precisely the reason for the antagonism directed at the people who hold on to the Rebbe's name and to his holy pathways. These people are assailed with great intensity precisely *because* they are still striving, hoping and struggling to escape from the great waters which are constantly flooding in upon them. This is expressed in the verse (Psalms 88:18), "All day they engulfed me like water; all together they surrounded me," and similarly (Psalms 69:3), "I have sunk in the deep mire and there is nowhere to stand. I have come into deep waters and the current has swept me away." There are many other similar verses. What can we return to God for all the favors He has bestowed upon us, that we merited to receive the Rebbe's holy words which can also give life to you and to people much, much worse than you? Had God not been with us in this, we would already have perished in our destitution. "If God had not helped me, my soul would at once have dwelt in the grave."

You should know, my dear son, that the great fear, dismay and depression that you experience as a result of your thoughts and your confused musing, serve to strengthen, God forbid, the confused musing and evil thoughts, as is written in the Rebbe's holy books, especially in Chapter 72 [of *Likutey Moharan* I] and in *Likutey Moharan* II (49, 51-54). Look carefully at these chapters. It is explained there a number of times that a person does not need to pay the slightest heed to these thoughts; he should not look at them at all. And even if it still seems to you that they are surrounding you and they will not give you a chance to breathe, you should fortify yourself determinedly to say words of Torah or prayer, business or the like, and do not look behind you at all. The crucial thing is not to be afraid in the least, because God is with you! As our master, teacher and Rebbe, of blessed memory, said (*Likutey Moharan* II, 48), "A person must pass over a very narrow bridge in This World. The main thing is not to be afraid." The most crucial thing of all, though, is the great power of our master, teacher and Rebbe, of blessed memory — and you merited not to oppose him! What is more, you merited to be at his holy gravesite, and in particular on Rosh HaShanah with the other members of his holy gathering! May your children, too, and all your offspring be counted among the holy gathering which is called in his name, of blessed memory!

You have plenty of things with which to pass the day. There are the three daily prayer services and the study of the *Shulchan Arukh*, Bible and the other holy books, if you have time. In particular there are the books of our master, teacher and Rebbe, of blessed memory, and the discourses in which I merited to explain his teachings and to develop new ideas based on them. "Study them over and over. Grow old and gray with them and do not depart from them. For there is nothing better." Whenever I write down the teachings that God helps me develop from the Rebbe's holy Torah lessons, it always occurs to me that you really need to hear *this* particular talk. Praise God, you have many of them in print or in manuscript and you will be able to receive more new ones from me, with God's help. You also need to engage in business; for "Torah combined with a worldly pursuit is good, as the effort expended in both of them causes a person to forget sin" (*Avot* 2:2). Remove grief and sighing from yourself with all your might! Trust in God's kindness that everything will turn out for the best. Practice "They will obtain happiness and joy; grief and sighing will flee," to drag the grief and sighing *themselves* into joy (*Likutey Moharan* II, 23). Say to yourself, "The worse I consider myself to be, God forbid, the more I can genuinely be happy that at least I do not oppose the Rebbe! What is more, I hail in his name and I am included among his holy gathering!"

There is no time to continue.

The words of your father, waiting for salvation.

Noson of Breslov

Really, still be happy!

456

With God's help, Wednesday, Emor, 5604, Uman.

Greetings to my beloved son, may he live, along with all his family.

I arrived here safely yesterday. Fortify yourself determinedly, my son, and bring yourself to joy however you can! "Do not be afraid or daunted. God is with us. For 'the whole world is full of His glory!'" These words were meant for you too, specifically, and for all of us; and while everyone knows this, it is necessary to review it many times every day. Most important, though, is the power of the tzaddik who revealed this. For only he in his great compassion instilled in us [this knowledge] that you and I can also give ourselves life with this, with "the understanding of the student" embodied by the verse, "My dead ones will rise. Wake up and sing, you who sleep in the dust!" (see *Likutey Moharan* II, 7). The likes of this have never been heard! How great are God's deeds which He has done and is still doing with us in this generation! "The choicest spice is silence," because "silence is a fence for wisdom," as is written there. Every single word of this teaching glows like a burning coal and is original, wondrous and awesome in the extreme, giving life to the spirits of the lowly and to the hearts of the downcast.

The truth is that I hadn't intended to write you anything about this now. But by the hand of God, I recalled these extremely holy and awesome words, and they are inspiring me tremendously right now. How great are Your works, God! Now that the Rebbe has already spoken these words in our presence and they have been transcribed by me into a book, and you have merited to hear them in writing and orally many times — certainly there is plenty of hope for our final outcome, for me, for you, and for all of us!

The words of your father, waiting for salvation.

Noson of Breslov

457

With God's help, Monday, Bechukotai, the 32nd day of the Counting of the Omer, 5604, Uman.

Warm greetings, blessing, success, life and all good to my honored and beloved friend, the learned man-of-standing, the venerable and generous Reb Dov Ber, may he live, along with all his precious children — to each one of them according to his own high level. And to my learned friend, the illustrious Reb Zvi Hirsh, may his light shine, along with all his precious children — to each one of them according to his own high level. And to my learned friend, the illustrious man-of-standing, Reb Avraham Ber, may he live, along with his wife and children, may they live, and to my learned friend Reb Abele, may his light shine, along with his wife and children, may they live. May God bless them in all their endeavors and grant them success in This World and the Next. May they continue to flourish to a ripe old age. Amen. May it be His will. And to all our precious comrades — to each and every one of them on his own high level — they all have my blessing for wealth, honor and good, long lives. Amen. May it be His will.

You should know, my brothers and friends, that I arrived here in Uman on Tuesday of last week and I immediately began to work at repairing our study hall. First of all, we had to work to get permission from the officials here. After much effort, God helped us and today the mayor of the city himself was at our study hall along with two other officials, and they granted permission to build the roof. We still have to obtain a license and with God's help we will receive it tomorrow. "It is good to thank God" for all this.

Now we must begin building the roof. At first I thought that I would only rebuild the upper part of the roof that caved in. Many people told me however that it is necessary tear out the entire roof and to rebuild it completely. I myself also understood that it is impossible any other way, but it is quite expensive. It cannot wait until I come to you, because in the meantime summer will pass and besides, when it comes to a mitzvah such as this, it is necessary to act as soon as possible. Furthermore, [we must act quickly] so that the woodwork and beams do not become damaged, God forbid. It is therefore imperative to begin at once — which is why I have just told you all this.

How surprised I am that I have not yet received even one *perutah* from you for this building! You already committed yourselves to the sums which appear on the list and you said that you would definitely send them immediately before Pesach or at least after Pesach. But there is no word and no money. I am therefore sending you the list of those who obligated themselves. See to it that they immediately pay off their pledges in full and without delay, God forbid, and send the money to my son, may he live, in Tulchin, so that that the building should not be halted, God forbid. You should know though that, even when they do pay off their pledges in accordance with the list, we will still be short of a great deal of money. The cost is high indeed, and you will certainly need to add more in accordance with what I will discuss, God willing, with Reb Avraham Ber when he is with me for this coming Shavuot. But surely we cannot abandon the building, God forbid, just because it is expensive to repair it. In the meantime, though, be sure that everyone sends what appears on the list; then we will know how much more will be needed. Be certain not to hold up the money that they committed themselves to on the list any longer.

Our holy building is a matter of no small import — it will benefit the greater community for generations to come for all time. It is impossible to fathom the enormous merit connected with this mitzvah for the wider community. It is absolutely without limit or bounds! Fortunate is the person who provides some truly significant support for this project according to God's blessing, to the goodness of his heart and to his own understanding of the greatness of our consummately holy and awesome master, teacher and Rebbe, of holy, sainted memory! Remember and remember well everything that I heard in the past from his holy mouth, everything that you yourselves have seen in his extremely holy and awesome books, and everything that has been spoken between us. For the holy work that the Rebbe is still doing with us to rectify us eternally "so that we do not go up in shame before God," is something very deep indeed.

The Knower of Thoughts knows that I am writing you all this in great sincerity. I know that I am not worthy of engaging in such awesome work, but God's thoughts are very deep. I am poor and destitute and my livelihood is extremely tight. I also need to marry off my sons, may they live. My son, David Zvi, may he live, who is a hunchback, has also been left a widower and I need to marry him off too. I have no power except in my mouth and my writing to awaken, arouse and encourage you [to help] in so great a mitzvah for the benefit of the wider community.

I trust your good hearts which have merited by His great kindness to be counted with us and to be included in the Rebbe's holy name which is also the Name of God — for His Name is associated with the name of the tzaddik (as in *Likutey Moharan* II, 66,67) — that you will certainly carry out these words of mine with the utmost swiftness and zeal. The more a person adds, the more Heaven will add to him wealth, honor and a good, long life forever, until he merits to gaze upon the "abundant good hidden away for those who fear You" and for those who are attached to them [the tzaddikim] body, soul and possessions, which is money. Then you will see the difference between the person who hailed in the Rebbe's blessed name and the one who opposed, mocked and disgraced the point of truth — "between the one who served God and the one who did not" (Malachi 3:18). Our Rabbis, of blessed memory, taught that this verse refers "to a person who reviews his study a hundred times in contrast to one who reviews it a hundred and one times" (*Chagigah* 9b). The same thing applies when it comes to charity "between the person who gives a hundred new rubles and the one who gives a hundred and one." For charity is above all else, especially charity such as this, which benefits the community and endures forever.

> The words of your true, eternal friend, sighing and downcast in the extreme over my soul's many troubles and over the troubles of the souls of Israel who lament their sufferings before me. I know their pain well. But I already know with the utmost clarity that the entire world is full of troubles, grief

and pain; and by His amazing kindness I merit to remember all the kindness and good that He has done for my soul in that He separated me from the Rebbe's misguided opponents and allowed me to hail in the Rebbe's blessed name and to engage in his holy work. This is my portion out of all my toil. This is my hope forever. And His kindness to me has been so abundant that I also merited to relate and to talk about His awesome wonders. Thus far has Your compassion helped me. Even when I am old and gray, God, do not abandon me, until I relate Your compassion to the generation. Let us be happy and rejoice in His salvation!

Noson of Breslov

458

With thanks to God, Wednesday, Naso, 5604, Breslov.

Let happiness and joy take over! To my dear, beloved son, may his light shine.

I received your letter today and I am prepared to fulfill your request to send a carriage for you Friday morning as you wrote in your letter. I would very much like, however, for you to be with us at the wedding, as well as for this coming Shabbat. It occurred to me yesterday to write you that you should definitely come for the wedding and not come for Shabbat and that you should postpone your Shabbat visit for the wedding. But I thought subsequently that it is possible that you will hear things which you need for your eternal goal on Shabbat more than at the wedding. In addition to this, there are many barriers to your coming to the wedding anyway. I therefore determined to take no action at all. I then received your letter, and at the moment I do not know what to write you about this. But you do understand for yourself, my dear son, that is appropriate that you be at the wedding as well. It does not look right to people that you, who are my son, should not be at the wedding, when our comrades, who are not related to me at all, are there. I know that this is very difficult for you, but nonetheless, if you could manage to be with us for the wedding and for Shabbat, it would be best. In any case, I will send the carriage as I mentioned. God will do what is good. You should send another letter before Shabbat. I am extremely busy and it is impossible to continue.

The words of your father, waiting to rejoice over His salvation.

Noson of Breslov

459

With God's help, Tuesday, Shelach, 5604, Breslov.

Life and peace to my dear, beloved son, may he live.

I arrived home safely yesterday and toward evening I received your letter informing me that the wedding is not to be held immediately. I am forced to travel this coming week to see to the building of the roof of the *kloyz*. This is an extremely urgent matter, as you know, and it is impossible to delay it any longer. As for the wedding that you are making, I obviously want very much to celebrate with you on this joyous occasion for your son, my grandson, may he live; but it is impossible for me to even speak about this at all right now. I must only do everything in my power to arrive quickly in Uman at least by this coming Shabbat, Parashat Korach. There I will think about the building project and the course my travels should take — and God's plan will emerge.

You, my son, may you live, do not worry about all this and do not engage in a lot of unnecessary thinking. Here you see with your own eyes that it is impossible for anything to proceed for you according to plan. You see that the world is full of sorrow and that you too endure what you do. In spite of this, though, you still think on each occasion that everything will proceed for you as you wish, according to plan. But you must subordinate your will to God's will and wait and hope at all times for God's salvation. While a person must certainly flee swiftly for his [spiritual] life as from a hunter's snare, still, even when it comes to one's religious devotions, I nonetheless heard from the Rebbe's holy mouth that in this matter "a person is told to wait."

You have already heard a great deal about this and much still remains to be said. Had God not helped us so that we rely on the power of the elder of holiness, I do not know if we would have the strength to cope with all spiritual and physical trials, that each one of us goes through. But, by God's compassion and amazing kindness, He already supplied us with the cure in advance of the blow inasmuch as we have a mighty refuge through whose power anyone can flee and escape to God, every day, from any place at all, from all the falls and spiritual rejections in the world and from everything that a person goes through. What is more, He opened our eyes and allowed us to see all this in the Book of Psalms and in the other holy books, as is written, "Although I walk through the valley of death, I will fear no evil; for You are with me." There are many similar verses. Fortify yourself, my son, and be strong! Trust in God's salvation and kindness — He will not abandon you or any of us! God's kindnesses never end and His compassion never ceases!

The words of your father, waiting for salvation.

Noson of Breslov

460

With thanks to God, Sunday, Chukat, 5604, Uman.

Let happiness and joy take over! To my dear, beloved son, the learned Reb Yitzchak, may his light shine, along with all his children, may they live; in particular to his son, the groom, my grandson, may he live. May He with Whom joy abides bring them to joy with His kindness — and me together with them. Let us be happy and rejoice in His salvation! Amen. May it be His will.

I arrived here last Friday. While I was still in Teplik, God had me incline toward the opinion of our comrades, my true friends, that I really must be at the wedding of your son, my grandson, may he live. I received your letter today and, the way I see it now, with God's help, I will indeed be at your celebration, where with God's kindness, we will delight in our mutual love.

Concerning the carriage for me, it is certainly impossible to wait until you come. Rather, I will either travel, God willing, on my own from here or you will tell those in Teplik to send a carriage for me before you arrive there. I have already discussed this with Reb Mordekhai, may his light shine, and you need not concern yourself with it at all. Under no circumstances, though, do I wish to attend the groom's festive meal [the night before the wedding] and therefore I will most likely not arrive until Tuesday morning, God willing. But even if I should come on Monday, I do not want them to pressure me in the least to join them at the groom's meal. I just do not have the strength for it. God is our salvation and our hope that all will go smoothly, with God's help.

So it appears that you "defeated" me, my dear son. Your desire and the desire of our comrades has compelled me to celebrate together with you, by God's salvation. Rejoicing in God will be our fortress! May you only merit, my dear son and friend, to "defeat" "the One Who spoke and the world came into being" (*Likutey Moharan* I, 124 and *Rabbi Nachman's Wisdom* p.176, #69), so that He will help you from now on to be as He wishes you to be at all times — to keep your mind from extraneous and unnecessary thoughts and to bind your mind at all times to the World to Come; to bring yourself to joy with all your might and to fortify yourself to always hold your ground. All this should be along the pathways of our master, teacher and Rebbe, of blessed memory, and the main way is through good desires and yearnings which you express in words from the depths of your heart. Thus you will fulfill (Psalms 13:1), "To the Victor, a Song of David," which our Rabbis, of blessed memory, explained — "Sing to the One Who is happy when He is defeated." Just fortify yourself determinedly to be happy with all your heart that we merited to be involved with holy, awesome words and conversations such as these! Praise God, we have someone to lean on — on the great power of the elder of elders of holiness! On this we rely forever!

The words of your father waiting for salvation.

Noson of Breslov

Greetings to all our comrades with a great love!

461

With thanks to God, Monday, Masei, 5604, Uman.

Warm greetings to my honored and beloved friend whom I love heart and soul; the learned, illustrious Reb Efraim, may his light shine.

You should know, my friend, that, praise God, I held the wedding for my son, may he live, and, thank God, everything went as it should have.

I arrived here on Friday, Erev Shabbat Korach. I cannot describe to you in writing the enormous anguish and uncertainty I experienced in connection with the building of the roof. But God's counsel has emerged, and it was decided to tear out the original roof completely. This is indeed what we did, and we have begun, with God's help, to build a totally new roof. You cannot imagine the enormous trouble and pain that this project is causing me, particularly because of its enormous cost. There are no workers available for hire and it is necessary to give them more than two gold pieces per day. Wood too is extremely expensive and right now I have absolutely no idea what to do.

Praise God, we have almost finished setting the beams over the actual study hall. They have not yet fixed the lattice work between the larger beams, though, and they are not available for purchase at all, even for a high price. Shingles are also not for sale and we have not even begun working on your father's house, may his light shine. God willing, I intend to start building the roof over your father's house tomorrow. We do not even have the wood that we need, though, let alone the lattice work, tiles and workers. And if it *is* possible with great effort to find them, they are extremely expensive. The cost of everything is extremely high and I have no idea what to do. "I raise up my eyes to the mountains — from where will my help come?" I do not have any time either.

The final word is — for God's sake, try with all your might to collect money however you can! When I arrived here before tearing out the original roof, they told me in your name that you promised to help from Kremenchug with the sum of twenty new rubles. Reb Avraham Ber, may he live, also promised to make an appropriate contribution from there. I was relying on this when I had the original roof torn out and took on the burden of an enormous expense such as this. Be sure now not to go back on your word and send at least the aforementioned sum. If there is not sufficient time to send it immediately, be certain at least to bring it with you when you come to Tcherin for this coming Shabbat Nachamu. For I intend to come there at that time, with

God's help; be sure to come there too with the money. Otherwise, I do not know how we will finish the building, and God forbid that we should abandon the project in the middle. One only encourages those who are motivated to act on their own, and especially when it comes to a project such as this. I am confident that you will carry out my words at once. Salvation is in God's hands.

Praise God, I have a great deal to say orally and in writing about the great and awesome exaltedness of building the holy study hall and I hope to God that you will see and hear what I have to say about this (see *Likutey Halakhot, Minchah* 7:69-71). Your eyes will see and your heart rejoice! Just fortify yourself mightly to have a large share in this and to contribute some really significant help. "The one who gets others to do charity is greater than the one who actually does it." May God repay your deed and may He help you and save you in everything in which you need to be saved. For He saves abundantly.

> The words of your true friend eternally, extremely busy and waiting to see you soon in joy. May you merit to carry out all the above and God will finish well for you.
>
> *Noson of Breslov*

462

With God's help, Monday, Devarim, 5604, Uman.

*Warm greetings, blessing, life and all good to my dear, beloved son,
the illustrious and learned Reb Yitzchak, may he live, along with all
his children, may they live.*

I received your lengthy letter yesterday, and I read it carefully twice. I do not understand, my dear son, your complaint
that I should judge you favorably. Could you even consider that
I do not always judge you favorably? This is all the more so since
nothing you have done to me is contrary to my will so I have
no reason to judge you favorably. I do not know who told you
on my behalf that I was upset with you, God forbid, because
you did something against my will, God forbid. All I said about
this was that I was a little sorry and that I felt great pity for you
and for those of our beloved, fine comrades who, like you,
sincerely and intensely yearn to be with me all the time. But then
the barriers array themselves so thickly that even for the wedding of my son, may he live, "a mountain stood between us"
and neither you nor your brother Reb Shachneh, may he live,
could be with me at the wedding. I never considered being
upset with you, though, God forbid. I only spoke in a general
way about how the barriers to holiness spread themselves out
in this world and about how they vehemently assail every
person. And even though a person *knows* about this, sometimes,
given his level, he cannot and *should* not force matters too much
in order to overcome them. There is a great deal to say about

this matter and most likely you have heard much from me about it already.

It certainly is true that I would rather you not be so busy with your job at the post office and that you would receive your livelihood in some less time-consuming way from another source, so that you could study and pray more and converse more with your Creator. But what can you do? "It is good to thank God" in spite of your job at the post office, you still travel for Rosh HaShanah each year, as well as for Shavuot and Shabbat Chanukah; and occasionally you also travel in the middle of the year as well. This is the entire holy teaching of *Azamra!*, "I will sing to my God with what I have left" (*Likutey Moharan* I, 282) and of "They will obtain happiness and joy; grief and sighing will flee" (*Likutey Moharan* II, 23) — namely, that a person needs to drag the grief and sighing into happiness and to turn everything into joy, that nonetheless, in His compassion, God did not [make him a gentile and so on]. And while I was somewhat pleased by your letter from which I understood that you are practicing *hitbodedut* and expressing yourself before God with some regularity (for this is the key to everything) — still, I do not want you to do so much needless, extraneous thinking. Just thank God Who has helped you thus far — thank Him for the past and request over the future for whatever you need in a general way and specifically, and express yourself before Him as I have frequently discussed. I would like to elaborate further, but I am extremely busy with the holy building.

I intend to travel this coming Thursday, God willing, to

Terhovitza for Shabbat; and from there to Tcherin for Shabbat
Nachamu. Salvation is in God's hands. May He guide me on
paths of righteousness for His Name's sake. Regarding my son,
your brother, Reb David Zvi, may his light shine, the pain and
anguish that I have over him is deep indeed, especially since I
have been informed that he is not feeling well. May God heal
him. I was also informed yesterday that your son, my grandson,
David Zvi, may he live, has no teacher and no study partner. I
am surprised that you said nothing to me about this. I will be
sure to speak with Reb Nachman and have him travel to Teplik
today to offer him some good advice on this matter. Most likely
everything will be fine. Do not be upset over this. I trust God
that Reb Nachman, may his light shine, will bring you a good
report on this matter. The final point is that the words of the
tzaddik, our master, teacher and Rebbe, of blessed memory, are
true, right, firm and established — that it is necessary to beseech
God for everything. We have no-one to lean on but our Father
in Heaven, and this is especially true for such a poor, destitute
and persecuted man as myself. But God's power to save is
abundant. May the Comforter of Zion and Jerusalem soon save
us and console us and bring us to joy over His salvation.

> The words of your father, extremely busy and wait-
> ing for salvation. Praise God, "in the straits God
> gave us relief" and the setting of the roofbeams is
> already completed. My upper room is already
> finished, and today they are placing the lattice
> work. God willing, tomorrow they will begin cover-
> ing it with the shingles. But there are still great

expenses involved in order to buy the tiles and to pay the laborers. God is our hope.

Noson of Breslov

463

With thanks to God, Tuesday, Erev Rosh Chodesh Menachem [Av], 5604.

Peace and life to my beloved, learned son, Reb David Zvi, may his light shine.

I heard yesterday that you are not feeling well and I have great pain and anguish over this. Even without this I feel enormously sorry for you, my dear son; and particularly so now, my dear son and friend. How my heart goes out to you! But I hope to God that He will soon save you, for He will not forsake you forever. Without a doubt you too, my son, are also God's handiwork about which it is said (Psalms 145:9), "His compassion is upon all His handiwork." He will not deal with us according to our sins, because His compassion is very great indeed. Just fortify yourself, my son, and really be strong! Remove anger from your heart! Hope to God and He will save you. I ask you, my dear son, to please carry out my words, as I have frequently discussed with you. I think about your well-being a great deal and I hope to God that He will soon save you. Be sure to write me a letter at once. Send it to your brother, Reb Yitzchak, may his light shine, in Tulchin, and it will reach me from there. I look forward to seeing a letter from you soon in Tcherin, where I plan to go, God willing, for Shabbat Nachamu.

I am extremely busy with the holy building and I have no time to continue at all.

> The words of your father who prays for you and waits for your salvation.
>
> *Noson of Breslov*

464

With thanks to God, Tuesday, Ekev, 5604, Tcherin.

Peace, life and all good to my dear, beloved son, the learned Reb David Zvi, may his light shine.

How very pained I am, my beloved son, that I did not receive a single letter from you about your good health! I received a letter last Sunday from my son, Reb Yitzchak, may his light shine, but he did not mention you specifically. He only included you together with the rest of my family. I am quite pained about this and I am longing for a letter directly from you. Therefore be certain to send me a letter at once. May God return you to your full strength and may He save you physically and spiritually in all that you need to be saved. Just fortify yourself really determinedly to keep yourself happy and to cast aside your bad thoughts! Do not think a lot at all. Just pass the day with the three prayer services, Torah study and reciting Psalms and converse at least a little with your Creator. You should also converse with others about whatever subject God presents you with. This will help open your mind. Then, most likely, the conversation will turn to the *takhlit*, the ultimate goal, and you will speak about the greatness of God which He revealed to us through our holy, awesome master, teacher and Rebbe, of holy sainted memory. His thoughts are very deep indeed and His greatness is unfathomable, so that there is hope for your final outcome too, my dear son — no matter what, no matter what. There is a great deal to say about this, but there is simply not enough time because the post leaves soon.

> The words of your father, waiting for your salvation and to hearing all good from you. Salvation is in God's hands.
>
> *Noson of Breslov*

To all our comrades — greetings and abundant salvation!

465

With God's help, Tuesday, Ekev, 5604, Tcherin.

Warm greetings to my dear son, may his light shine, along with all his family and children, may they live. Life, blessing and all good!

I arrived here safely on Wednesday, Erev Tishah b'Av. I cried on Tishah b'Av and, by His compassion, I merited to rejoice on Shabbat Nachamu ["The Shabbat of Consolation"]. "For You, God, have helped us and consoled us." There is no time to write much at all at the moment, as the post is leaving soon. I received your letter last Sunday and I was pleased. I was quite irritated, though, that you did not write me individual greetings from my son, Reb David Zvi, may his light shine, because I heard in Uman that he was not well. Thus I was anxiously waiting to receive a letter from him in his own hand or at least to hear from you about his health and whether he had recovered his strength. I am extremely pained about this right now and I am waiting to hear good news about him. Salvation is in God's hands.

> The words of your father who is extremely busy. It is already close to noon and I have not yet put on my *Rabbeinu Tam* tefilin. I hope in God's salvation that everything will be for the best.
>
> *Noson of Breslov*

466

With thanks to God, Thursday, Reay, 5604, Tcherin.

Warm greetings, life and blessing to my dear, beloved son, the apple of my eye; the learned Reb David Zvi, may his light shine.

I arrived here yesterday from Kremenchug and I found what I had been hoping and waiting for — your letter informing me about your good health and that, by God's kindness, the seeds of your salvation have begun to sprout and you have begun your speedy recovery, with God's help. I came back to life! For how very deep my grief and pain were when I heard in Uman that you were not well. And when upon my arrival here I received a letter from your brother, my son, Reb Yitzchak, may he live, and he did not mention a word about your health, then my suffering and anguish swelled beyond all calculation. What can I give back to God for the past, since you informed me yesterday in your letter that, praise God, you have begun to recover your strength?! May I only merit to hear soon the good report that, praise God, you have completely recuperated. Amen. May it be His will.

As for the most important thing of all, there is your terribly bitter lament which you voiced in your letter, referring primarily to the pain of your sins brought on by the enormous provocation of the Evil One. For the evil thoughts attack you furiously and *they* are the essence of the evil impulse (*Likutey Moharan* I, 49). It is true that I hear your cry and I know your pain, both past and present. How my heart goes out to you! My insides shudder! Your pain is mine, and my pain and anguish are very great indeed. But it is with precisely this fact that I console and encourage myself — that by God's wonders and enormous kindnesses you are still crying out with an anguished, bitter lament such as this which reaches all the way to Heaven! Know and believe, my dear son, that God and His true tzaddikim also hear, understand and are listening to your letter's cry and wail too, and they are thinking about your salvation. As for the salvation being so long in coming — this whole matter contains many deeply hidden things. God's thoughts are very, very deep and the delay is certainly from our side inasmuch as we do not rouse ourselves as we should to overcome the evil thoughts. Besides this, God desires the prayers of Israel, even of the most inferior Jew, and He desires that you pray a great deal and cry out to Him more and more. All the same, though, even your bitter cry up to now has not been lost.

Now, my dear son, begin to understand afresh the lesson on the verse "*Azamra!* I will sing to my God with what I have left" (*Likutey Moharan* I, 282), and make a new start at accustoming yourself to apply it anew every day! Out of my love for you and out of my obligation to fulfill "Tell them to your children and your children's children," I will now teach you anew a few words of this lesson. I will do so in Yiddish, so that the words will enter your heart and you will be able to practice them simply and straightforwardly.

This is what our great and awesome Rebbe, of holy, sainted memory, used to say: "When a person sees that he is very inferior indeed, it is forbidden for him to fall. Rather he must encourage himself and reflect, 'Have I never ever done anything good? Did I never perform a single mitzvah? Well, I do fast on Yom Kippur; and also on Tishah b'Av and all the other four fast days too, even though it is very painful for me. I also go to the mikvah on occasion. And even amidst all my wrongdoing, God save us, I really *am* trying and I very much want to rescue myself! No matter what, I still have some good points in me in that I have done the will of the Creator a number of times!' In this way a person must encourage himself and absolutely never despair..." So it is written in the book [*Likutey Moharan* I, 282] in the Holy Tongue. Look it up. It is clearly explained there. I only went over a few points in Yiddish to put the words anew into your heart. But if, God forbid, the evil one still attacks — well, it is necessary to go back and to apply this teaching again and again, every single day all the time. Then, in the meantime, God helps tremendously.

It is particularly important to rouse oneself to articulate and express all this before God and to say, "Master of the Universe! However I am! However I am! You know my pain and I know my pain! Still, though, You did an eternal kindness with me and You created me from the Seed of Israel and You did not make me a gentile. Still, they performed a Brit Milah [circumcision] on me and they spilled my blood on the eighth day. Then in *cheder* I learned *aleph-bet, siddur, Chumash* and Talmud. How many slaps and how much pain I suffered from my teachers! And I have also worked hard many times on myself. What can a person do? 'I want to do Your will, but the leaven in the dough (the evil urge) holds me back!'" (*Berakhot 17a*). If the holy Tanna [Rabbi] in the Talmud was not ashamed to say this, we certainly do not need to be ashamed to cry it out before God with all kinds of cries and entreaties!

Just the way you cry out to me in your letter so many times, "Bitter!" "Bitter!" "Bitter!" "Bitter!" "*Gevalt!*" "*Gevalt!*" — so do you need to cry out to God with all your heart every day. And if, God forbid, God forbid, the Evil One still assails you, you just have to keep on crying out more and more like this, time after time, until God looks down from Heaven and sees. He will not ignore you forever. What is more, we have an ancient father, the elder of elders, whose power is great and awesome in the extreme. It exceeds all limits and bounds! I promise you, my dear son, that no matter what, no matter what, the Rebbe will definitely effect a wondrous spiritual rectification for you. Just fortify yourself determinedly to fulfill my words and to thereby prevail to bring yourself to joy.

Remember well everything I have said to you recently and everything you have heard from me in the past. Really force yourself to study the Rebbe's books every day whether much or little. At least do not let a day pass without studying the Rebbe's books and the *Shulchan Arukh!* Then God will help you to study more each day and also to express yourself before Him every day, a little or a lot, as a child before his father. The rest of the day force yourself to be joyful any way you can. I hope to God that the verse will be fulfilled for you (Job 8:7), "Your beginning was painful and your end will be sublime." The most important thing is that you subordinate your own ideas to mine; for my ideas are those of our holy, exalted Rebbe, of holy, sainted memory. He is your life.

I would have wanted to elaborate, but the time for Prayers has arrived. I hurried to write you immediately before Prayers, because this letter is the essential fulfillment of the commandment to recite the *Shema*, "Hear, O Israel!" For this letter fulfills, "you shall instruct your children in them" and "teach them to your children" (from the first and second paragraphs of the *Shema* respectively). This is particularly true for *these* words which flow forth from the source of life, from the consummately exalted "flowing spring, the source of wisdom." They can inspire even you and people thousands of times worse than you! Know and believe, my son, that people much worse than you have already been with me, and they drew close to God as a result of words such as these which I received from the Rebbe. Some of these people have passed on in peace to life in the World to Come and eternal life is their portion through the power of the Rebbe. Those of them who are still alive are righteous people and their final outcome will certainly be good, with God's help. It is impossible to elaborate on this any further in this context.

The words of your father writing in tears and also in joy, because of my hope for a good end for all of us. You, I and all Israel will enjoy a good end through the holy tzaddik, the grandfather of grandfathers in whom we take shelter. Ultimately, everyone will be rectified. But how great are God's kindnesses that we know about the one who is engaging in our rectification and we do not oppose, God forbid, the one who is working to save us eternally! *Ashreinu Ashreinu!* Happy are we! Blessed is our God... [Who created us for His glory and separated us from those who err]!

Noson of Breslov

467

With God's help, Thursday, Reay, 5604, Tcherin.

Greetings to my dear son, the learned Reb Yitzchak, may he live, along with all his children, may they live.

You have before you the letter that I wrote to my son, Reb David Zvi, may he live (see the previous letter). I received a letter from him yesterday and I was delighted, as I had been hoping for it very much. I had intended to send it to Breslov, but I just now decided to send it to you because these words are also meant for you, my dear son. I myself also need these words very much. They must be new for every single person, each and every day. Be certain to send this letter at once to my son, Reb David Zvi, may his light shine. Send it with a trustworthy man and closed with your seal, such that it will be delivered directly into his hands as quickly as possible. You will understand all this for yourself. I received your letter yesterday immediately upon my arrival from Kremenchug and I was pleased. I already sent you my letter along with the sum of one hundred silver rubles when I arrived here on Tuesday the week of Parashat Ekev and I am expecting to receive an acknowledgement of this here soon. Then I will answer you with a proper letter. At the moment I am writing you in connection with the aforementioned letter to my son, Reb David Zvi, which is relevant to you as well. There is absolutely no time to write more, even if it *is* quite necessary. I have already written you a great deal though and I must discuss a number of matters here concerning the *kloyz* (study hall) in order to complete it in the best possible way.

> The words of your father,
>
> *Noson of Breslov*

468

With thanks to God, Thursday, Rosh Chodesh Elul, 5604, Tcherin.

May the One "Who makes a path in the sea and a road through the mighty waters" quickly show us a path and road to teshuvah [repentance]. May He write and seal us for a good year. To my honored, dear and beloved son, the learned Reb Yitzchak, may he live, along with all his children, may they live.

I received your letter yesterday. I will write nothing new at the moment, as I am in a great hurry to travel to Medvedevka for this coming Shabbat and from there to Uman. I want to arrive there in Uman, with God's help, for the Shabbat following, Shabbat Parashat Teitzei. May God direct my steps to good. May He have compassion on you and on all of us and may He banish grief and sighing from us. May we merit to rejoice at all times in the salvation and great kindness that He has bestowed upon us by His consummately wondrous and awesome kindnesses of which "thought has not the slightest grasp." In them we trust that He will still grant us eternal good in the end. Let us be happy and rejoice in His salvation! Praise God, I have spoken many words of Torah, words of truth, on recent Shabbatot and I rejoiced and danced over His salvation. Would that sadness might vanish from us completely that we might prevail with all our might and rejoice any way we can to fulfill "I will rejoice and be happy over Your kindness!"

> The words of your father waiting to see you in joy this coming Rosh HaShanah. Rejoicing in God will be our stronghold forever!
>
> *Noson of Breslov*

Greetings to all our comrades with a great love; in particular to my illustrious friend, Reb Nachman, may his light shine, grandson of our master, teacher and Rebbe, of blessed memory. I certainly have not forgotten you, God forbid. You are engraved on my heart and mind at all times, but we have no-one to lean on but our Father in Heaven. I have done and, with God's help, I will do everything in my power to benefit you. But the essence of my hope is in God alone. He has abundant power to save you and all of us. Just really fortify yourself determinedly in Torah study, prayer and in conversing with your Creator and come for Rosh HaShanah — no excuses. Thus you will enjoy good forever.

Noson, the same

469

With God's help, Thursday, Rosh Chodesh Elul, 5604, Tcherin.

Greetings to my dear, beloved son, the learned Reb David Zvi, may he live.

I was delighted to receive your letter yesterday. I was extremely pained, however, when you wrote that you are not feeling well. May the Master of Compassion quickly heal you. May you get up on your feet and "may your feet stand on a level place" physically and spiritually. May you merit to go to the study hall and to pray there with concentration. Make a resolution to pray right away in the morning and not to do a lot of talking before praying. Just make a determined effort every morning to pray immediately with the congregation. Do not talk with your tefilin on, not even your *Rabbeinu Tam* tefilin. Only after praying and studying, in the middle of the day, may you converse and speak as you wish in order to sharpen your mind. Accustom yourself to speaking with our comrades every day. Most likely you will discuss the ultimate goal, the greatness of our master, teacher and Rebbe, of blessed memory, and the greatness of his awesome Torah lessons, stories and conversations — all of which are the greatness of the Creator.

I already wrote you a somewhat lengthy letter. Would that

you might carry out my words, which emanate from the Rebbe's words, and adhere to them all the days of your life so that you may enjoy good in the end. At the moment there is no time to go on, as I am in a great hurry to set out for Medvedevka for this coming Shabbat. I plan to travel to Uman after Shabbat and I want very much to arrive there for Shabbat Parashat Ki Teitzei. May God guide me on paths of righteousness for His Name's sake.

> The words of your father who prays for you, waiting for salvation.

> *Noson of Breslov*

I was surprised that you forgot to write regards to me from my son, Yosef Yonah, may he live. If it is possible for him to write at least a couple of lines by himself with someone else's instruction, particularly that of his writing teacher, Reb Moshe, may his light shine — that would be excellent. But at least send greetings from him to me in Uman. Send greetings to my modest wife, Dishel, may she live, and to all my family, may they live. Greetings as well to my son, Nachman, may he live. I received your letter and I was delighted. Be sure to write me in Uman as well. Peace, life and all good. For God's sake, be diligent in your studies and concentrate when you pray, especially now during the month of Elul and the holy Days of Awe! Who will not experience fear during these days?

It is impossible to write much now. Remember your Creator in the days of your youth, my son, that you may enjoy a good end.

> *Noson*, the same

Greetings to my son, Yosef Yonah, may he live. For God's sake, be a man! You have to know that you are not a little child. Fortify yourself and put your mind into your studies. Concentrate when you pray and pronounce every word clearly. Think about the ultimate goal. I think about you a great deal. But you also have to take pity on yourself, especially during the days of Elul and Rosh HaShanah.

> The words of your father, waiting to see all of you with all good in This World and the Next forever.
>
> *Noson*, the same

470

With God's help, Sunday, Tavo, 5604, Uman.

Warm greetings and life. May you be written and sealed for a good year. To my dear, beloved son, the learned Reb Yitzchak, may he live, along with the rest of his family, may they live.

I arrived safely here in Uman last Thursday night and I found your extremely long letter regarding the *shidukh* [marriage arrangement]. I immediately wrote a letter to Tcherin and I sent it with my carriage driver who brought me here from there. I told them that it is impossible for you to bring your daughter. You really are in the right too, as I discussed with them there face to face. Even if you wanted to set aside what you think, it is still impossible to set aside what your wife and relatives think. Most likely you already wrote them as is fitting. Now we must only man our posts and see how God's salvation will conclude the matter. I was quite irritated with you, my son, for becoming so upset, for forcing the issue so and for having so much anguish over something which is hidden from our view. Nothing is more concealed from a person than matters relating to marriage matches. Therefore, even if the prospective match was the richest person of the most noble descent in the whole generation, it would still be inappropriate to force the issue. Who knows how the matter will turn out in the end? Therefore, do not force anything. Just rely on God. If God means it to be, He will conclude the matter in the best possible way immediately or at a later time. "The word of our God will stand forever." I also received your letter today concerning the *shidukh* and I have already given you an appropriate response.

There is no time at all to continue, as the bearer of this letter is in a hurry.

Noson of Breslov

471

With God's help, Thursday, Tavo, 5604, Uman.

Warm greetings to my learned son, Reb Yitzchak, may he live, along with all his children, may they live.

On Sunday of this week I sent you a letter with a man from Tulchin. I informed you that I received two letters from you here and I responded to you appropriately. I have nothing new to report at the moment. I expect our people from Tcherin to be here tomorrow, God willing, and if I receive any news from them in connection with the marriage arrangement, I will inform you as is fitting. I already wrote you, warning you not to be pained over this matter at all. Simply rely on God. He will bring it to a good conclusion.

May God save us in His compassion and show us the path to *teshuvah* [repentance]. May we merit to attain the mystical meaning of the month of Elul on the practical level, to fulfill "Who makes a path in the sea and a road through the mighty waters." This means to be "knowledgeable in *halakhah*" as is explained there, to fulfill "If I ascend to Heaven, You are there; and if I go down to hell, here You are" (see *Likutey Moharan* I, 6). It is all through the power of the "new light" who revealed all this! He engaged all his days in "repentance on repentance for his former conception of Godliness." How much truer is this now that he has ascended to his eternal rest, to "the day which is entirely Shabbat!" Would that he might emanate upon us from there the holiness of Shabbat until we too merit "the day which is entirely Shabbat." There is a great deal to say about this right now. May we only merit to fulfill the Rebbe's words properly, as God and he wish us to. Then we will enjoy good forever.

The words of your father waiting for salvation.

Noson of Breslov

Greetings to all our comrades with a great love; in particular to my illustrious friend Reb Nachman, may his light shine, grandson of our master, teacher and Rebbe, of holy, sainted memory. I very much yearn for him to come here for this approaching Rosh HaShanah. It will benefit him in This World and the Next. It is impossible to write much. May God allow us to prepare ourselves as we should for Rosh HaShanah and to feel from now on "the power of the holiness of the day. For it is awesome and frightening indeed" (from the Rosh HaShanah Liturgy). No matter what, *Ashreinu!* How fortunate we are that we are part of the holy gathering which assembles in the name of our master, teacher and Rebbe, of holy, sainted memory! We already heard from his holy mouth that "nothing is greater [than to be with me for Rosh HaShanah]" (*Tzaddik* #117).

The words of your father waiting for salvation.

Noson, the same

Letters from 5605 (1844-45)

The year in review

This was the year of Reb Noson's passing. The compiler of *Alim LiTerufah* ("Eternally Yours") writes:

These are the letters of our teacher and rav, our pride and strength, the apple of our eye, Reb Noson, of holy sainted memory, from the year 605 of the Sixth Millennium. It was in this year that he passed away on the 10th of Tevet (December 20, 1844) which fell then on Friday, Erev Shabbat Vayigash. May his merit protect us. Amen, selah.

472

With thanks to God, Friday, the Ten Days of Repentance, 5605, Uman.

May the One Who is constantly doing new things grant us a good new year both physically and spiritually. To my dear, beloved son, the learned Reb Yitzchak, may he live, along with all his children, may they live.

In my house just now were *etrogim* from Reb Yaakov Weisman. I nearly bought one of them for three and a half new rubles, though he was not entirely satisfied with it; but then I decided to rely on you instead. For I hope to God that through your good desire and yearning you will certainly buy me a fine, valid *etrog*. It is all in God's hands. Therefore, if you have not yet bought one, do so at once. I already conveyed the information to Reb Nachman from Heissen and you will also understand for yourself own how to proceed by God's salvation. Then God's plan will emerge. The truth is that I would be willing to pay even six new rubles or more, provided that it be worth the price. But I hope to God that, since *etrogim* are presently available, you will buy me a fine, valid *etrog* for a reasonable price. Be sure to send it to me quickly so that it will reach my home before I arrive next Thursday. You should also send me a good, beautiful *lulav* and three *hadasim*. You should handle this all in the best way possible and charge me however you wish.

May the Master of Salvation and Compassion have pity and compassion on us so that we may merit to cry a great deal on the holy, awesome and fearsome day that is coming upon us, peace, i.e. on Yom Kippur. May we likewise merit to express our hearts and our sins before Him until He looks down and sees from

Heaven and opens up the path of *teshuvah* (repentance). This path of *teshuvah* is the holy path that our teacher Moshe forged during these forty days (from Rosh Chodesh Elul to Yom Kippur) which our awesome Rebbe, of holy, sainted memory, revealed in this generation based on the verse "If I ascend to Heaven, there You are; if I go down to hell, You are here." A person needs to be extremely knowledgeable in this indeed, as is written there on the subject of "knowing how to ascend and descend" (*Likutey Moharan* I, 6:6,7).

Ashreinu! Ashreinu! How fortunate we are! We can really say this thousands and tens of thousands of times inasmuch as we merited to hear awesome words such as these! May we only merit to fulfill them and to have God open our hearts to His Torah and place love and fear of Him in our hearts. Thus may we prevail over all the thoughts which confuse and distract us, may we never fall for any reason, and may we be truly knowledgeable in all the above, in accordance with God's will and the will of those who fear Him who revealed all this and more. It is for this very reason too that I did not buy an *etrog* here now — namely, because it is still prior to Yom Kippur. Perhaps I will be worthy *after* Yom Kippur of a more beautiful *etrog*, as the Rebbe revealed (*Rabbi Nachman's Wisdom* p.202, #87). Even though it appears that this letter will not reach you until after Yom Kippur, you should still pay close attention to these words. For the crucial thing is to draw these pathways of *teshuvah*, i.e. this "knowledge," into the whole year.

Due to the honor of Shabbat it is impossible to continue any longer. I already spoke on Rosh HaShanah about how the essence of this pathway of *teshuvah* is enhanced by the holiness of Shabbat. This is particularly so now, as Shabbat-Shuvah (the

Shabbat between Rosh HaShanah and Yom Kippur) is approaching. For the essence of the holiness of Shabbat is to attain *teshuvah* amidst joy; because the essence of *teshuvah* is joy, to rejoice in God wherever a person may be. Praise God, I have a great deal to say about this. But now, because of the honor of this Shabbat, it is impossible to continue. May God in His compassion seal us for good, long lives and for peace and may He truly bring us back to Him soon.

The words of your father waiting for salvation.

Noson of Breslov

Warm greetings to all our comrades with a great love! And greetings to my learned friend Reb Yaakov, may his light shine, and to all our comrades! All these words were meant for them as well and they too ought to read this letter. Perhaps they will fortify themselves from now on not to waste their lives, God forbid, and to begin again to attach themselves to me anew. For there is no refuge they can flee to except me. Then all of us together will flee and escape to our rock and our fortress who in his great power will draw us close to God. The Rebbe's power to save all those who take shelter in him is extremely great and awesome indeed in This World and the Next! They will do what they deem best.

The words of the one awakening and encouraging them for their own true, eternal good.

Noson, the same

473

With thanks to God, Hoshana Rabba, Erev Shabbat, 5605, Breslov.

My dear, beloved son.

I received your letter before *Hodu* (Morning Prayers) and I was pleased by your heart's desire for the true good. It stirred me to say the *Hosha Na!* ("Save, please!") prayers with extra enthusiasm, since I felt your pain, along with the pain of all our comrades and of all Israel. They are all going through twice as much as you are, though there are countless differences and variations among individuals. *Ashrekha!* Happy are you, my son! Happy are all of us that we came into the world at a time when a new light such as the Rebbe was revealed, a holy, awesome light such as this, the light of lights! His greatest praise is silence!

What else shall I tell you now at so pressured a time? For there is the honor of Shabbat and the Festival and the bearer of this letter is in a hurry. Just fortify yourself determinedly and bring yourself to joy with everything I just said, because God is with us! Do not fear, be afraid or frightened at all! God will not abandon you in This World or in the Next! For this one (the Rebbe) went out before us and he said explicitly before his ascent to the sublime, supernal heights, "What is there for you to worry about seeing that I am going before you?" (*Tzaddik* #122). It is now time to rejoice on Shemini Atzeret and Simchat Torah. Remember what I said on Rosh HaShanah about Shabbat, with regard to concluding the Torah reading with Parashat Bereishit on Simchat Torah. All the work we engage in from Rosh HaShanah until now is all in order to draw forth the holiness of Shabbat. This is one and the same concept as "being knowledgeable in *halakhah*," whereby every person any time, wherever he is, can fulfill "If I go down to hell, You are here"; and in his place too he can rejoice in God, the Torah and in His true tzaddikim. Thus he can turn all the grief and sighing into great joy that, yes, even *I* with everything that I go through, still hail in the name of a holy and awesome light such as this! Happy are you, Israel!

The words of your father,

Noson of Breslov

Greetings to all our comrades with a great love; in particular to the grandson of our master, teacher and Rebbe, of blessed memory! Happy are you, Israel!

474

With thanks to God, Tuesday, Lekh Lekha, 5605, Breslov.

Greetings to my dear, learned son, Reb Yitzchak, may he live.

I received your letter yesterday. I had already heard a little about the salvation of your son, my grandson, David Zvi, may he live, but I did not believe it. For I myself was in Teplik between Yom Kippur and Sukkot and spoke with him face to face, and he did not mention anything about it. Now "it is good to thank God" for all the good He has bestowed upon us. It is impossible to elaborate on this right now, though, as the bearer of this letter is in a hurry. Please let me know if your son, my grandson, Michel, may he live, has completely recovered his strength yet. May God rescue you from all pain and fear and may you merit to rear your sons and your daughter to long, good lives amidst satisfaction and joy.

But you already know, my dear son, that the world is replete with suffering, as is written (Job 14:1), "Man was born to toil; short-lived and full of grief." All the philosophers acknowledge this too. What they do not know, however, is the ultimate purpose for which man was created to toil. "But we are Your People, the Children of Your Covenant, the Children of Avraham...*Ashreinu*! Happy are we! How good is our portion!" (from the Morning Prayers). For we know the absolute truth about the eternal goal: that man was created in order to know God, Blessed be He — and for this it is well worth enduring this suffering. What is more, the very fact that a person knows about and believes in this tempers the suffering and enables him to turn everything into joy!

The primary way of doing this is by bringing oneself to joy that we are from the Seed of Israel and that we know about and believe in the true tzaddik who actually *attained* the eternal goal. No matter what, through him we will certainly merit to have a good eternal end, to gaze upon the pleasantness of God! And compared with the tiniest point of *this* awesome expectation and hope, all the world's toil and suffering is naught. What is more, praise God, "He will not send His hand into the grave" (Job 30:24) and "In suffering You gave me relief," so that within the straits themselves there are many great "expansions" (*Likutey Moharan* I, 195). Therefore just really be happy! Just happy...! Be healthy and joyful all the time and accustom yourself to constantly turn all the grief and sighing into joy, as we have already discussed extensively. For it is good to thank God for already providing us with the cure in advance of the blow through our holy and awesome Rebbe, of holy, sainted memory, and there is hope for our final outcome!

The words of your father,

Noson of Breslov

475

With God's help, Thursday, Lekh Lekha, 5605, Breslov.

Warm greetings to my beloved son, may he live, along with the rest of his family, may they live.

I received your letter just now. I will not respond to it, however, as I already sent you a letter through Reb Nachman from Heissen. I am pained by what you wrote, because it appears that you have not yet left behind your fears concerning the various matters in which you are involved. But see, my dear son, how correct I am in what I always say about the bitterness of the affairs of This World. It is all rooted in what they [our Sages] said (*Zohar* I:241), "Were it not for the salt, the world would not be able to endure the bitterness."

It would be appropriate for you to receive hints from this by which to bring yourself to joy at all times that we merited to know...etc. Come and look upon the might of your master! For we know that the days of Chanukah are approaching! Chanukah embodies the concept of the dedication of the Temple which is effected in accordance with our *Selach Na!*,

"Please forgive!" plea on Yom Kippur. No matter what, Israel as a whole certainly effected some pardon and forgiveness through their plea of *Selach Na!* Thus there will certainly be a sprouting of the seeds of salvation on Chanukah, and likewise a beginning of the dedication of the Temple. This in turn will cause "the illumination of son and student" to shine forth eternally and to radiate His Godliness to "those who dwell on high" spiritual levels and to "those who dwell down below" on low spiritual levels; and they will be included in one another. Then God's glory will fill the whole world and we will all recognize His greatness and exalted glory (*Likutey Moharan* II, 7). Furthermore, "in the place of His greatness, there we find His humility" through which He pitied us and shone upon us lights such as these! Let us be happy and rejoice in His salvation!

The words of your father,

Noson of Breslov

Thanks to His Holy Name for your sons' salvation, may they live. So may He always save you and rescue you from all pain and fear and may He strengthen your heart and the hearts of your children, may they live, for His service. For this is our life forever.

476

With God's help, Wednesday, Vayeira, 5605, Breslov.

Greetings to my dear, beloved son, may his light shine, along with all his family.

I received your letter yesterday and Reb Sh. has not yet arrived. I had been waiting for him to come before preparing a letter to you, because then I would know what to write you about your business. The time for reciting the Morning *Shema* and for the Morning Prayers has now arrived but your enormous yearning for my letters compels me to put pen to paper. I do not really know what to write you. After everything that you, I and all of us have endured, it is necessary to repeat the Rebbe's awesome words anew (Rabbi Nachman's Wisdom #3), "God is very great and we know nothing at all. Things are taking place in the world and people know absolutely nothing at all." He concluded this conversation by saying, "The main thing is never to despair of crying out, praying, supplicating and entreating." One screams. One pleads, etc.

These words have been giving me vitality for a long time now; and, not only that, but they help me to speak with people and to shine points of the absolute truth into them! How great are God's deeds! If you listen to and really think about this aforementioned holy conversation, you too will be able to feel in your heart what it is impossible to articulate, as in "Her husband is known in the gates (*ShAaRrim*)," " God is known to each person according to what he conceives (*meSHAeR*) in his own heart" (Zohar I:103). For the Rebbe spoke this holy conversation *after* he revealed his awesome and exalted Torah lessons and stories, his revelation of Godliness, his profound, awesome and wondrous advice, the likes of which have never been revealed, and after he revealed the cool, fresh, running water of the well-springs of salvation. After all this, *then* he cried out that "we know nothing at all!" If you really think about all this, you will be able to say with new enthusiasm and feeling "God is great and highly to be praised; His greatness is unfathomable!" Similarly, in every place where the greatness of the Creator is mentioned, we can understand through this perception that, by God's compassion, He will open up to us the Light of the Infinite until we merit to speak our words with great fervor and self-sacrifice.

It is impossible to explain this matter any further even in person, let alone in writing. "Lord, my God, You are very great!" I now understand this verse for myself in the following way. "Lord, my God..." — even the revelation of Your Godliness and greatness that You illumine within *my* heart, as in "*my* God"—even there "You are very great!" How much more must Your *actual* greatness be, since I know that Your greatness is absolutely unfathomable, as discussed above! It is impossible to explain all this and it is practically impossible even to write it down; but because of your enormous good desire I simply could not restrain myself.

But now that God has sent these words to my pen, my dear, beloved son, really take them to heart and do not say that you are far from them, given your deeds and how busy you are with business affairs. God forbid that you should tell yourself such a thing! To the contrary! *This* is God's enormous greatness, that in His compassion He informed us through the true tzaddik that "His greatness is unfathomable" and that there is hope every moment of every day for every single person. For He already supplied us with an eternal cure in advance of our crushing blows, God spare us, i.e. the spiritual blows, which are the greatest suffering of all, as each person knows in his own soul. But in direct response to this, this entire awesome conversation left the Rebbe's holy mouth, this conversation which begins, "God is great and we know nothing at all," until at the end he said "The main thing is never to despair of crying out...," as I quoted above and as I merited to hear directly from his holy mouth.

While all this that he spoke in my presence contains extremely profound meaning, as far as it concerns *us*, he said it only in order that we too should believe in God's enormous greatness and thereby fortify ourselves and never despair of crying out through whatever should come upon us, upon our children or upon all future generations. "God is great and we know nothing at all. There is a phenomenon that everything is turned to the good." The very fact that I am now writing you these words, my dear son, is also a result of God's enormous greatness. Fortify yourself determinedly, my son and friend! Seize happiness and joy and turn all the grief and sighing into joy at all times!

The words of your father inspiring himself with all the above.

Noson, the same

Loving greetings to all our comrades, in particular to your son, my dear grandson, David Zvi, may he live. Write me about how your son, Michel, may he live, is doing. Greetings as well to the grandson of our Rebbe, of blessed memory, Reb Nachman, may his light shine. He too should read this letter and he should let me know when he sets out for his safe journey. If my friend, your in-law, is there, send him my loving greetings. All these words were also meant for him and for all our comrades who desire the truth. Fortify your hearts and be strong, all you who hope in God!

477

With God's help, Monday, Erev Rosh Chodesh Kislev, 5605, Breslov.

To my dear son; the customary greeting.

I sent your letter to Reb Sh. in Uman and it has most certainly reached him. For I sent along with it another letter to Reb Chaim Graniver, who is one of our comrades from there, and I received a response from him last Friday. There is nothing new at the moment. "God is great and highly to be praised!" Recall the letter which I wrote you some days ago which speaks about the conversation in which the Rebbe said, "God is great and we know nothing at all" (see previous letter). My vitality now is only through this — but it is impossible to speak about it, especially in writing.

Fortify yourself determinedly, my son, anew all the time! Through all the various bitterness that you and I experience, it is necessary to bring ourselves to joy all the more, and to turn all the grief and sighing into joy! For what would we have done, God forbid, if amidst bitterness, grief and sighing such as this, we were to be opponents of the Rebbe, God forbid, God forbid? We would be completely without hope, God forbid! But now, now, there is plenty of good and wondrous hope for all of us! Without a doubt there is good hope for me and for you. Hope to God and He will save you. And no matter what, really be happy!

Noson of Breslov

478

With thanks to God, Sunday, Vayeishev, 5605.

My dear, beloved son.

You are receiving the watch. Try to have it repaired immediately so that it will be returned to me today by the bearer of this letter. May God shine the light of the holiness of the approaching holy Chanukah upon us and by His kindness may He send His light and His truth. Let us be happy and rejoice in His salvation! You are also receiving letters from Tcherin which you should deliver to the appropriate people. I have conveyed additional information to the bearer of this letter.

The words of your father waiting to see you soon in joy.

Noson of Breslov

Greetings to all our comrades with a great love! I hereby enjoin Reb Nachman, may his light shine, to take a few hours out of the day to stand over the watchmaker and to make sure that he completes the repair today and that he does a good job. You should also go with him and ask the watchmaker to fix the watch at once. I assume that you will handle everything in the best possible way, since you know how much I need the watch all the time.

Noson, the same

* * *

[Publisher's note: following are several undated letters, printed in earlier versions of the Alim LiTerufah.]

[Compiler's note: This addendum was found in Reb Noson's handwriting. The beginning and the end of it are missing.]

What can I say? The distress and bitterness of the world that one hears in these times cannot be expressed in writing. Evil and bitter, it cuts to the quick. Every single person is full of suffering and distress and no-one has any idea what to do. But not a single one of us wants to take up the craft of our ancestors and cry out to God. For, because of our many sins, the bitterness and suffering have become so overwhelming, God forbid, that people cannot even cry out to God. May God on His own in His abundant compassion just take pity on us and open our eyes, rejoice our hearts and bring us back to Him in perfect repentance so that we will all merit to see the coming of the redeemer speedily in our times. Amen. May it be His will.

[Publisher's note: Because this letter refers to the printing of the Likutey Tefilot, *it appears that it was written sometime between 1819 and 1824, when Reb Noson had a printing press in his home. There is also a reference to Reb Noson's nephew, Reb Isaac, who passed away sometime in 1830-1831.]*

My dear son.

I have nothing to write to you now. When I left my house I had not thought to write to you. But while writing a few words to my nephew, Reb Isaac, may his light shine, I remembered your tremendous desire to receive my letters. So I decided to send you regards.

I feel very bad over the fact that you weren't happy when you were in my house and you were terribly broken-hearted. It was hard for me to bear it. Nevertheless, I know and believe that God's compassion is still on me and on you and on all of us. He certainly won't forsake you forever and, no matter what, your end will be a good one!

Now, my son, hearken to my voice, to what I am commanding you; bring yourself to joy in any way you can, especially in these coming days of the month of Adar, when merriment is to be increased. Start *now* to make an Achashveirosh skit, a rich-man poor-man skit, a summer-winter skit and other types of skits and merriment.

The paper and ink seem to be fine. I don't see any way to get olive oil. Send it quickly either Monday or by post — without delay. That way, I won't have to think about it on Friday, please God, at all. Meanwhile, you profited greatly through the paper and ink. This entire letter! I had not thought to write at length, but your strong desire prevailed. The ink "flows" through the pen on such very fine paper.

Thank God Who has helped me till now. This, too, is one of the aforementioned "salvations and expansions" as in (Psalms 4:2), "In my constrictions, You gave me relief." In truth, it is a large expansion and a wondrous salvation because our letters are precious remedies. They all flow from the "wellspring from God's house" which "all its fruits are for eating and its leaves are for healing" (cf. Ezekiel 47:12). "Leaves" refer to the paper which are leaves and pages upon which are written all the holy books which are our remedies and life, forever.

Noson, the same

Regards to my friend, the learned, esteemed Reb Menachem Mendel, and his brother, my friend, the learned Reb Shlomo, may their light shine, and to my nephew, my friend, the son of my dear friend, Reb Yeshayah, may his light shine.

I have written to you several times to send me money for the printing. I even received an answer that you *want* to send but you weren't all together then. Now I'm reminding you again. Arouse your warm hearts and send me some money for the Prayers. That way, you will also merit to have a portion in this tremendous mitzvah. You will also receive the prayers in return for your payment. Your eyes will see and your hearts will rejoice.

The words of their true friend,

Noson, the same

While writing this letter I received your letter today with the sum of five rubles from Reb Yeshayah, may his light shine. May God repay his deed. There is nothing for me to add because I already warned you strongly to come immediately to Uman for this coming Erev Rosh Chodesh. Do this without any changes. Even if, God forbid, your father-in-law is delayed and does not come to his house by the time you receive this letter, I call upon you not to wait for him at all. Just hire a carriage immediately and travel to Uman for Erev Rosh Chodesh Nisan without delay. Because it is close to Shabbat, it is impossible to continue.

Peace and joy and life,

Noson, the same

[Compiler's note: This letter was sent to one of our comrades. The beginning is missing.]

...I also send you greetings with great love. Before Pesach, I wrote somewhat at length. Afterwards, I received your letter from your in-law, Reb Yoel, may his light shine. I was surprised that you hadn't received my letter. I am even more surprised that I only received one letter from you. Because of this, you missed an opportunity in that I didn't write to you.

Also, this winter, I was bedridden in Uman and stayed there more than five weeks. Afterwards, I was in Terhovitza and was travelling for more than seven weeks. I didn't see any letter of yours there. Your father, my friend, was looking forward eagerly to your letter and was disappointed. Actually, in this regard, you are not fulfilling your obligation towards your father at all. Then I arrived home very weak and found your letter at the home of Reb Noson, son of Reb L., which was written several weeks ago. I didn't know then where you were. I returned home close to Purim and sent you the abovementioned letter between Purim and Pesach. I still don't know if you received it. I have nothing to add now to that letter. Just carry out what I wrote there and send me what you promised in the letter through the abovementioned Reb Noson. Also, try as much as possible to collect from our comrades and especially from my friend, Reb Zvi b'reb M. Breger and from my friend, Reb Leibele b'Reb Ch. I am sure that you will do everything you can for my sake in the best possible way. May God Who is good, finish for you for the best.

About the matter that you wrote, that your in-law should advance the time of the wedding to before the time of the agreement, he already said that it is impossible. He was in my house and excused himself greatly. He said that, with God's help, he would make the wedding at the agreed-upon time. Maybe he could advance it to this coming Elul. I think you should come here, without fail, for this coming festival of Shavuot, and then you can finish everything for the best. Also, the fifty rubles which you already remitted is on deposit with me as a surety but the time for payment has come. I don't want to be involved any more but I don't want to abrogate the deposit until you come yourself and deposit it with whomever you want.

For all these reasons, I have nothing more to say. Just carry out my aforementioned request to send me whatever money you can from yourself or from others. After that, hasten yourself to prepare to come here for this coming festival of Shavuot. This will be good for you in all respects, physical, spiritual and financial, and for the good of the couple, may they live. May the Master of salvation and consolation, console and save you, materially and spiritually, so that you should merit to escape and draw near to God from all your troubles until everything turns into good.

There is much to write on this subject but neither time nor the page is sufficient! Also, I am hoping that, with God's help, you will be coming. Then, face to face, we will discuss God's salvation as much as He will laden us with His never-ending kindness and wonders. May we be happy and rejoice in His salvation.

The words of your true friend, eternally hoping first
for your answer and then to see you soon, in joy.

Noson of Breslov

Warm regards to your whole family, your son the groom, may he live, and my friend, your father-in-law. He too should send a sum as I wrote in my previous letter. Greetings to all our dear comrades with great love. Whatever money you collect, should only be sent to my son, Reb Yitzchak, may he live, in Tulchin. I am also sending this letter to Tulchin to be sure that it reaches you with God's help.

The account of Reb Noson's passing

[Editor's note: The following account was written by our comrades in Breslov to those in Tcherin describing the passing of the light of our eyes, the tzaddik, foundation of the world, our teacher, Reb Noson of Breslov, of sainted memory, who passed away in the year 5605, on Friday, Erev Shabbat, the 10th of Tevet.]

With thanks to God, 5605.

May He Who said "Enough!" to His world say "Enough!" to our troubles! May God comfort us. Woe for the calamity that has stricken us! We have been left alone like a mast on a mountain top, like a flagpole on the top of a hill! For, because of our sins, our splendor and pride, the crown of our heads, our souls' beloved, was taken from us — our master, teacher and rav, Reb Noson, of sainted memory — on Friday, Erev Shabbat, the 10th of Tevet, Parashat Vayigash, an hour before the arrival of Shabbat. May we be an expiation for his rest.

His condition began to deteriorate on Saturday night, Motzay Shabbat Parashat Mikeitz. That Shabbat, i.e. Parashat Mikeitz, when he came to the Third Meal to teach Torah, his opening words were these: "Even though it is embarrassing to say — since every speaker says it — it nonetheless needs to be said. You should know that we all must have our last moments and die, and we will all have to lie with our feet to the door."

He said these words with great awe. He then taught the lesson "Rabbi Shimon rejoiced" (*Likutey Moharan* I, 61) on the subject of advice, of having faith in the Sages and about the printing of books. He also taught the idea that when the soul ascends on high, its true perfection is that it should remain down below as well (see *Likutey Moharan* II, 7:4). Afterwards he was extremely happy.

That Friday night prior to this he gave a lesson about the Menorah and he danced by himself. After leaving the table he spoke about the Yom Kippur service. The words left his mouth like bolts of fire as he said, "The High Priest, when he entered the Holy of Holies, stood in the place where he stood and entered the place where he entered. See before Whom you are entering! 'One, one plus one...' (Yom Kippur Musaf Liturgy). And a Torah scholar is greater than the High Priest, as is written, 'She (the Torah) is more precious than pearls'" (*Horiyot* 13a). Prior to this he related a dream he dreamt which hinted at his passing. On Motzay Shabbat Parashat Mikeitz he entered the room where we had held the Third Meal and taught a lesson connected to Parashat Mikeitz. At the conclusion of the lesson he gave an explanation of the Mishnah (*Avot* 1:6), "Acquire a rav (teacher) and buy, *K'Nei*, a friend." This is what he said, "'Acquire a rav'; and if you do not know who the rav is, '*K'Nei* a friend' — the *KaNeh*, the pen, should be your friend. A person must draw himself close to a rebbe. And when there is no rebbe he should attach himself to the pen (i.e. to the rebbe's writings)."

Reb Noson wept as he recited Havdalah, and in the middle of the night he grew very weak. His strength waned with every passing day. On Monday, Reb Zev Lubarski came to him. Reb

Noson spoke to him about the Rebbe's Rosh HaShanah, exhorting him in the strongest terms to travel to Uman for Rosh HaShanah. That Wednesday night after the Evening Prayers we were standing before him. The aforementioned Reb Zev, who had also come, was standing to the side and Reb David from Tulchin was standing in front of him. Reb Noson said to Reb David, "Do not block Zev. At least let him gaze at me. The Rebbe also once told someone, 'Look at me. It will be of great benefit to you.'" "We must get together," Reb Noson said. Reb Zev asked him, "Where?" "In the Next World," he responded.

He then told an awesome story about the *Sefer HaNisraf* ("The Burned Book"), which was burned while the Rebbe was in Lemberg. Reb Noson transcribed the book from the Rebbe's dictation in three and a half hours. "I walked out afterwards," he said, "as if from the *Idra*" [The *Idra* was where Rabbi Shimon bar Yochai revealed some of the deepest mysteries of the *Zohar*.] Reb Noson then said, "It was only by Divine help that I just told you this story."

At midnight he recited *Tikkun Chatzot*. After reciting *Chatzot*, about three hours before daybreak, he took up his pen for three and a half hours and composed part of a Torah discourse based on the Mishnah, "One is permitted to water a dry field during the Intermediate Days of the Festival..." (*Moed Katan* 2a; which was incorporated into his final discourse — see *Likutey Halakhot, Rosh Chodesh* 7).

Later Reb Meir Yehudah came to him. Reb Noson said, "Even if a person is the worst sinner, the most important thing is that he hold onto the Rebbe. Then he will certainly repent and be rectified." On Wednesday a number of our comrades were standing in his presence and he said, "Your main job will be to print books. 'Let your wellsprings flow outwards!'" He also spoke about "the 72 strings" (*Likutey Moharan* II, 8).

Thursday morning two hours before daybreak Reb Meir Yehudah and Reb Leibtze came to Reb Noson and he said, "The angel Dumah comes to a person after he is buried, splits open his stomach and dumps its contents onto his face (see *Shabbat* 151b). Oy! Especially when the person's stomach is full of medicines, this punishment is like a burning fire! But the Rebbe will certainly rectify everything."

In the morning during the Morning Prayers, Reb Noson grew extremely weak. It was then that the *tzaddeket* Adil, the Rebbe's daughter, came to him. She said to us, "Why are you silent?! You must cry out in prayer for his recovery." But Reb Noson did not agree because, he said, he has many enemies. Rather, he instructed us how we should pray for him. He said that we should ask in our *hitbodedut* that it be counted to his merit that he wrote down the Rebbe's teachings, arranged them properly and made them distinctive; and that even now he still wants to print. "Your very lives depend on me," he said.

Reb Zvi from Teplik also came to him and Reb Noson asked him if he had received the money from the landowner yet. Reb Noson said to him, "Give me your money and I will watch over it for you until the World to Come." "My ancestors accumulated down below and I have accumulated up above" (*Bava Batra* 11a), he said. He then instructed us to recite many Psalms "however you can."

Thursday night we read Reb Noson two of the Rebbe's stories, #1 and #2 (see *Rabbi Nachman's Stories*). Prior to daybreak he told us to bring him hot water for a bath. Before it was brought he spoke a great deal — it was almost as if he were giving his last will and testament. "You must hold yourselves together with a great love. You are good, *kosher*, people but you are *shlamazelnikers* (losers)!"

He suddenly said to all those present, "Three tragedies occured in the month of Tevet. What were they?" No-one remembered and he answered himself, "Ezra the Scribe died, the Torah was translated into Greek, and the city wall was breached (i.e. the Babylonian king, Nevuchadnezzar, laid siege to Jerusalem). Well, when Ezra the Scribe passes away and *treif posul* (i.e. atheism, heresy and false ideologies) get the upper hand, as we find today when there are thousands and tens of thousands of *treif posul*... I trust, though, that one page of the Rebbe's teachings will be enough to rectify everything. I therefore instruct you that your work should be to print the books, to fulfill 'Let your wellsprings flow outwards.' You must be strong with money, desire and effort!" He said to his son Reb Yitzchak, "You too must give five hundred silver rubles for this. If not, then give sixty silver rubles."

He also said, "Even with the harsh and bitter punishments that exist, in the end they still want to oppose such a Rebbe as this! *Oy!*"

In the morning Reb Noson put on his tzitzit and tefilin and prayed with all his might. He said the *Selichot* (penitential prayers for the fast day) and he cried during the reading of the Torah. After prayers Reb Noson studied, finishing the commentary of the *SHaKh* on a section of the large *Shulchan Arukh*. Those around him suggested that he study in the small [abridged] *Shulchan Arukh*. "It is an effort for you to study in the larger edition," they said. But Reb Noson replied, "Do not be so loyal to me." Afterward he recited Psalms. He then told Nachman, the son of Ozer, to bring him *kol tuv*, "all good," but he did not know what Reb Noson meant. He explained, "Bring me the *Tanakh* (Bible) — this is "all good."

Later on he said that if two men would come in with a fiddle and dance for him, it would certainly make him feel good. He said that he would not drink anything else, even tea. Two hours later, though, he told his son, Reb Yitzchak, to go to the house and bring Shabbat rolls — just make sure they were prepared specifically for Shabbat. He ordered those around him to set up a table for him on the chair and Reb Noson himself sat on the candle chest. With great difficulty he ate a small piece of bread with a tiny amount of sauce and compote and, when he finished, he said that it is permissible to recite the Blessing After Meals on a nearby bed. During the Blessing After Meals he said, "May the Merciful One draw upon us the holiness of the Land of Israel." Afterwards he said, "I had not planned to eat, but I changed my mind."

Later on he sent for candles and he said, "The Shabbat candles, the Festival candles and the Chanukah candles are all one concept! I have mountains upon mountains of the most wondrous, amazing teachings on the subject, but I just do not have the strength to say them."

He subsequently addressed Reb Nachman from Tulchin and quoted the verse, "'Go to Yosef and do whatever he tells you' (Genesis 41,55). The main thing is to be attached to tzaddikim."

He later told all of us to go to the mikveh and we went. When we returned from the mikveh his condition had greatly deteriorated. The *tzaddeket* Adil came to him and asked, "What? Has your condition worsened?" Reb Noson answered, "It is with great kindness."

He did not speak with us any more. We only heard him saying, "May God bless you and keep you," the blessing "Who brings on sleep...," "the Gracious One Who forgives abundantly," "Who sanctifies the Shabbat," "Blessed are You in holiness" and *Echad*, "One." This lasted for about an hour and a half.

He passed away in a state of great calm and serenity moments after the time for lighting the Shabbat candles. He was buried on Motzay Shabbat, amidst great honor, even from the *mitnagdim*. I will not elaborate any further in writing. So much could be said about this that the skins of all the rams of *Neviot* could not contain the account.

Please, please, our friends and brothers! Fortify yourselves mightily to support our master and teacher's household! Let the gold flow from your pockets to publish his holy books! This is the thing he stressed most of all! May God comfort us and gladden our broken hearts. For as you all know, Reb Noson's sole desire and yearning was to rejoice in God and in His holy Torah.

From all our comrades in Breslov, 5605

Letter from Reb Naftali

Student of Rebbe Nachman

Thursday, Parashat Teitzei

My beloved brother and friend from youth.

I heard about what happened to you — "I heard and my heart shuddered. My lips, they shook!" How I feel for your bitter pain! How pained I am for you, my brother! My sweet love for you is fixed in my heart from our youth, so that in my own heart I feel your bitter pain. But we must take solace, as it is written (Isaiah 40:1), "'Take comfort, take comfort, My People,' says God." The Torah is eternal and applies to every person at all times; and now too it says, "Take comfort, take comfort." From the time that I heard and was grief-stricken over your pain, I have been sick at heart and sighing very much.

But this is my consolation: that I have known you from my youth and I know that implanted deep in your heart is the point of true faith in God, His Torah and in His greatest tzaddikim who are "the wellsprings of salvation" (see the Targum on Isaiah 12:3). With their words a person can indeed take comfort and encourage himself at all times to fulfill the holy verses with which Jeremiah consoled himself following his own terribly bitter lament (Lamentations 3:18-32): "I said, 'I have lost all expectation and hope in God'. But I will say in my heart — 'therefore I will have hope. God's kindness never ends. His compassion never ceases...' Even if He brings on grief, He later takes pity in keeping with His compassion and enormous kindness." So may it be with you. And may the prophecies and consolations which Isaiah spoke for future generations also be fulfilled for you (Isaiah 66:13), "As a man's mother comforts him so will I comfort you, and in Jerusalem you will be consoled." May you also be encouraged in this way. Fortify your heart and be strong in the hope that you will merit to go, amidst abundant displays of relief and favor, to the holy city of Jerusalem! Amen. May it be His will.

In the innermost depths of our hearts you and I both know and feel the point of holy faith which was implanted there from our youth in that we merited in our youth to draw near to the light of lights, the purest of the pure, and the greatest of the great of the tzaddikim — our master, teacher and Rebbe, the "the flowing spring, the source of wisdom." This is true wisdom dressed and wrapped in pure, true faith; and this point of holy, honest faith, of sainted memory, is the source of wisdom and faith. It is from him that the point of true faith took root in us, to believe and "to declare that the word of God is right, my Rock, in Whom there is no injustice" and that through everything that comes upon a person he may draw closer to God with the songs, praises and expressions of thanksgiving spoken by the sweet singer of Israel [King David] in the holy Book of Psalms.

What more can I say about this, when you know it all very well? I have been so deeply involved for so long now with these wellsprings of holy Torah wisdom which the Rebbe left after him as a blessing and a remnant for the generations to come. He in his clear wisdom informed us on the verse "She discerns that his enterprise is good" (*Likutey Moharan* I, 285) that even if a person merely tastes the pleasant wisdom of these holy, lovely Torah teachings — if his ears only heard them in his youth from the mouth of the true tzaddik and wise man — then [the verse continues] "her candle (i.e. the light of these teachings) is not extinguished at *night*" — i.e. even amidst all the darkness and spiritual rejection which every person experiences. Therefore awaken this holy vestige and come here and visit the Rebbe's holy gravesite.

The Rebbe promised us that, if we say Psalms at his holy gravesite — especially the Ten Psalms [of the Tikkun HaKlali] (see *Rabbi Nachman's Tikkun*) — he will shelter and protect us forever and for all eternity. Certainly after what you have gone through in your old age, it would be correct for you to come here [and do this]. While it is certainly difficult for you to break down the barriers and come for Rosh HaShanah, you should at least be sure to prevail, with God's help, and come for a day during the approaching holy month of Elul. It is unnecessary to say any more to an intelligent and enthusiastic person such as yourself. I will only add briefly the words of the Tekoan woman (Samuel II, 14:14), "All of us will die; and as water which runs onto the ground cannot be gathered up again, [so it is with us and our lives]. For God lets no one escape it." I am therefore urging you to do good and to seriously think about strengthening yourself and drawing close anew to the Rebbe's light both in deed and in word by coming to say Psalms at his holy gravesite. Perhaps you will merit to pour out your heart before God — the Rebbe's holy gravesite is a place particularly appropriate and well-suited to this — and to speak out all that you have gone through from the very beginning. Deep in your good heart you understand well that this is indeed your obligation in both the physical and spiritual realms.

The words of your true friend always, [writing you]

out of the great love for you which is implanted in my heart. I know from reliable tradition that in the very end, after our flesh disintegrates and our spirit returns to God, we will all gather together in the place of the source of our vitality, of blessed memory. I therefore encourage and fortify you, before the day flees and the shadows lengthen, to come to the holy gravesite and to be written and sealed immediately for a good life and for peace in the physical and the spiritual, as you yourself wish.

Naftali of Uman

Letters of Reb Noson's son, Reb Yitzchak

Compiler's note: Since most of this holy book consists of letters which our teacher, Reb Noson, of sainted memory, wrote to his son Reb Yitzchak, of blessed memory, I thought it would be an excellent idea to print here as an appendix some letters by Reb Yitzchak, of blessed memory, which I have in my possession. These letters, in Reb Yitzchak's own handwriting, were sent to me by his distinguished grandson, the illustrious Reb Nachman Sternhartz from Tulchin. Much can be learned from them in terms of drawing close to the true tzaddik and love for our Holy Land. For "even the mundane conversations of Torah scholars deserve study." This is particularly true for these letters, which are full of words of fear of Heaven, wondrous encouragement, and holy advice for the service of God emanating from "the flowing spring, the source of wisdom." May it be God's will that their holy words constantly be engraved on our hearts and that they manifest themselves in actual practice and deeds to benefit us all our lives. Amen. May it be His will.

1

With thanks to God, Friday, Vayakheil, 5592, Tulchin.

To my honored master, father, teacher and rav — peace and life forever.

"My life for my petition and my daughter for my request." I ask you please to pray that God should send her a complete cure for all her pains and that she should quickly recover her strength. My eyes are lifted to God alone and to the prayers of your exalted holiness. Thank God, I have merited thus far to rely only on God and not on any intermediary by the use of physical remedies. It was not for nothing that God had you send through me the letter you wrote to Kremenchug to the Rebbe's daughter [Sarah] about the need to stay away from the doctor. At that time [the importance] of guarding oneself from cures on the natural level was engraved upon my heart anew. I really drummed into my head what was written there! Thank God for that! All this was only decided in my *own* mind though. I still had to persuade my wife to agree — and this I effected only through my prayers. For that whole week I prayed, "Master of the World! Save us from physical remedies!" and, thank God, I succeeded. My trust is in God that He will soon cure her completely. I have a great deal to write about this, but time does not allow because of the honor of Shabbat. The bottom line is, "If we had come into the world only to hear this, it would have been reason enough!"

I already wrote to your honor that some of the Rebbe's teachings are deeply implanted in my heart. This matter [regarding doctors] is one of those things that I merited to really hear, to take to my heart and to never forget. I have heeded this well indeed, both on the physical and the spiritual level — I understand [the reason] for it in terms of the physical and, besides that, I believe in the words of the Rebbe, of blessed memory. In spite of all that is happening, with God's help, I studied many times more this week than I have in times past. May God allow me to always carry out your holy advice from now on and forever. How anxiously I await your holy response! Please, please, my master and father, may his light shine, give me life physically and spiritually, and quickly give me a fitting response!

> The words of your son, waiting for salvation soon through the prayers of your exalted holiness and yearning to receive your answer to all my letters and to merit to genuinely fulfill it from now on and forever eternally.
>
> *The insignificant Yitzchak*

2

With thanks to God, Sunday, Pikudey, 5592, Tulchin.

I prepared this letter (see Letter #1) to send on Friday, Erev Shabbat, but it was delayed until now when I received your holy letter. What can I say? What can I say? I found there what my soul loves. So may God bring me to joy to truly fulfill your holy words. What can I say to you, my master, father and teacher, may his light shine? In recent times the advice you wrote in the past about crying out and beseeching has taken on a new potency for me — i.e. the

advice that, no matter what, a person must cry out and request
[from God] and that, no matter what happens, a person always
accomplishes something by this. For even in the meantime
[when he has yet to be answered] the cry is still not lost, God
forbid. On the contrary, he really does accomplish!

I saw this now specifically when I witnessed God's kindness to me in connection with the recovery of my daughter
and especially with regard to our having avoided the doctor.
The latter of these two I effected only through prayers and
supplications — with crying out and requesting — by just
asking God for an unearned gift. Thank God, I also accomplished through this advice a great deal in connection
with what I myself am going through. For in this matter this
advice is certainly good, seeing that, in itself, the crying out
is good. How deeply the words of your exalted person entered
my heart when you wrote about the great inherent value of
good desires! This alone helps me in that I give myself life by
my holy yearnings and desire for the truth, i.e. by the fact that
at least I have holy *desires*.

I spoke about this quite a bit this past week with my friend,
Reb Mordekhai, may his light shine. Thank God Who has
helped me thus far in that there are a number of points from the
Rebbe's teachings that I have really absorbed from your
honored person and on which I am indeed quite steadfast. May
God allow me to apply them at all times and to truly fulfill them,
"to study, to teach, to keep, to do and to fulfill." May I merit to
come to the true, eternal goal in this world, as the Rebbe, of
blessed memory, wishes me to do. There are a great many things

I would like to write to your honor, but it is simply impossible due to lack of time. Basically, in my opinion, there is no father in the world who fulfills "teach them to your children" the way that you, my honored father, fulfill this commandment with me. For the main thing to teach is advice and pathways by which one can fortify himself in the service of God. Thank God, I have already received from your holy exaltedness a great deal of holy advice and many pathways by which to fortify myself in the service of God no matter what. So may God allow me to constantly hold vigil at your doors day after day and to carry out all of your holy words in the physical and the spiritual so that I may merit to apply myself diligently to Torah study and prayer and not to stray left or right from your holy will. Rather may I always fulfill all that I hear from your mouth, in holiness and purity and in joy and wholehearted gladness.

> The words of your son, hoping that the verse, "a wise son brings joy to his father," will be fulfilled through me in all respects.

The insignificant Yitzchak

My wife, may she live, my daughter, may she live, and my son David Zvi, may he live, all send loving regards. All our comrades send regards.

3

[This letter is from Reb Noson's son, Reb Yitzchak, to Reb Nachman of Tulchin, in Uman.]

With God's help, Wednesday morning, Toldot, 5621, Tulchin.

Life, peace and abundant lovingkindness to my honored and beloved friend, the illustrious, distinguished and learned Reb Nachman Ha-Levi, may his light shine.

I received your letters from [Parashat] Vayeira and [Parashat] Chayey Sarah in good order and I read them carefully. While I was greatly pained by the distress and suffering you are experiencing, I inspired myself tremendously with the beautiful words with which you are strengthening yourself. The whole world needs to hear this! For it is well known that situations like these occur throughout the world. But *they* have no way of mitigating [the suffering] and strengthening themselves! This can only be accomplished in the spiritual realm where there is an overall mitigation [*hamtakah*] by the tzaddik, the foundation of the world. For he, in his great power, sweetens the bitterness of the entire world. God had pity on us and allowed us to draw close to his holy light and to receive wondrous advice from him on how to encourage ourselves amidst the great floodwaters which are rushing in upon us. We must praise the Master of All for all the good He has bestowed upon us! What can I say? What can I say?

I just now studied the lesson *Azamra!* (Likutey Moharan I, 282) and I realized anew the preciousness of this holy teaching. I literally received new life as a person who drank a life-giving elixir. I literally came back to life! In addition to this, there is, with God's help, the glimmer of understanding that I have in my heart of how very high the words of this teaching actually reach. And we, with God's help, rely on this holy *chazan* [prayer leader] who "sees in what place the children are reading" (see *Azamra!*). May God be with us and may we merit to hold onto this prayer leader all of our lives in This World and the Next forever and for all eternity. Then our final outcome will certainly be good and wondrous indeed! The most important thing is that we should merit to fulfill the Rebbe's holy advice and to adhere and to practice this awesome teaching of *Azamra!*

May we likewise merit to fulfill all the Rebbe's holy teachings, especially as they were explained to us by his holy student, my honored master, father, teacher and rav. I hope that their holy merit will protect us and rescue us from the great floodwaters and that we will merit to hold our ground in Torah, prayer and good deeds and to strengthen ourselves in life with all our good points. For this is [also] a result of the pursuit of the "elder" and there is no other strategy but to hold onto our good point. Then we will certainly be safely rescued. May God be with us from now on and forever.

I was extremely surprised by what you wrote me that, since you are distressed over the matter of your daughter-in-law, you are entertaining the notion that you were mistaken from the beginning. I cannot understand how your honor can think such a thing. To all appearances [everything seemed to be well]. She was the daughter of our friend Reb Nachman, may his light shine, the daughter-in-law of our friend Reb Efraim. Reb Efraim [even] sent me a letter concerning this matter to the effect that, by arranging a marriage with her, our friend Reb Nachman did just what he himself had considered and that this was really the most obvious place for her. *Nu?* So what shall we do now, God spare us? Why should your honor think such foolishness and make yourself needlessly miserable over the past. "Trouble is bad enough in its hour," and, in this matter, he is not an "only child." The same thing takes place in practically every household. God in His abundant compassion tempers the pain in every situation. He will also show him compassion and temper it for the best. This is all happening for the sake of your son's free will. May God strengthen his heart in Torah, prayer and good deeds. God will surely help him so that all will be well. May God quickly bestow upon him domestic peace.

> With this I will close and say farewell. Your beloved friend, waiting to hear from you about displays of relief and salvation. Amen. May it be His will.
>
> *Yitzchak*

As for supporting the *kloyz* (the study hall in Uman), I certainly very much wish to furnish it with the best appurtances. But how can I describe to you the enormity of our needs here? Our friend Reb Itzele is presently naked and bereft of everything. In addition to this, ever since the end of the Festival, his family has not been well; and now today he too is not well. Our friend, "the holy fruit," Reb Nachman, is also extremely pressured in his livelihood and he has no-one to help him. You are also aware of the situation of my son, Reb David Zvi, may he live. May God have pity on me and abundantly bestow all good through me. Nonetheless, my friend, I have taken this matter to mind and I will be certain to think about how I can have a good share in this. May God grant salvation such that I may perform His will in this, as this is indeed my good intention.

My friend! It seems to me that your honor told me that you too have some connection with the marriage arrangement being made in Constantine. I am therefore informing you that our friend Reb Nachman is ready to travel to Costantine in the days ahead in order to finalize the match, God willing, with our friend, Reb Itzikele. They have already reached agreement by way of letter and there remains only to close the match. He wrote there yesterday that he is traveling to him to finalize [the *shidukh*], God willing. I too, as you might have expected, also wrote as was fitting. I would thus like to remind you that if you intend to have any share in the match you should write them immediately to remind them of this. You can also mention me. For the truth is that I was the real matchmaker here, as Reb Nachman knows. I wrote about this matter from the outset and I am also doing so now. Nonetheless, I have decided, for a number of reasons, not to ask directly for any remuneration. You, however, can hint to them from afar on my behalf.

Your friend, the same

4

[This is a letter which Reb Yitzchak, of blessed memory, wrote to his sons about his arrival in our Holy Land, may it be rebuilt and established.]
With thanks to God, Friday, Erev Shabbat Matot-Masai, 5628, here in the holy city of Zefat, may it be rebuilt and established speedily in our times. Amen, selah.

Let the mountains bear greetings and blessing to my honored and beloved sons, may they live, along with their wives and all their children, may they live. May they all receive blessing from the Life of Life from now on and forever.

I wrote you a lengthy letter from the holy city of Haifa. Now I thank God for all the good He has bestowed upon me. Thank God, I received all my belongings with nothing missing and with God's help I experienced amazing acts of lovingkindness in all these matters. "Its beginning was suffering and its end — tranquility." Praise God, I arrived here last Tuesday towards evening and, by God's kindness, the people here welcomed me with great honor. Many people even came out to meet me. I did not rest for the first 24 hours after my arrival as a number of honorable people came to greet me. They all treated me with great love and they blessed me that I should settle well here.

When I came to pray in the synagogue of the honored ARI, the person in charge, the honored Reb Pinchas from Kaliban, welcomed me at once and had me stand right next to him. The wealthy and distinguished Reb Chaim Leib from Kaminetz also prays there and he came to my place immediately and greeted me lovingly. His roots are in the city of Mohilov and his love for my honored master, father, teacher and rav, of sainted memory, and in particular for my holy, honored grandfather, Reb David Zvi, of blessed memory, is deeply engraved on his heart.

What can I say? What can I say? God is great and highly to be praised! How great are the wonders He has done with me! It is all through the merit of the great Eshel tree, "the flowing spring, the source of wisdom," of holy sainted memory, and of his holy student, my honored master, father, teacher and rav, of blessed memory. So may God continue to help me and may their great merit stand me in good stead and give me success here in achieving my eternal goal and in following their holy pathways. May I merit to make a fresh start in serving God, to hold vigil at the doors of Torah, prayer and good deeds and to add greater life and vitality every day. What can I tell you, my sons? How good and pleasant it is to live in this Holy Land! It is impossible to imagine. There are a number of hours when I must practice the holy teaching of "lest they be destroyed" (as a result of experiencing too much holiness, as in Exodus 19:21). May God help me improve my pathways of holiness for many long, good years to come. Amen. May it be His will.

I do not yet have a place to live. I am presently staying with our beloved friend, Reb Meir, may his light shine, from whom I am renting a room on a short-term basis. My windows open to a view of the holy gravesite of the tzaddik, the holy Tanna Rabbi Shimon Bar Yochai, and I can at this moment see his holy gravesite. May his merit protect us. May God pity me in His abundant compassion and provide me with a proper dwelling. While there are many places available for rent, I need a special room in which to pour out many supplications before God. May I find by His kindness a proper dwelling. God is my hope that He will also send me true salvation in this matter for my own good.

I did not intend to write you a single word today as I am still extremely busy. It is just that the courier to Beirut suddenly appeared and I thought I would at least inform you of my safe arrival here. I do not have time to continue or to address anyone individually. God willing, by the time the next courier leaves, which is in about two weeks, I will prepare letters to each place and to each person as is fitting. Right now I have still not rested from my exhaustion after the donkey ride which really took a toll on my body. In spite of this there were also wondrous displays of kindness in this area as well. May God have compassion on me and may the approaching holy Shabbat come with rest, love and peace. With this I will close and say goodbye.

> The words of your father and friend, happy and glad every moment with his whole heart that I was privileged to come here and blessing you with all good, physical and spiritual, that you will enjoy good all your days. Amen. May it be His will.
>
> *Yitzchak*

I ask you very much to please extend greetings for me to each and every one of my friends, may they live, with a great love. Tell them that, God willing, next time they will all receive individual letters from me with love. Please write to Tulchin and inform them of my safe arrival. God willing, in the course of time I will write to everyone as is fitting. May God grant them the best of everything. Warm greetings to my fine friend, the outstanding and distinguished Rav Yaakov Teitelbaum, may his light shine. I could not withhold the favor from you [of greeting you]. Practically not an hour passes that I do not mention you. My love for you is engraved upon my heart, since you had a large share in my coming here and in enabling me to merit true good such as this. May God be with you, your children and your sons-in-law in all your endeavors so that you

may enjoy good all your lives from now on and forever. Amen.
May it be His will.

> Your true friend, happy and glad over my arrival
> in the Land.
>
> *Yitzchak*

5

*With thanks to God, Tuesday, Ekev, 5628, here in the holy city of Zefat,
may it be rebuilt and established speedily in our times. Amen, selah.*

*From the depths of my heart I send greetings to my dear, beloved and
cherished sons, the learned, distinguished and honorable Reb David
Zvi, may he live, and to the learned and distinguished Reb Michel,
may he live. May God fortify your good hearts in Torah, prayer and
good deeds and may He bless the work of your hands that you may
flourish all your days. May you live for many long years in good and
pleasantness, [blessed] with children, life, and ample sustenance all
your lives. Amen. May it be His will.*

I informed you immediately from the holy city of Haifa of
my safe arrival there. Subsequently, when God brought me here
to the holy city of Zefat, I informed you again of my safe arrival
along with that of all my belongings, with God's help. As I
instructed you, as soon as my son, Reb David Zvi, may he live,
arrives home from Odessa, you should send me a letter with the
first post to give life to my soul. I imagined last week when the
courier arrived here that I would certainly be receiving your
letter, but I did not merit it. This is the reason that I could not
send a letter to you with that courier. Therefore, my sons, may

you live, I am warning you from now on — at no time should you delay sending your letters to me. For with every letter you send me you give life to my soul and thereby truly fulfill the commandment to honor your father. Do as you see me do and always read my letters carefully so that you may answer me appropriately on every point.

I informed you in my letter from here about my safe arrival and I wrote you that, with God's help, I was honorably welcomed. Similarly, with God's help, on Shabbat Parashat Matot-Masai we had a joyful Shabbat in the house of Reb Meir, may his light shine, and a number of honored people, in particular from the *kollel*, sent me liquors. The house was full of people throughout Shabbat. With God's help, I pronounced a blessing in heartfelt joy that I merited to come here.

Friday, Erev Shabbat, was the *yahrzeit* of the honored tzaddik, foundation of the world, the ARI, of holy, sainted memory, and I visited his holy grave for the first time. How can I possibly describe to you, my sons, the sublime preciousness of his holy grave along with those of all the other holy people buried there? May their merit protect us. I found there men, women and children crying out and pleading in prayer for their very lives. As soon as one of them left, another came and the cries that were heard were from the depths of the heart. I too was there with my own prayers and requests and, with God's help, I expressed my heart there. From there I went to the grave of the holy tzaddik, Rav Pinchas Ben Yair, may his merit protect us.

What can I say? What can I say? I walked back to my house literally like a man walking on air. I did not know where I was.

For me everything was connected with the holy grave of "the flowing spring, the source of wisdom," of holy, sainted memory. It was literally as if I was standing right there [in Uman]; and the truth is that they are all one. *Ashraiy!* How fortunate I am! How good is my portion! My lots have fallen in pleasant places! For I merited to enter into the shade of "the flowing spring, the source of wisdom," of blessed memory! It was he (the Rebbe) who instilled this lovely sensation in my heart through his holy student, my honored master, father, teacher and rav, of blessed memory. May it be God's will that I merit to pass my days and years in this Holy Land engaged in Torah, prayer and good deeds in a spirit of joy and gratitude.

I have so much in my heart to say about this, but it is impossible to bring it from potential to actual and to actually articulate it. With God's help, the land is bountiful and there is plenty of good, healthy food. But would that we might soon merit that the land not be in such ruins! You cannot imagine it! What can I say to you, my sons, may you live? I would certainly go to the holy grave of the ARI every day, but the walk there is treacherous and it is still difficult for me to go there alone. May God only give me the strength to go there every two weeks at least. Praise God, last Monday, the 15th of Av, I was also there in the afternoon and I took a man with me as a watchman. It was even more precious to me than the first time, but I arrived weak and exhausted. And where am I going to find a man to my liking to take with me every time? This applies particularly to the holy gravesite of the honored Tanna Rabbi Shimon Bar Yochai, whose gravesite stands literally in front of my eyes. My soul yearns to fly there, but travelling there requires greater preparation and a longer journey, comparable to our journey from home to Uman. How can I describe to you the road to his gravesite? It is mountains, valleys and hills strewn with rocks large and small. In short, one must just yearn and long for this good. By God's kindness I am prepared with God's help to go there, God willing, for this coming Erev Rosh Chodesh Elul. May God be with me and may He save me with all good. Amen. May it be His will.

You should know that last Thursday, praise God, I moved into the house which I rented for us. Neither of us were well during those days and I endured great anguish over this. With God's help and through His abundant kindness we recovered our strength after Shabbat Nachamu. The essence of the anguish that I suffered was over how to escape from the doctor and particularly for my wife, may she live. I just could not prevail against all the people who were coming to her. Here people use medicines even more than the people outside of the Land. For "God made everything with its counterbalancing opposite" (i.e. just as the Land of Israel is holier, so there exist there stronger forces opposing holiness), God spare us. But by God's compassion on me through the power that I received from the mouth of my honored master, father, teacher and rav, of blessed memory, I was saved from everything. May God be with us from now on and forever and may He save us from all illness. May He give us strength in all our 248 organs and our 365 sinews for many long good years to come.

Beyond this, God abundantly bestowed His kindness upon

us and He provided us with a maid for our house. She is a righteous and healthy woman and she takes care of all the domestic responsibilities. She bakes, cooks and runs all the necessary errands. My wife, may she live, could not even get out of bed. Even now, when with God's help she has recovered her health, she is still not able to go to the market. The aforementioned woman does not even receive a salary from us; she just gets room and board. I cannot describe to you the tremendous kindness that God has done for us by providing us with her. May God place it in her heart to indeed stand by her words as we agreed. My expenses at present are somewhat high as the people here think that I am rich. I guess this must be my *mazal*, with God's help. I trust God that He will provide me honorably with all that I need.

I ask you, my sons, may you live, to look out for me in all respects. My friends from Tulchin promised to help me here and you should prudently and consistently demand from them that they indeed do so. You should do the same with all our comrades, may they live, in whatever place, and in particular with my close friends and comrades, may they live. Perhaps God will be gracious to me so that I will merit to have my own house. I very much need this in order that I may have a special place for my devotions, and in rented quarters it is impossible to obtain this. All the buildings here are structured in a disorderly fashion. Only when a person purchases a dwelling for himself does he redesign it as he wishes. I cannot elaborate on this for you. I am certain that you will understand for yourselves how to proceed in this matter for my benefit. May God give you success in this.

For God's sake, whatever money you have to send me here, you should send directly to me, Reb Yitzchak Sternhartz from Tulchin. Be sure to specify "Sternhartz." Likewise, all the letters and even, God willing, when Reb Sander sends money — as presumably he will send to Reb Nachman — you should send everything to me and I will deliver it to him without delay. This is what Reb Nachman wants as well. For, with God's help, a perfect love, fraternity and companionship exists here between us. Thus far Reb Nachman has done nothing without the knowledge of our friend, Reb Meir, may his light shine. Do your utmost, with God's help, to have a respectable sum sent to me immediately after Rosh HaShanah for me, for our comrades, and for other people here. In particular you should remind our friend, Reb Zvi M.Z., may his light shine, about his donation that he sends here every year at this time, and presumably you will incidentally mention me as well.

I ask that you read all the letters enclosed here and that you deliver them to each one of the appropriate persons. The reason for this is that I may have written something to someone that you there find undesirable and I want you to be able to withhold the letter [if you wish]. In my opinion I have written appropriately, but I cannot impose my own will from such a distance against the judgment of people there. In short, I am relying on you so that everything, God willing, will be handled in the best possible way. From now on I will write no letter to any person without first receiving a letter from him — then I will be forced to give him an appropriate response. But now for this first time, it seems to me that I am obliged to do this. Many people asked me specifically to write them a letter and I promised them that I would. Thus I am now compelled to keep my word. From now on though, why should I write letters, especially since I have no time for it? I am waiting anxiously at all times to merit to hear good news of your success from the time that I left you and how the matter is proceeding in all respects. Most important, I am waiting to hear about how *you* are doing and I am praying for you about this every day. May God be with us and may He allow us to hear all good from one another.

I hereby bless you both right now that you should merit, God willing, to be in Uman for this coming holy Rosh Ha-Shanah. May God rescue you from all formidable impediments, God forbid. Rather, let everything be by His kindness, as on every Rosh HaShanah, and may you mention me there at all times. I too will make good mention of you here, since my soul is bound up with yours. Would that I might hear, God willing, word of your safe journey and arrival home! This would indeed give me joy! May God be with us and may he grant us salvation. Amen. May it be His will.

6

With thanks to God, Thursday, Reay.

The second courier came last Sunday and, praise God, I received your letter from Thursday, [the week of Parashat] Balak. Your lovely words brought light to my eyes and you really uplifted me; for how I yearned for your letter! While I was indeed distressed by what you wrote about the mail to Odessa getting lost, I cheered myself with the fact that, praise God, you bear no blame, God forbid. With God's help, this matter will certainly be properly rectified. The same thing happened a number of times when I myself was [in charge of the post office] and everyone knows that we are not responsible for the mishap. We must only petition God that no mishap occurs through any fault of ours, and then, with God's help, He will certainly save us from this.

I was certainly quite pleased with what you wrote me that, thank God, you have a free loan fund for what is necessary for the store. Nonetheless, my dear sons, in this area too, one must be extremely careful not to do a lot of borrowing [or lending]. For even without an *iska* [interest] agreement it is still necessary to pay a person for his time. I am confident though that you will be cautious in this respect on your own. May God grant you success and may I merit to receive a report of your well-being. For God's sake, do not worry! Trust in God's kindness at all times — He will not abandon you. And, for God's sake, be sure to have peace reign among you. This will perfect my joy.

The mail has been held up for more than five weeks and I am therefore uncertain as to whether or not this letter will reach you before you travel to Uman for the coming holy Rosh Ha-Shanah. I have thus written you a separate letter directly to Uman to my friend Reb Nachman HaLevi and I enclosed the letters for Tcherin; I also wrote you greetings there as well. Thus you may receive my letter there. Read it and be sure to carry out what is written there. Most likely you will in any case speak with our dear comrades, may they live, to my benefit and in particular, my friend, Reb Yitzchak, the son of Reb Gershon, may his light shine. God willing, when you arrive safely from Uman, you will presumably have something to send me here. It could be, however, that it will not be ready to send off right away, as it may be necessary to wait for the money from Tcherin which is customarily sent after Yom Kippur. The same thing applies to Terhovitza as well. Most likely our friend Reb Zvi, M.Z., will send his contribution then as well. Let me know [at that point], by letter, the sum that you have in your possession and do not wait until you [actually] send me the money. For I am yearning to receive your response to this letter.

Even apart from this, any time at all that you send money here, you should send a separate letter ahead directly to here via Beirut [informing me that you are doing so]. The money takes longer to arrive and in the meantime I will be anxiously awaiting your letter. For despite what I said, that I would not be longing for your letters, the truth is that I do and this is how it has to be. I trust that God in His kindness will save me in this matter. But now, at the start, I still need the letters, as an intelligent person can easily understand. As time passes and I sate my soul upon the preciousness of the Land, presumably I will come to true mental clarity, with God's help, which will exert a positive effect in this area as well. Beyond this, my sons, may you live, I have a tremendous amount to say due to my heart's enormous enthusiasm for living in this Holy Land, but it is impossible to express it in this context. Praised be God for the great kindness He has done for me!

The words of your father blessing you with all good and desiring to hear and to tell all good about us and about all our brothers, the Children of Israel. Amen. May it be His will.

Yitzchak

Greetings to my modest, dear daughter-in-law, Esther Sheindel, may she live, and to my dear, fine granddaughter, the bride Adil, may she live; to my dear, lovely grandson, Nachman, may he live, to my bright granddaughter, Batia, may she live, and to my bright young grandson, Shachneh, may he live.

Greetings to my modest, dear daughter-in-law, Rachel, may she live, to my dear, lovely grandson, Aharon, may he live, and to my dear, lovely grandson, Naftali, may he live. My precious children! Believe me, I do not forget you even for one moment and I pray to God for you every day. May He only accept my prayers. I implore you, do not worry but live [together] in peace. God certainly will help you and, God willing, you will be healthy and strong and you will see joy and satisfaction from your children. May God help me to hear all good from each one of you individually, and in particular may I soon merit to hear the joyful tidings about the wedding of my dear granddaughter Adil, may she live, to her groom from Teplik amidst joy and contentment. This will certainly give me new life.

The words of your father wishing you all the best. Be healthy and happy.

Yitzchak, the same

My wife, may she live, sends you all heartfelt greetings. Thank God, she is very happy that she merited to come here and she wishes you all the best. The way she misses the children is beyond anything in this world and she anxiously waits every moment to hear all good from them. Be healthy and happy.

From me, your mother,

Davrish, wife of Reb Yitzchak Sternhartz

[Publisher's note: apparently, Reb Yitzchak's wife also signed the letter. Her name, as signer, appears several times in the text.]

Greetings to my dear friend, the learned and illustrious man-of-standing, the honored Reb Yaakov Teitelbaum, may his light shine. This entire letter of mine is in front of you and you know everything. How can I express the great love for you which is fixed in my heart such that I cannot forget you for even one moment? You were my primary supporter who encouraged me to come here and the merit that you have for doing this is very great indeed. For, with God's help, the great and lovely preciousness of this Holy Land is inscribed in my heart. It is just impossible to imagine. And at every moment I constantly give thanks to God for this good, this kindness, that you did for me. It is for this reason that I asked your honored person to distinguish me with your good words in a letter to give life to my soul.

The words of your comrade and genuine friend who mentions you for good in his prayers.

Yitzchak

My sons, may you live. You should send greetings for me to all the wealthy citizens there, and especially to those who came to my aid and who also promised to help me in the future. In particular you should do so for our friend, Reb David Shore, may his light shine, since in Balta he affectionately blessed me for my journey.

Also, act for the sake of the mitzvah and speak there with Reb Chaim Lerner and his son Reb Y. They have a relative here, Adil, the daughter of Reb Chaim, and she is poor and destitute. It would be appropriate for them to send a gift to her for her sustenance. It will be counted as a great mitzvah.

You should also tell my friend, Reb Yisrael Kitzes, may his light shine, that it would be fitting for him to take pity on his step-mother. The pitiful state she is in is just unimaginable. She is sick in bed, God spare us, and she is in the *hekdesh* [a free hospice]. Why should he withhold his help from her? For the sake of the honor of his father, of blessed memory, he should be sure to honor him in this and it will bring him success.

His friend, encouraging him to do good.

Yitzchak

To my brothers and comrades, my honored, dear friends who pray in the study hall in the new city in Tulchin. Greetings from the Land of the Living! May you all have God's good blessing all the days of your lives in the spiritual and the physical. May your honor and *mazal* always ascend with children, life, and abundant livelihoods for many good years to come. Amen. May it be His will.

What can I tell you, my friends? This Holy Land is full of all good. Really, nothing is lacking. Only, by our many sins, everything is in ruins. Anyone who sees it is sick at heart, until God looks down from Heaven and sees, takes pity on us and quickly brings us our redemption and our righteous Mashiach. May it come speedily, in our times. Amen, selah. Then we will merit to see the building of the House of Our Splendor, the joy of all the earth. In the meantime, it is good to live here in one's old age. Thank God, there is plenty of good food to eat. In particular, there is the inspiration of seeing the resting places of the honored "holy ones who are in the earth." This part is absolutely indescribable. I give thanks to God every moment that He has bestowed His kindness upon me and brought me here. I long and hope to God that He will allow me to settle well here, to begin to hold vigil anew at the doors of Torah and to pass all the days and years of my life in Torah, prayer and good deeds, in wholeheartedness for many long, good years to come. This is what I have longed for all my life. Thank God, I am already here, and I trust God that everything will fall properly into place.

Your friend, blessing you with all good and mentioning you for good all the time in my prayers with love. May God allow us to hear all good from one another about ourselves and about all our brothers, the House of Israel.

Yitzchak

7

*With God's help, Sunday, Noach, 5629, the holy city of Zefat, may it
be rebuilt and established speedily in our times. Amen, selah.*

*From the Land of the Living I call forth greetings to my beloved, dear
sons whom I love as myself, the learned distinguished and honored Reb
David Zvi, may he live, and the learned, distinguished and honored
Reb Yechiel Michel, may he live, along with their wives and children,
may they live. May they all receive blessing from the Dwelling Place
of Blessings for all good, spiritual and physical, for many long, good
years to come. May I constantly merit to hear tidings of their good
salvation from now on and forever. Amen. May it be His will.*

I received your precious letter from Tuesday, the first day
of this past Rosh Chodesh Elul, safely, on the morning of holy
Hoshana Rabba, when I was in the synagogue. My yearning
was so great that I was not even able to read it. Tears streamed
from my eyes out of my great love for you and because I had
merited to see your handwriting. My yearning for this letter had
grown so overwhelming that I could no longer endure it. I gave
thanks to God and I was unable to settle my mind until the
Blessings before the Reading of the *Shema*. At that point I
pushed everything out of my mind and finished my prayers.
With God's help, I recited the *Hallel* and *Hosha Na!* prayers with
heartfelt enthusiam and after prayers I walked home and had a
taste of liquor and cake as is customary.

I then opened your letter and read it twice over slowly from
beginning to end. I was filled with great joy, and as a result of
that letter I was happy all day on Simchat Torah together with

our comrades, may they live. While I did find in your words some things about which I am quite distressed, all the same, with God's help, the measure of good is greater inasmuch as I did merit to hear how you are doing. Besides, we have always known that it is impossible for things to proceed smoothly and that waves must inevitably pass over every single person. Even in the Holy Land they are not exempt from this! The main thing though is to look at the favors which God in His great mercy so kindly and abundantly bestows upon us each and every day, which are beyond all calculation. Our hope is to God that He will save us from now on and forever in all that we need to be saved, spiritually and physically. Amen. May it be His will.

You should know that I sent you a letter from here immediately upon my safe arrival, as I wrote to you on the letter to Reb Yaakov David. I was quite surprised that you did not receive it then together with Reb Yaakov David's letter, since I sent them both on the same day. It included some urgent words of inspiration for you, as well as some urgent letters for Uman to be sent on to Teplik and Terhovitza. I am therefore waiting to know if you received that letter which was written on Friday, Matot-Masai. Subsequently, you should know, I sent you a long and urgent letter which I began on Sunday of Parashat Ekev and finished on Thursday, Parashat Reay. I also enclosed a letter there to each and every person individually, and, most important, a response to our friend, Reb Zvi M.Z., aknowledging receipt of the money.

There I described to you everything I experienced from the day of my arrival up to that time and I personally closed the letter inside the large package going to Beirut. I also sent a letter separately to Uman to our friend Reb Nachman. I enclosed other letters there too, as well as greetings to you, because I thought that perhaps the [first] letter might arrive in Tulchin at the time that you, God willing, were in Uman. I therefore sent directly to Uman as well so that you would also find a letter from me there and I instructed Reb Nachman to show you my letter. So now, my sons, may you live, in this letter I described to you everything and you can imagine how anxiously I am waiting for your response to it. You should also inquire in Uman as to whether the aforementioned letter of mine was received, as it included some urgent matters. May God Who is good finish for me from now on and forever.

You should know that after I wrote the aforementioned letter and properly sent it off, I again was not well. This presented a problem as far as my traveling to Miron for Rosh Chodesh Elul was concerned and I had been longing terribly to do this. With God's help, though, that Sunday before Rosh Chodesh He alleviated my pain and I summoned my strength and traveled there. I arrived there toward evening and out of the great excitement and yearning that I felt there I did not even notice my condition at all. Whatever I was capable of doing I did.

I was reminded again and again of God's kindness and I asked myself how it could be that a person of my modest worth could merit to arrive at this place and to say the awesome prayer about Rabbi Shimon Bar Yochai (in *Likutey Tefilot* II, 47) at his holy gravesite. I poured out my heart in earnest prayer a great deal at his holy grave and a little at the grave of his son, the holy, honored Rabbi Elazar, may their merit protect us, and also at the grave of the holy Tanna Rabbi Yitzchak Nafcha. Afterwards I went to the holy grave of the holy Tanna Rabbi Yochanan HaSandlar and there too my heart opened up in prayer. From there I went to the holy cave of the honored Tanna, Hillel the Prince, and of his illustrious students. The tremendous inspiration and excitement that I felt there are just indescribable. I gave praise and thanksgiving to God constantly that I merited to be in the lot of "the flowing spring, the source of wisdom," of holy sainted memory, and of his holy student [Reb Noson]. For it is by their great power that I merited to taste the holiness of that place. I was overflowing with joy and, with God's help, I made favorable mention of you all there in my prayers. I had compiled a notebook of all the names, listing them in order. I read out every one of the names from my book and I prayed and asked for everything that I could for them. May God hear my prayer and may He grant us His salvation, that we may enjoy good all our days from now on and forever.

Afterward, I returned home from Miron and it was then that I felt how weak I was. Riding on the donkey was particularly difficult — you cannot imagine it. With God's help I arrived home safe and unscathed, albeit utterly exhausted, and I did not feel well that whole week following. But, with God's help, through the enormous inspiration and excitement that I felt because I merited to be in Miron, I was happy all the time and I accepted everything with love. After that my heart was really stirred to apply myself diligently to my studies, but I was unable to actually realize this in deed due to my great weakness.

From Shabbat Parashat Shoftim I recovered my strength somewhat though I was still not able to really sit down to my studies. My desire to do so, though, never left me, and, with God's help, I fully recuperated about halfway through Elul. Halfway through the month I went to the holy gravesite of the ARI along with all the other holy sites there which I had not yet visited. I also immersed myself in the holy mikveh of the ARI and I arrived home full of yearning. With God's help, from that time until now I have been applying myself diligently and studying a great deal. My wife and I both, thank God, are healthy and, praise God, the holidays passed joyfully. It is impossible to give all the details, but essentially, "God is great and highly to be praised!" I give Him thanks at every moment for the kindness that He did with me by bringing me to this point and for letting the lovely holiness of this Holy Land be implanted so incalculably deep in my heart. May I only merit to constantly hear from you in letters filled with good news. Then my joy will indeed be complete. For, as far as what's happening with me is concerned, with God's help I have found ways of overcoming the distractions. But my pining for your letters I just cannot put out of my mind — only, when by God's compassion, I forget. For my love for you is engraved upon my heart.

How I longed to hear all about our holy Rosh HaShanah in Uman and about where we ended up praying! How inspired I was to hear that the matter is approaching a gratifying conclusion. Would though that I might soon hear about the complete salvation: that our holy building has been completed!

[Publisher's note: the *kloyz* built by Reb Noson in the 1830s was rebuilt in the late

1860s. Reb Yitzchak was eager to hear the news that repairs and renovations were finished.] No prayer left my lips without my mentioning this matter, particularly at all the famous sites. I also prayed a great deal for you, that you should both merit to be in Uman for Rosh HaShanah among our holy gathering and I look forward to hearing good news about this. I bound myself from here, life, spirit and soul, to our holy gathering. I was particuarly stirred in this direction when I was at the holy gravesite of the ARI on Erev Rosh HaShanah and in his holy merit I bound myself from there to our holy gathering. May God be with us from now on and forever and may He allow us to hear all good from one another so as to give each other life. Amen. May it be His will.

You should know, my sons, may you live, that I have considered the matter of my expeditures and, after all the economizing, I am required to spend four silver rubles a week. I already wrote you that I must keep a maid, as my wife, may she live, simply cannot do everything; especially since this is something new for her. By God's compassion, He provided me with a woman who works in my house only in exchange for her board. So may He continue in His kindness to me and fortify my heart to trust that He will never abandon us. At present, I am not worrying about this in the least, since, praise God, for the time being I have enough to cover my expenses. I am informing you about this though so that you will know to exert yourselves to my advantage with all your ability in this matter. Furthermore, I have an opportunity to buy a house, which is something I deeply yearn for in order that I might have a special room for my devotions. But I am unable to determine how to proceed in this matter until I receive information from you about my income and about when it will be reaching me. My wife gives me whatever she has, but it is a small amount. We need no less than twice that. The money that I have I am unable to give [for the house] as long as I have no new income from you, since I need this money available now for my own daily expenses. May God in His great compassion take pity on me and save me to my benefit.

8

Today is Wednesday, Lekh Lekha.

The courier from Beirut arrived today and, praise God, I received what my soul loves, your precious letter, from Friday Erev Shabbat Nitzavim. How I longed to know whether you received my letters from Parashat Ekev and Parashat Reay! My dear sons, you really gave me life! May God give you life. Particularly uplifting was the good news I found there about our holy building in Uman. So may God continue in His kindness so that our holy gathering may grow larger and larger, and may you merit all your days to be among our holy gathering there on Rosh HaShanah. I too from here will be counted there among you in life, spirit and soul through the merit of the "holy ones who are in the earth." Now I long to know if you received the letter that I sent at that time directly to Uman to our friend Reb Nachman. I enclosed some urgent and important letters there, as I did not know if [my other letter to you] would reach you [at home] before you set out. Thus I am anxious to know if it was received on time, that is, when you were there. May God allow me to hear good news.

My sons, may you live. I read your letter twice over and I found it pleasing on every point. You breathed life into my every limb! May God in His great compassion take pity on me and may I merit to constantly hear good news from you. Particularly pleasing was the good report about holy Rosh HaShanah in Uman and about your safe arrival home whereupon you found the business in order. May God grant you success so that you may always fulfill the dictum, "Torah study in conjunction with a worldly occupation is good." May your Torah [study] be at fixed times and may you follow all the holy pathways of the honored "flowing spring, the source of wisdom," of holy sainted memory, which we received as an inheritance from my honored master, father, teacher and rav, of blessed memory.

The most important thing, though, is that you encourage yourselves with all your good points! And you can encourage yourselves constantly with the fact that there is now a new way for you to fulfill the commandment of honoring your father — namely, by working to help with my sustenance here. Thus you can be sure that whatever good God allows me to attain here will also be counted in your favor. For (Deuteronomy 33:18), "Rejoice Zevulun in your going out and Yissachar in your tents" applies to this too [Zevulun earned money to support Yissachar in his Torah study]. Even though you cannot supply all my needs from your own pockets, whatever is accomplished through your agency will be counted to your merit. Do not take lightly the matter of encouraging yourselves with this! All the more so, since I am not seeking extras,

God forbid, but just bread to eat and a place to rest. As far as clothing is concerned, thank God, I still have sufficient.

My primary orientation is my work toward the true goal. God knows my heart and in His great compassion He has already helped me tremendously in this. Most of all He has helped me have an inkling of the uniqueness of this Holy Land and I inspire myself with this every single moment. The longer I am here the more I change, and in all I see here God has allowed me to find wonders, so that the holiness of the Land has become implanted deeply in my heart. But it is absolutely impossible to speak about this at all. For "each person understands it according to what he perceives in his own heart."

Therefore, my beloved sons, may you live, for God's sake, derive inspiration from the fact that God has presented you with a great opportunity such as this. You, my son Michel, may you live, in your last letter you lamented before me how terribly busy and harried you are [by your worldly affairs] and I know the pain you have over this. I too was tested in this way and quite likely even more so. My dear son. You should know that not once, not twice and not several times, but times without number, I expressed a similar lament before my honored master, father, teacher and rav, of blessed memory. On each occasion he answered me, "You do not know what God wants of you! The main thing is that you lift up your eyes to Heaven in all that you do and whenever you are able to grab some good, do not refrain from doing so. The main thing is good desires and, especially when you are going to the post office, lift up your eyes to Heaven. Let your whole desire and orientation be for the true good and, as for what is happening to you, you have no idea at all. In the end, God willing, all will be well."

Please, my dear son! Most likely you have also heard this from me in person, but perhaps you have forgotten, so I am repeating this good advice for you again. What is more, all the good of my master [Reb Noson] is before you — i.e. all his holy books — and in them you can find rest and tranquility for your soul. My sons, may you live! My brothers and friends! For God's sake, fulfill "each man will help his brother" and fortify one another! This goes for business, for encouraging yourselves with all the good that you merit to grab from amidst of your worldly occupations and for being happy at all times. And in the merit of this, God will give you success in all your endeavors both spiritual and physical so that you may enjoy good all your days. My eyes will look on and rejoice!

Beyond this, my sons, may you live, what more can I say to elaborate? Thus far has God's compassion helped us. So may He constantly add to His kindness to us and allow us to hear all good from one another. When I receive a letter from you after your arrival home from Uman, then most likely I will compose a lengthy letter to you. As of now, though, you have not yet written me a proper response to all the requests that I put forth in my letter you received from Parashat Reay. I ask you and caution you in the strongest terms to read my letters carefully and to answer me on every detail. This is extremely important, as there were a number of letters [enclosed there] and it is crucial for me to know if all of them were received and then delivered or sent on to the appropriate individuals.

I was quite surprised, my sons, that I did not merit to receive one word or even a greeting sent through you from my two beloved friends, our friend, Reb Yaakov, may his light shine, and our friend, Reb Zvi M.Z. I do not know what to think about this and I am a little bit discouraged by it. But I trust God that their love for me has not been severed, and especially not that of our friend, Reb Yaakov, may his light shine, who merited to help me so much. May God grant him success. My love for them is engraved upon my heart and I remember them constantly in my prayers for their good. So, my friends, my sons, may you live, you should send them loving greetings from me. When I am honored by them in any way, I will certainly repay them many times over. May God forever grant you abundant well-being and please answer me on this matter explicitly so that I may know. Beyond this, may God place love and fear of Him in our hearts all our days, so that we may merit to walk the straight and true path.

> With this I will conclude and say goodbye. Your father, who loves you and whose soul is bound to yours without a moment's interruption, blesses you for all good. May God send true salvation.
>
> *Yitzchak*

Greetings to all our friends, may they live, to all our comrades, may they live, and to all those who come to our study hall. When I receive responses from them to my greetings which I sent them in my previous letter, then most likely I will honor them with my letters. May God give them abundant well-being and success forever. I received the note of our venerable, excellent friend, Reb Naftali, may his light shine, and I was pleased.

Do not forget to tell me where the children, may they live, are studying this winter so that I may have the satisfaction of knowing.

9

With God's help, Wednesday night, Vayeitzei, 5629, here in the holy city of Zefat, may it be rebuilt and established speedily in our days. Amen, selah.

From the Land of the Living I call greetings to my honored, beloved and precious sons whom I love as myself, the learned, distinguished and illustrious Reb David Zvi, may he live, along with his wife, may she live, and their children, may they live; and to the learned and distinguished Reb Yechiel Michel, may he live, along with his wife, may she live, and their children, may they live. May they all receive blessing from the Life of Life, that they may merit abundant good, both spiritual and physical, in This World and the Next forever. May my eyes see it and rejoice! Amen. May it be His will.

I thank God with all my heart that I merited to receive two letters from you this week — one on Monday through our friend Reb David, may his light shine, and another today through the courier together with the sum of 146.32 silver rubles and your report about our holy building in Uman, about holy Rosh Ha-Shanah, about your journey there and about your safe return home. My spirit came alive within me! So may God continue to allow me to hear about your salvation and well-being at all times.

This would indeed give me joy. What pleasure I had from hearing about your holiday celebrations in the study hall and in your homes together with all our friends, may they live. My hands are stretched forth to God that He will always bestow His favor and lovingkindness upon you and that you will enjoy abundant domestic peace and blessing. May "your homes be meeting places for sages" wherein are heard words pertaining to the eternal goal. Amen. May it be His will.

I wrote you a long letter during the week of Parashat Lekh Lekha. At the moment I have nothing to add until the arrival of a proper answer from you and until I see what you send me in the first mailing which you promised me in the two aforementioned letters. I was extremely pleased that you wrote me that you received all my letters. For with this I have acquitted myself of a great burden and now I have nothing further to do. God knows how much uncertainty I felt and I experienced numerous doubts about every single letter — this is why I wrote that you should read all the letters. It just seemed to me, though, that I had to write *once*, in particular at the beginning, to inform people, as they requested, of my safe arrival here. At the same time I also discussed the issue of helping to support my living here. This is why I was so interested to know whether the letters were received by each one of these people; for then I would know that I had fulfilled my obligation.

So now you really uplifted me by informing me that all the letters were received. I know that I must put no trust in any natural means, but rather that I must cast myself only on God's providence whereby He watches over every creature. In His compassion may He also sustain me comfortably all the days of my life in this Holy Land along with my wife, may she live, for many long, good years to come. By God's help, I took my life in my hands that I may hold vigil at the doors of Torah study and He has sent diligence into my heart for all my studies. The preciousness of this Holy Land grows increasingly dear to me all the time. Especially when I am at the holy gravesite of the ARI, of holy, sainted memory, and at the other holy sites, I experience a wondrous new vitality. It is entirely the result of our holy pathways which flow forth from "the flowing spring, the source of wisdom," of holy, sainted memory, which we received through my honored master, father, teacher and rav, of blessed memory, may his merit protect us. May God be with me now and forever and may I add new holiness and purity every day until I soon merit to come to the eternal goal in this lifetime. It is for this that my soul has longed all my life right up to this very day. So may God favor me with this good and may He bring me to joy with my good point from now on and forever. Amen. May it be His will.

> With this I will close and say goodbye. The words of your father, praying for you every day and blessing you with all good, spiritual and physical; waiting to hear from you and to also give you good news about us and about all our brothers that we may enjoy good all our days.
>
> *Yitzchak of Breslov*

How very delighted I was to hear that you brought your

sons, may they live, to Uman for Rosh HaShanah! I gave thanks and praise to God for this. May God strengthen their good hearts, starting now, to follow the straight path and may they merit all their lives to be among our holy gathering for many long, good years to come. Amen. May it be His will.

I hereby extend greetings to my modest, fine daughter-in-law, Esther Sheindel, may she live, to my dear granddaughter, the bride, Adil, may she live, to my dear grandson, the charming, pious Nachman, may he live, to my bright granddaughter, Batia, may she live, and to my young grandson, Shachneh, may he live. How grieved I am over the pain my daughter-in-law is experiencing! I pray for her all the time. I hope to God that He will soon save her and send her a complete recovery. For God's sake, do not let her become downhearted over this in the slightest and do not employ any medicinal dressings. Just wait for God's salvation through which He in His kindness will protect her from all disease and heal her completely. May I soon merit to hear news of her true salvation.

Greetings to my modest daughter-in-law, the fine Rachel, may she live, to my dear grandson, the charming, pious Aharon, may he live, and to my dear grandson, Naftali, may he live. I constantly mention them for good in my prayers and I look forward to hearing all good from them. May God be with us and save us.

My wife, may she live, extends warm, loving greetings. We received all the cake through Reb David and we were delighted! We wish you sweetness and good always with happy hearts and pray that we merit to hear all good from you. The words of your mother, praying for you always. May I soon merit to receive good cake from the marriage of my granddaughter, the bride, Adil, may she live.

> The words of,
>
> *Davrish, the wife of Yitzchak Sternhartz*

Greetings to my distinguished son-in-law, Reb Yaakov Michel, may his light shine, to my dear, charming grandson, Chaikel, may he live, to my dear granddaughter, Chanah, may she live, and to my dear grandson, David Zvi, may he live. I was amazed that I did not receive a single word from him. After he promised me that, God willing, he would write me a long letter after Rosh HaShanah, in the end I did not receive even a greeting from him. Thus I have nothing to write him. I mention him and his children, may they live, for good every day in my prayers. May God allow us to hear all good from them — this would indeed give me joy. Greetings to all my dear neighbors, may they live, and in particular to my friend, the young man, Reb Yaakov, may he live; and warm greetings to all our comrades, may they live. What is this that I do not hear a single thing from my friend Reb Hirsh Leib? Please let me know how our friend Reb Matil, the grandson of the late Reb Moshe Chaim, of blessed memory, and his sister, may she live, are doing. Let me know what is happening with them. I mention them in my prayers all the time. If there is an improvement in their situation, you will give me life [by telling me]. May God grant them true salvation.

My friends, my sons, may you live. If you ask our friend, Reb Chaim Krasinstein, if he is willing to accept a bottle of goose oil for Pesach for me [and he agrees to take it], see to it that you make me about 10 pints of oil for Pesach and send it to me through him. This is something which is very expensive here and it is not readily available. Even olive oil for Pesach is difficult to find. Besides this, though, thank God, there is excellent food and [even] delicacies here for an extremely low price. There are lemons and oranges — two and half *gedolim* for two large ones or four small ones. There is choice olive oil.... But a person still has free will to complain, God forbid, if he wants to. *Ashreinu!* Happy are we! How good is our portion that the lovely holiness of this Land has entered my heart! May God be with us from now on and forever. Amen. May it be His will.

You should read the letters for Odessa enclosed here and then seal them so that they will safely reach the proper people. Perhaps God will favor me so that merit will devolve upon them through me for their good.

Your father, the same

10

With God's help, Friday, Erev Shabbat Tzav, 5629, the holy city of Zefat, may it be rebuilt and established speedily in our days. Amen, selah.

From the depths of my heart I call forth greetings to my precious sons whom I love as myself, the learned and distinguished Rav David Zvi, may he live, along with his wife and children, may they live; and to the learned, illustrious Reb Michel, may he live, along with his wife and children, may they live. May they all be blessed by the Life of Life Who should favor them with all good, physical and spiritual, so that they may enjoy good all their days from now on and forever. May my eyes see and rejoice! Amen. May it be His will.

While I do not have anything new to tell you right now, since I have not yet received your response which I so long for to my long letter from Parashat Shmot, I nonetheless wanted to uphold what I wrote, that there should be communication between us every month. In addition to this I urgently need you to send the letter enclosed here to our friend Reb Moshe M., may his light shine, in which is enclosed for him the response from his brother-in-law, may his light shine, from the holy city of Tiberias. How tremendously you uplifted me when you sent me greetings in the letter of the aforementioned Reb Moshe! You literally brought me to life! For I found there more to be happy about than in the previous letter.

My beloved sons! Fortify your hearts and be strong! Trust God; He will not abandon you. You can learn from my case about God's great lovingkindness and wonders inasmuch as He allowed me amidst great floodwaters such as these to come here to tread upon this holy soil. What can I say? What can I say? If all the seas were ink it would still be insufficient to describe the great preciousness of this Holy Land! And, with God's help, my affection for the Land just continues to grow. What can I give back to God for all the kindness He has bestowed upon me? "Who has performed and accomplished this Who calls forth the generations from the 'beginning'," in whose holy shade we take shelter? (see *Likutey Moharan* II, 67). For not by my own power or actions was I worthy of this; but only through the power and merit of the great Eshel tree, the tzaddik, foundation of the world, "the flowing stream, the source of wisdom," of holy sainted memory, may his merit protect us, and through that of his holy student, my honored master, father, teacher and rav, of blessed memory. It was he [Reb Noson] who instilled in me [the will] to turn to the Rebbe's holy pathways and to follow all the holy advice which emanates from him. This is what helped me fortify myself for so many years in my desire [to come here]. Then, through their great power, God had compassion on me and I merited to bring this from potential to actual — to take my life in my hands and come, with God's help, to this Holy Land.

So may their great merit stand me in good stead, so that God will have compassion on me and allow me to go this year with my wife to the holy city of Jerusalem (may it be rebuilt and established speedily in our times. Amen, selah) and to be there among those who make the pilgrimage for the coming holy festival of Shavuot. At present all my thoughts are centered on this, although how exactly I will manage to do it is still concealed from me. For my livelihood now is extremely tight. Nonetheless, I trust in the kindness of God Who has accomplished so much with me that He will also perform this kindness. I have no strategy right now except prayer and supplication and, most of all, to be strong in my desire. For I do want this very much indeed! May God favor me and bestow this kindness upon me at its proper time just as He has given me good thus far, and may I soon merit to inform you good news regarding this. Amen. May it be His will.

Praise God, the days of Purim passed joyfully. I celebrated in my house together with all our comrades and a few others, and there was a quorum of ten at the holiday meal. My sons! How can I describe to you the enormity of the wondrous kindness that God has done for me in connection with the purchase of my house? With God's help, we have a nice, spacious area in which to get together and speak about the good treasures that we have [i.e. Rebbe Nachman's teachings]. All this is in spite of the fact that I am now forced to endure significant pressure with regard to my necessities. What is more, Pesach is rapidly approaching and it is necessary to buy new utensils. Everything is expensive too. For a half *fud* of potatoes here I had to pay 70 silver *kopeks* of pure silver. Money is extremely tight and, with God's help, I have never yet been tested [with financial pressure] such as this. May God send me good salvation from now on. In the meantime, what consoles me in my destitution is that I see myself dwelling in a marvelous house such as this! Then I give thanks to God for His kindness to me. My hands are spread forth in prayer for His kindness that in the course of time I will be saved in this [other] area too, and that He will remove me from my straits and send me abundant sustenance, so that we may enjoy good all our days. Amen. May it be His will.

What more can I tell you, my sons, may you live? Were it in my power, I would send you all the good of this Land. It is an absolute wonder to me! May God let me live for many years in good and pleasantness. I hereby bless you that you too should merit in your old age to take up residence together with your wives, may they live, in happiness in this Holy Land. Meanwhile strengthen yourselves determinedly to engage in Torah, prayer and good deeds as much as you possibly can.

May God bestow abundant blessing upon you and provide you with all good — children, life and ample sustenance — such that you will merit to provide me here with all that I need to live comfortably.

I am forced at present to strengthen myself in trust very much, since temporarily my situation is extremely tight indeed. The sum that I received from you together with the five rubles from our friend Reb Zvi M.Z. does not cover my present expenses and I was forced to borrow ten silver rubles which I doubt will last me even until this coming Rosh Chodesh Iyar. You, my dear sons, as much as you can, do not withhold this favor from me! I cannot explain the details of my situation to each person; but you, in person, can raise the matter with each person according to his own situation. May God bestow favor and grace upon you so that your words are accepted for good. Enclosed here are my letters to Uman. Read them in their entirety and afterwards seal each one properly and send them off quickly. You may add to and embellish them as you deem best. May God finish well for us. The days of Pesach are now approaching. May God be with us and may we merit to receive them in holiness and in purity and to fulfill all the holy commandments which are performed then. It is most important to avoid even a trace of *chametz*, leaven, on the physical level; and, especially on the spiritual level, to merit to banish from ourselves all our heart's foreign thoughts and to have holy thoughts from now on and forever. With this I will close and say goodbye.

The words of your father and friend blessing you
with all good and looking forward to rejoicing in

the joy of the coming holy Festival. May God allow
me to hear word of your joy on Purim and Pesach.
Then my heart too will rejoice!

Yitzchak

Warm greetings to my daughter-in-law, the modest Esther
Sheindel, may she live, and to my excellent granddaughter,
Adil, may she live; to my fine, distinguished grandson, Nachman, may he live, to my bright granddaughter, Batia, may she
live, and to my bright, young grandson, Shachneh, may he live.
And warm greetings to my modest daughter-in-law, Rachel,
may she live, to my fine, distinguished grandson, Aharon, may
he live, and to my excellent grandson, Naftali, may he live. How
tremendously you uplifted me when you wrote that your sons
are walking on the straight path. You literally brought me to
life! Would that I might always hear only good from you! What
shall I write you? I wish you all good and may what I request
for you always come about. I ask you, do not worry; put your
hope in God that everything will always be well.

The words of your father blessing you with all good
from the depths of his heart.

Yitzchak

My wife, may she live, sends greetings with a great love.
Thank God, she is enjoying living in this Holy Land, especially
since the purchase of our own residence, even though she too
is forced to endure much pressure and hardship. For even
though I do have an old woman as a maid, she still must do

[much] herself. This is particularly so in the matter of Pesach when a woman must do things in which she has never been tested before. Nonetheless she accepts it all with genuine love out of affection for the Holy Land. May God soon help us to live here in prosperity.

Davrish, the wife of Reb Yitzchak Sternhartz

Warm greetings to all our dear comrades, may they live, to all our neighbors and in particular to our friend, the young Reb Yaakov, may his light shine; and to our dear friend, Reb Avraham Meir, may his light shine, and to his son, Reb Yitzchak, may his light shine, to all our friends, may they live, and to all those who come to our study hall. Time does not allow me to write any more than this to each one of them. When I receive letters from them, I will certainly answer them fittingly. May they all receive blessing for all good from the Dwelling Place of Blessings. They are all engraved upon my heart to mention them for good.

Yitzchak

11

With thanks to God, Sunday, the 29th day of the Counting of the Children of Israel, 5629, here in the holy city of Zefat, may it be rebuilt and established speedily in our days. Amen. May it be His will.

From the depths of my heart I call forth greetings to my precious sons whom I love more than my own heart and soul, the learned and distinguished Reb David Zvi, may his light shine, along with his wife and children, may they live, and the learned and distinguished Reb

Yechiel Michel, may his light shine, along with his wife and children, may they live. May the Life of Life bestow upon them blessing, life and all good, spiritual and physical, that they may be planted in the tent of Torah, prayer and good deeds. May God's blessing be upon them with abundant blessing and success that they may enjoy good all their days. Amen. May it be His will.

I received safely your fine letter from Parashat Pikudey and Vayikra along with all the letters. How can I tell you what a great mitzvah you did by uplifting me the way you did! A thousand thanks, my sons, for this. So may God fortify you at all times in your good will and may I constantly merit to hear news of your success to inspire me.

How very thrilled I was to know about your rejoicing with our comrades, may they live, in your home this past holy Purim and how for the whole of Purim you ate your meals together as a group. So may God help you to have peace reign strong among you all your days amidst good and pleasantness. This would truly make me happy. I was surprised that you did not mention that our friend Reb Nachman, the son of Reb Y. TZ. and Reb Zvi Aryeh were present at your celebration. I assume they were together with you. Please let me know about this.

You wrote me that my letter reached Uman at the correct time when the well-to-do people, may they live, were there. I was surprised that I received no response from our friend Reb Nachman through our friend Reb Itzele. It would appear from this that there have been no new developments to my advantage. Well, it is all from God and my hope is in Him that He will save me. I assume that when there *is* a new development to my advantage, you will inform me of it immediately.

In connection with the fifty silver rubles which are due as a payment on my residence and what you wrote, that in your opinion, my wife, may she live, should pay this sum — I already wrote you that I never thought otherwise. I did not even give the initial one hundred silver rubles with a whole heart. It was only that our comrades encouraged me in this for my own good. Now, with God's help, I am grateful indeed to them for this. My wife, may she live, would certainly be happy to have this sum come out of her money. But at present the man here who buys this type of jewelry is not available and it is necessary to start now to pay *iska* [a certain type of interest charge permitted under Jewish law] about which I am somewhat distressed. Perhaps God will grant, though, that what you wrote me will come about, that our dear friend, Reb Abele, God willing, will soon be here. This will really be perfect for me. For then I will send the jewelry back with him to you and there will certainly be a buyer for it there. Thus the matter will turn out well.

Right now I am extremely happy, my beloved sons, may you live, that you sent me the sum which I requested. With God's help, this will cover the expenses of my holy journey to the holy city of Jerusalem for the approaching holiday of Shavuot. I will economize on my expenses so that I will have enough left over for my sustenance until the arrival of the payment which is owed to me on my account. May God favor me with His good kindness so that everything will come at its proper time in accordance with His will. May I merit to diligently proceed in my studies and may I succeed in my holy task — to effect my request for myself, for you, for all those who are with us and for all our brothers, the Children of Israel. May I merit to reach the eternal goal in this lifetime in this Holy Land. Amen. May it be His will.

I am indeed distressed by the tightness of your livelihood. But thank God for this kindness, that business is always slow during the wintertime. God's kindnesses never run out and He is my hope that business will pick up and that you will receive bountiful blessing and success. My hands are stretched forth in prayer for you to God again and again each and every day. My request is set down before him that He will save you in all matters for your good and in particular that He will open your good hearts with Torah, prayer and good deeds. This is all I want. You are my good portion and lot and my love for you is bound upon my soul. I cannot forget you even for a moment. Would that I might find favor and grace with God so that He will hear my prayer at all times to save you in all areas so that you may have good all your days! May I always merit to hear from you the sounds of Torah, prayer and good deeds amidst a bountiful livelihood and that you are raising up your sons and daughters to Torah, *chuppah,* and good deeds for good, long lives. Then my joy will indeed be complete. For their good is really my good.

My son, Michel, may you live. You expressed to me at great length your pain over how little you are engaging in Heaven's work due to your involvement in business. What can I say to you, my dear son? My heart sheds rivers of tears over this. But, my dear son, as you already know, this is just not the way. The most important thing is to make yourself happy with all the good points, and especially with the desire! With God's help, you do at least constantly have good desires. This is the main thing! In the end it will all certainly be for good. You can see from my case in particular the great value of yearning. From what you know of me you will be able to understand that it was only through good yearnings that I came, to merit to be upon this holy soil amidst the sweep of pain and sorrow that has passed over me during the time that you have known me.

Do not forget, my dear son, that I went out into the world right after I turned twenty. But I always allowed you to hold vigil at the doors of Torah until the time I left you [for *Eretz Yisrael*]. You can be confident in this power that God will not abandon you. Do not abandon your good yearnings even for one moment! In the meantime you will certainly grab some good as well. For God undoubtedly helps all the time and "no good desire is ever lost" (*Zohar* II, 150b). What is more, all our treasuries [i.e. Rebbe Nachman's books] are before you and you will be able to find in them comfort for your soul.

I already wrote you this on one occasion and I will repeat it again; you can really encourage yourselves with the fact that you have a great merit such as this of being involved in supporting and sustaining me here in this Holy Land. You can receive vitality from this as if you were constantly engaged in Torah and devotion; for we are all one soul. You know what my heart's intention was in coming to "the place of my vitality" and by God's kindness I am succeeding in doing God's desire. For at all times my heart is burning inside me to reach the ultimate goal and, with God's help, I do not waste my time on anything. My only desire is to study God's Torah as much as I possibly can. It is impossible for me to speak about this very much, but because of my love for you I am forced to encourage you a little. I have said enough for an intelligent person to understand. You, my sons, may you live, can be very happy indeed over this, since in a number of respects those who support Torah study are considered to be above those who actually do the studying and we are as one person.

May God be with us and may He direct us at all times on the straight and true path to discern His will. May we constantly draw happiness and joy upon ourselves along all the holy pathways which were fixed in our hearts by the true luminary and tzaddik, foundation of the world, our honored master, teacher and Rebbe, "the flowing spring, the source of wisdom," of holy, sainted memory, which we received through his holy student, my honored master, father, teacher and rav, of blessed memory. May their merit protect us. *Ashreinu!* Happy are we! How good is our portion that we merited this good lot that we have! May our portion be with them from now on and forever and may we merit to increase our understanding and knowledge of this so that we really understand the enormity of our success in this respect! Thank God, I feel this to a greater extent here and with a clearer understanding. May God in His great compassion have pity on us and abundantly bestow His compassion upon us at all times. May He allow us to hear good news from one another about ourselves, our families and about all our brothers, the Children of Israel, may they live. Amen. May it be His will.

I received the note from our friend, Reb P., may his light shine, and, with God's help, I am prepared to do as he wishes and distribute his sum to worthy poor people. May God grant his wish and allow him to give more and more charity to this Holy Land. I was surprised that I was not honored with a single word from his dear father, my close friend, Reb Zvi Hoizner, as you wrote that he is ready to answer me. This is particulary surprising since I made a request of him as a favor to Reb Yaakov David, may his light shine, that he encourage his [Reb Yaakov David's] son, Reb Ozer, may his light shine. I asked you as well to do this for his benefit and I have received no response from you concerning this matter. Reb Yaakov David comes to me constantly about this. His poverty is extremely dire and I cannot bear [to see] his pitiful state. Therefore, if his salvation from his son has not yet reached you, be sure to work on this for his benefit with all your might. It will be considered as a great mitzvah.

12

With thanks to God, Friday, Erev Shabbat.

Praise God, I arrived back from the holy [Lag b'Omer] festivities yesterday toward evening. My sons, may you live! How can I possibly describe to you the enormity of this event? I bless God with all my heart that He has helped me to this point. This is a fine "wedding" indeed! It is worth traveling from the four corners of the earth to witness this and to see the intense holy faith that all our brothers, the Children of Israel, may they live, have in it. People come from the ends of the earth. They spend vast sums without shedding a tear. There were even a number of honored men from Cherkassy. They just rejoice the whole night and, immediately in the morning, go on their way.

The enormous impediments to this journey that we had here today were just unprecedented. It rained here for two days straight, Wednesday and Thursday. The people who live here could not remember when there had been such rains at this time of year. None of the residents of this city left [for Miron] until the morning of Lag b'Omer. It was not possible to go there at night, as the courtyard is under the control of the Sefardim and all the houses there are rented out to well-known wealthy Sefardim from other countries who come here every year. The Sefardi women also fill the study hall from wall to wall. But every year, when the sun shines, all the people of Zefat stand outside on the rooftops and inside the courtyard and set up makeshift *sukkot* for themselves. On this day, however, this was just not possible due to the incessant rain, and they built a large fire here [at night] instead. The fire here was lit amidst great rejoicing next to the synagogue of the honored ARI, of holy, sainted memory, and it was visible all the way to Miron. Praise God, we danced a great deal in the middle of the pouring rain and subsequently in the synagogue, all with love and affection.

Early in the morning of Lag b'Omer the people here began travelling there [to Miron] in the pouring rain. What can I tell you? Had I not seen it with my own eyes I would never believe it. All of them, men, women, children, even infants, were drenched by the rains. But the entire journey was full of joy out of the great affection that they have for this event. Some of the Sefardim left before they arrived and there was room to get into the study hall. First everyone said what was in his heart in prayer at the gravesite and they wept many tears from the depths of their hearts. Subsequently, with God's help, the joy reached the very heavens. There were clarinets and drums and they all sang wonderful songs. The boys also take their [first] haircuts, what they call here *"chalake."* It is the most splendid thing. They have songs for this and they dance amazing dances with the children. My soul nearly left me over the beauty of the event. The children here are amazingly bright — I have never seen anything like it.

In short, the works of Rabbi Shimon are wondrous indeed and I, praise God, merited to stand right there next to the *tzion*. I said our holy prayer written about his enormous holiness (Likutey Tefilot II, 47) and I lifted my eyes up to Heaven and gave praise and thanksgiving to God that a person of my level could merit to stand on this day at his holy gravesite. I expressed myself in prayer from the depths of my heart and I mentioned all the people that I have on my list. Afterwards I danced, thank God, a great deal with joy in my heart until in the middle of the dancing I sat myself down on the mule for the trip back. My wife, may she live, was also with me and, praise God, we arrived home safely and without mishap. We were only tired and weary. May God give us strength to come to Jerusalem, the holy city (may it be rebuilt and established speedily in our times.

Amen, selah!), as we wish. Praise God, I hired mules today for the journey there, God willing, this coming Monday. May it be His will that it will be at a propitious time, that the journey will proceed smoothly and that we will merit to arrive there without any distress on the road, God forbid. May we have the strength to do what we wish to do there and may we merit to arrive home safely as well without any distress on the road, God forbid. Rather, may everything pass in peace and tranquility that we may enjoy good all our days. Amen. May it be His will.

My heart is full of things to say about this, but it is impossible to bring them from potential to actual [and to articulate them]. My sons, may you live! *Ashreinu!* Happy are we! How good is our portion that we merited to take shelter in the shade of the wings of our honored master, teacher and Rebbe, "the flowing spring, the source of wisdom," of holy, sainted memory, and of his holy student, my master, father, teacher and rav, of blessed memory, who instilled in us at least the knowledge of what to yearn for! And they left all our treasuries as a blessing after them, and in particular that fundamental blessing, the Rosh HaShanah gathering. This is something absolutely amazing and new! Do not forget what is written at the conclusion of the Rebbe's holy words about the revelation of the tzaddik, Rabbi Shimon Bar Yochai, i.e. the words "et cetera." Take note of these words "et cetera" and you will understand a little of what I said above. I have said enough for the knowledgeable to understand. May God be with us from now on and eternally to remain in this lot of ours forever. Amen. May it be His will.

I was a little bit surprised not to have received a single word from our friend, Reb Zvi M.Z., but of course it is all from God. I trust in Him that He will not abandon me. I am presently waiting to receive the sum that you sent me so that I will not need, God forbid, to borrow for my expenses. I am quite averse to doing this. I must prepare my letters now; and if I receive the money, God willing, through the next courier, God willing, I will inform you of it with a few lines on a separate page. There will not be time [then to write a full letter] because of the departure of the caravan. I am also extremely busy right now, as you can understand. This journey [to Jerusalem] is almost more onerous for me than my journey here from outside the Land. May God in His abundant compassion take me safely on this journey with absolutely no distress on the road at all. May He bring me safely for next Shabbat to the holy city of Jerusalem (may it be rebuilt and established speedily in our days), healthy and strong as we should be and, once there, may I merit to immediately express thanksgiving and gratitude to God for all the wondrous kindness that He constantly does for me. Now too I am confident that He will fulfill my heart's requests for good. With this I will close and say goodbye. My soul is bound up with yours and I mention you at all times in my prayers for good.

> The words of your father blessing you with all good, spiritual and physical, and waiting at all times to hear report of your success in This World and the Next.

> *Yitzchak*

Greetings to my modest daughter-in-law, Esther Sheindel, to my fine granddaughter, Adil, may she live, to my precious grandson, Nachman, may he live, to my bright granddaughter, Batia, may she live, and to my young grandson, Shachneh, may he live.

Greetings to my daughter-in-law, the modest Rachel, may she live, to my precious grandson, Aharon, may he live, and to my lovely grandson, Naftali, may he live. Believe me, my beloved children, I do not forget about you even for a moment. May God help and may all that I request for you be fulfilled. I ask you — do not worry! God will help. Everything will come at its proper time in accordance with His will.

My wife, may she live, sends you all greetings with a great love and wishes you all the best. Her love for you exceeds all measure, especially her love for the children. She too is traveling with me to Jerusalem. May God give her a good trip. She petitions God for you all the time and hopes to always hear good news from you. She asks you to let her know about how the couple, Sesia, may she live, and her husband, Reb Moshe, may his light shine, are doing, and also about their daughter, may she live, and about how their livelihood is going. This will really make her happy.

Davrish, the wife of Reb Yitzchak

Greetings to all our comrades, may they live, to all our friends, may they live, and to all our neighbors there; in particular to our friend and neighbor, the distinguished young man, Reb Yaakov, may his light shine. I received his note with the one silver ruble and I have placed it in my bosom to leave it at some holy site on my way to the holy city of Jerusalem, may it be rebuilt and established speedily in our days. Amen. Besides this, I have all the names that he gave me written down in a book and will mention them in prayer at all times for good.

Our friend Reb David Reide asks you to arouse all his family there, may they live, and in particular the well-to-do Reb Zvi Tabachnik, may his light shine, to take pity on him and to help support him in his livelihood because his situation is pressured in the extreme. Why should they distance themselves from him so much, especially since he is a God-fearing man? They should endeavor to help him. Let me know what is happening with this matter. Please extend greetings to all those who study in our study hall, to each one of them with great love.

Your loving father,

Yitzchak, the same

13

With God's help, Friday, Erev Shabbat Parashat Bemidbar, the 48th day of the Counting of the Children of Israel, 5629, here in the Holy City, Jerusalem — may it be rebuilt and established speedily in our times. Amen, selah.

Let the mountains bear greetings and blessing from the Land of the Living to my beloved sons, my heart's delight, the learned and distinguished Reb David Zvi, may his light shine, and the learned and distinguished Reb Michel, may he live. May the Life of Life bestow all good upon them, both spiritual and physical, that they may enjoy good all their days together with their wives and children, may they live.

*May they merit to have "two tables," both Torah and wealth, at one
and the same time. Amen. May it be His will.*

I will proclaim God's kindnesses and all the good that He
has bestowed upon me! Blessed is the One Who has kept us
alive, sustained us and brought us to this time! Praise God, I
arrived here safely last Friday around midday. Here I found
what my soul loves — that is, our dear comrades, may they live
— and I merited that day to pray the afternoon prayer and
Kabbalat Shabbat by our Holy Place, our House of Splendor [the
site of the Holy Temple]. My heart was certainly wrenched within me
by the great bitterness of the Destruction [of the Temple]; one
who sees it is deeply affected. Woe for the calamity that has
overtaken us! It is impossible to describe. But in spite of all this,
when I saw the crowds of our brothers, the Children of Israel,
may they live, praying there, men, women and children alike,
all pleading and petitioning from the depths of their hearts for
their souls' redemption, I thought, "This is my comfort amidst
my destitution; because from this will ultimately spring forth
the redemption — may it come speedily in our times. Amen,
selah. God's ways are hidden from us."

I prevailed with this thought of mine and I attached myself
too to all the holy groups of our brothers, the Children of Israel,
may they live, and I prayed with them. Nonetheless my spirit
did not return to me. We then went to our house and we began
encouraging ourselves with the true hope that we believe that
by God's kindness the righteous redeemer will come speedily
in our times, until we came to joy and danced before Kiddush
amidst our hearts' longing. Praise God, the entire Shabbat

passed joyfully. Subsequently, on Sunday, we traveled together to the holy city of Hebron.

Sunday evening we reached the house of the [grave of the] tzaddeket, the Matriarch Rachel, of holy, sainted memory, and we spent the night there. From midnight until morning we poured out what was in our hearts in prayer and first thing in the morning we prayed the morning prayer with a quorum. There I found some solace for my soul. We arrived in the holy city of Hebron on Monday, Erev Rosh Chodesh, late in the day. We immediately went to the mikveh and then went to pray the afternoon prayer at the Cave of the Patriarchs.

What can I say? What can I say? It was exactly the same as our Holy Place [the site of the Holy Temple] and in my heart there was not the slightest difference between them. We were there approximately two hours and, although a few "precious stones" were thrown at us, it was still with kindness. On the day of Rosh Chodesh we went around to all the holy places until at last we came to the cave of Yishai, the father of [King] David, and of the tzaddeket Ruth. There my heart really opened up, since I recalled the enormous holiness of the teaching that our master, teacher and Rebbe, "the flowing spring, the source of wisdom," of holy, sainted memory, revealed on the verse "And Boaz said to Ruth" (Likutey Moharan I, 65). Ashreinu! Happy are we! How good is our portion that we merited to enjoy true good such as this! We came to heartfelt joy.

On Wednesday morning we traveled back [toward Jerusalem] and we came again to the house of our mother, Rachel, at the early time for the afternoon prayers. I prayed the afternoon prayer there and, praise God, we arrived here safely. Thus far has God's compassion helped me. It would be impossible to describe to you the great suffering I have had on the road from the time I left my home in the holy city of Zefat until today. In short, the way is full of miracles, not subject to natural laws at all. Rather, God in His compassion sent His messenger before us and guided us through this whole journey. Natural laws had no influence at all. So may He save us in His compassion and fulfill our requests to Him concerning all of us, and may He allow us to celebrate the holy Festival of Shavuot in heartfelt joy. May He also take us back the same way, so that we may come to our home in the holy city of Zefat without suffering on the road at all. May we merit to reach there with "our bodies, our possessions and our Torah learning intact" (Rashi, Genesis 33:18). Amen. May it be His will.

We also went yesterday to pray the afternoon prayer at our Holy Place. This time my heart opened up and I expressed myself before God regarding the general and the particular. I mentioned all the names of all our friends as they appear on my list and we stayed there until night. Praise God, it was quiet [there] and we will most likely go there again today for the afternoon prayer, Kabbalat Shabbat, the [evening] prayer and to count the *sefirah* for the 49th day [of the Omer]. May it be His will that we merit to experience the illumination and holiness of the holy Fiftieth Day, the day on which we received our holy Torah. May we merit to accept upon ourselves anew the holiness of the holy Torah, to place it in our hearts from now on and forever so that we may enjoy good from now on and forever.

May it be good for us all our days — true good for our eternal goal. This would really give us happiness and joy. Amen. May it be His will.

There is of course a great deal in my heart to say about this holy journey, but my mind is not yet clear due to the hardships of the road. However, because of my great love for you, I wanted to inform you of my safe arrival here and of all that I wrote above. I intend to stay here by God's kindness until this coming Sunday, Parashat Behaalotekha. Then we will turn our steps toward home, toward the holy city of Zefat. It is possible that we will travel by way of the holy city of Tiberias and out of my love for them, I will go together with them. When by God's compassion we arrive safely home, I will write you at length concerning all that is in my heart and I will enumerate for you all the holy sites which I merited to visit and which, with God's kindness, I will merit to visit again. Meanwhile, my beloved sons, give praise and thanksgiving to God Whose abundant compassion has helped us thus far. What can I say? What can I say? "Who has accomplished and performed all this Who calls forth the generations from the beginning?" It is only the holy merit of the Rebbe and of his holy student, my honored master, father, teacher and rav, of blessed memory, which has favored me with this great kindness. So may his holy merit stand me in good stead from now on and forever to attain what my soul seeks, the eternal goal, in this lifetime, in this Holy Land. May I merit to hear good tidings and news of your success amidst good and pleasantness. This would really bring me joy.

The words of your father and friend, praying for

you every moment, all the time. May God in His abundant compassion hear my prayer for us, for all those who are with us and for all our brothers, the Children of Israel, that we may enjoy good with redemption, salvation, and compassion. Amen. May it be His will.

Yitzchak

My wife, may she live, sends heartfelt greetings. She, thank God, is just delighted that she merited to come here and to visit all the holy sites. She prayed that you will always enjoy good. The distractions that I had over her on this journey were with great kindness. May God favor me in the future so that everything will be with His kindness for our good.

Greetings to my dear son-in-law, Reb Yaakov Yechiel Michel, may his light shine, along with my precious grandchildren. My love for him has not left me and I remembered to mention him in prayer at all the holy sites. May God in His abundant compassion save him for good.

Greetings to all our friends, our comrades and our neighbors, may they live. May they all be blessed and visited with the good that I asked for them. When God allows me to quickly arrive safely home, with God's help I will set down greetings to each one of them individually in accordance with what God places in my heart.

The words of your true friend,

Yitzchak

I must also mention for good the name of my soul's friend, who is as dear to me as a brother, the learned, distinguished and honored Rav Yaakov Teitelbaum, may his light shine. My brother and friend! What can I say? What can I say? How great are the favors and kindness that you did for me by helping to support me thus far! So is my love for you engraved upon my heart and I absolutely cannot forget you. May God grant you success as your heart desires until you merit in this lifetime to attain the true goal amidst abundant peace and blessing. May I merit in my lifetime to see you "planted in your tent" along with your wife, may she live, in this Holy Land amidst heartfelt joy.

The words of your friend like a brother,

Yitzchak

Send greetings for me to our dear, excellent friend, Reb Nachman Tulchiner, in Uman. Inform him of my safe arrival here and of all that I wrote above. God willing, I will write him individually from my home. I received his letter through our comrades and his true words inspired me.

The words of the same

I too wish to send greetings to my friends and comrades, my dear brothers — how good and lovely their names are — Reb David Zvi, may his light shine, and Reb Michel, may his light shine. I wanted to inform them of how we are doing and that on Wednesday [of Parashat] Bechukotai I arrived together with the rav of our camp and our friend Reb Yaakov, may his light shine, the son of Reb Zvi, here in the Holy City of Jerusalem — may it soon be rebuilt and established. Amen. May it be His will.

I ask you to send greetings to our illustrious friend Reb Nachman HaLevi, may his light shine, who lives in Uman and to all our dear comrades. May God allow us to welcome the coming holy Festival and may we merit to receive the Torah — to keep, to do and to fulfill it and to celebrate and rejoice in its light.

The words of your long-time friend,
Avraham Abba Rabinowitz of Tcherin

Please send greetings to our dear comrades in Breslov.

14

With God's help, Tuesday, Ekev, 5629, here in the holy city of Zefat — may it be rebuilt and established speedily in our times. Amen, selah.

Peace, abundant salvation and all good to my dear, beloved sons, may they live.

On Thursday, Devarim, I wrote you through the post. I informed you of my concern over the delay in your letters in that I have yet to receive a letter from you after the one that you wrote me on Thursday, Tazria. I reiterated this [in a letter] last week sent through our dear, distinguished friend, Reb Meir, may he live, who set out from here. Most importantly, I instructed him verbally. Since then I have been waiting and yearning for the courier to arrive this week. Perhaps he would gladden my heart with the receipt of your letter. The courier arrived yesterday, but my hopes have been disappointed.

How can I describe to you how very worried I am over this? It is only by the kindness of God Who gives strength to the weary that He also gives me a little strength to soften the pain that I have over this. For the time being I cannot find fault with you, God forbid, since after I instructed you to send me a letter every month you have certainly been doing so. Who knows what is responsible for this delay? May it be His will that it be for the good. I am most certainly suffering over the delay in the arrival of the money. The sum with which our honored comrades favored me was indeed a great kindness from God and had it not been for this I do know what would have happened to me. But this sum is already gone. The kindnesses and wonders that God has done for me in this area have been abundant indeed until now and I trust that, with God's help, He will not abandon me.

All the same, I *am* presently suffering over the money's delay. This however is not one thousandth of my yearning to see your handwriting. This would really put new life into me! As a result of my weakness over all the above I did not intend to write through this post. I thought, though, that since it seems to me that you have certainly already sent me your letter with the money, as I again urged from the holy city of Jerusalem, and since it was apparently delayed on the way, it is crucial for you to know about this so that you can see to rectifying matters and to ensuring that the money reaches me quickly. For you should know that I am presently at the point where I am forced to fulfill, "Bless God day by day" — and I really mean "day by day"! I have said enough for an intelligent person to understand.

Please, my sons, may you live, heed my words! Be sure to think about me and help support me in my livelihood here as much as you possibly can, both by sending me your money on time and also by ensuring that I will have some income from our friends for my sustenance here. I considered writing some letters in connection with this to our friends in Tulchin, but my mind is confused right now. What is more, I do not know what is happening there and perhaps they have already sent me some gift. Thus I have no way of addressing them, especially since I have already written them a number of times and as yet have received no answer from them. I have also not received a response from our family in Uman. In short, I am totally in the dark about everything and I cannot approach [anyone] again until I receive some answer about this and know if anything positive has been achieved in this area. May God in His abundant compassion take pity on me and may He favor me with His great kindness so that I merit to succeed in my task of striving for the eternal goal and to rely on Him that all will be well. May I merit to rejoice in His great kindness that He has graciously allowed me to be one of those who dwell in the Holy Land. This now is my portion, the reward for all my toil! This alone gives me life right now.

You should know that I sent you seven letters this summer: 1) on Thursday, Shemini, through Reb Yoel Zvi [this letter is not extant]; 2) on Friday of that same week through the post; 3) before my journey to Jerusalem, may it be rebuilt and established speedily in our times. Amen, selah; 4) on Friday, Erev Shabbat Bemidbar, from that Holy City; 5) through our friend Reb Abele, may his light shine; 6) on Tuesday, Chukat, through the post; 7) on Thursday, Devarim, through the post. This is in addition to what I sent through our dear friend, Reb Meir, may his light shine, and as yet I have received no response even to the first of them. May God favor me with His great kindness and quickly save me in this matter.

In my letter from Parashat Chukat I gave you a list of my friends who helped me when I traveled here — I thought that it might perhaps be important for you to have. I am enclosing here a list of a few of our comrades, may they live, so that you will have it in front of you to help you remember. I discussed this with our dear friend, Reb Abele, may his light shine, and he told me explicitly that he can do something to help me during our holy gathering [at Rosh HaShanah]. He is extremely busy [then], but he promised me that if your sons rouse him in this matter he will certainly help you with all his might to my advantage. For he saw and understands my situation. Thus you will understand how to proceed and may God give you success. For I rely on God alone in this entire matter. May God Who is good show me favor.

You should know that at present I have in my possession one *rendel* of cash. In addition I must pay for various items bought on credit to the sum of three *rendelach* and a little more; and there are two more weeks until the next courier comes. It is also time to prepare wood and coal for the winter, and the Holidays are rapidly approaching. With all this, my sons, may you live, the delay in your letter surpasses everything. I have informed you of all this in order that you should know my situation. I already wrote you that my expediture for necessities is not less than four silver rubles a week in the local currency which cost five silver rubles *depoziten* [currency exchange] and I cannot economize any more. On eating and drinking I can cut back as much as possible, but on other things I am simply unable to. I must keep a maid, which is a matter of life and death, and the same thing goes for washing clothes and the like. Even with this, my wife, may she live, still must do more housework than she has the strength for, though it impossible to explain this in this context.

I discussed all this with our friend, Reb Abele, may his light shine, as you will hear from him. May God put counsel into your hearts so that you will know how to proceed to my advantage. Beyond this I have nothing to say. Even all this I have written against my will; rather necessity has compelled me. The holy days of Elul are approaching. May it be His will that we merit to receive them as we should, to strive with new zeal toward the eternal goal until we merit to come into the days of holy Rosh HaShanah with a proper countenance. I hereby bless you that you should merit to be in Uman for the holy Rosh Ha-Shanah, with your sons, may they live, to be counted among our holy gathering which congregates there to bask in the shade of "the flowing spring, the source of wisdom," of holy, sainted memory, who resides there. May my lot be with them. With this I will close and say goodbye.

The words of your father who loves you, waiting to hear good news of your journey to Uman. May your

journey there and back go smoothly, as both you
and I wish. Praying for you,

Yitzchak

My wife, may she live, sends you heartfelt greetings and
yearns with all her heart to hear good news from you. Thank
God, she is a great help to me here. God's kindnesses to me have
indeed been abundant in this respect. Her whole orientation
and goal is that it be easy for me to engage in my service of God.
May God be with me from now on and forever that we may
enjoy good all our days. Amen. May it be His will.

Davrish, the wife of Reb Yitzchak Sternhartz

My sons, may you live. I was surprised that I did not merit
to hear if, during the course of the year, you were in Uman for
some Erev Rosh Chodesh as you were accustomed to do when
I was there. Sometimes you would even go twice during the
year. Please let me know the good news about this and may God
give you success in the future so that you will be able go there
whenever you wish. This would really give me joy and uplift
me.

Greetings to all our friends, may they live, and to all our
comrades, may they live, with a great love! With God's help,
when I receive, God willing, a letter from one of my friends I
will be certain to respond at once as he wishes. May God give
you the success which you and I, your genuine friend, wish.
With love,

Yitzchak, the same

Send greetings for me to our dear, honored and illustrious friend, Reb Nachman HaLevi [of Tulchin], may his light shine, in Uman. My sons, may you live. It has long been my custom, since the passing of my master, father, teacher and rav, of blessed memory, may his merit protect us, to give a *pidyon* [redemption] every Erev Rosh Chodesh to our friend, the aforementioned Reb Nachman for the sake of the needs of all of us. Last year as well I gave him 18 gold coins, as you know. Now, since my letter [from you] is concealed from me, I cannot know if my present situation allows me to give 18 gold coins. Therefore, my sons, may you live, I am relying on you to give him money for a *pidyon* on Erev Rosh HaShanah for the sake of the whole group [of us]. You should give as much as you deem appropriate — the more the better. The most important thing is that it be specifically with silver coins. Whatever sum you give I will take on my account. May God Who is good redeem us from all evil. May He draw blessing and kindness upon us and may He allow us to hear all good from each other. This will give me life.

Greetings to our dear friend, Reb Nachman Ch.B.R. with a great, eternal love!

You are receiving enclosed a note which will allow you to receive five good *lulavim* from our friend and relative Reb Lipa Manales, may his light shine. You may do with them as you see fit. It may be necessary to give a gift to someone and you will be able to do so. It would certainly be particularly appropriate to favor our dear friend, Reb Yaakov Teitelbaum, may his light shine, with something like this since, if it is received there intact, it will be considered a very great gift indeed. For even an insignificant thing which grows here in the Holy Land is more precious than anything which grows outside of the Land, and especially when it is used to perform a commandment. You should do as you deem best for our interests.

You should know, my sons, may you live, that my affection for this Holy Land grows greater and greater all the time. It is the essence of my vitality. The whole reason that I wrote at such length in my letter is because of the love for you which is bound to my soul which desires and longs to know how you are doing. As for my livelihood, I trust God that He will not abandon me and that everything will come in its proper time; that I will merit to perform the commandment of putting a fence upon the roof of my house as soon as possible and that I will yet have some small room for my devotions. I have a good place to build it too with a window as is fitting. I therefore ask you not to worry about me. As for what is happening with you, you should trust in God at all times that He will not abandon you. May God fortify you in Torah, prayer and good deeds and may I merit to always hear good from you — true, eternal good in This World and the Next. Amen. May it be His will.

> Your father blessing you with all good and waiting
> for your good response to give me life.
>
> *Yitzchak*

There is a note enclosed of which you should make one identical copy. Put one of them on the holy *tzion* and give the other one to our friend Reb Nachman HaLevi along with the *pidyon* for the whole group of us. May God give us long life with good and pleasantness. Amen. May it be His will.

Yitzchak

15

With thanks to God, Thursday, Parashat Ekev, 5629, the holy city of Zefat — may it be rebuilt and established speedily in our times. Amen, selah.

I call forth greetings from the Land of the Living to my soul's friend, my heart's beloved, the learned, distinguished and illustrious man-of-standing, may his fine name be praised, Reb Avraham Abba, may his light shine.

May you receive blessing from God to be visited with good in all your endeavors until you merit to gain true good in This World and the Next from now on and forever. Amen. May it be His will.

My friend. I imagined that I would receive your letter from Odessa as you promised, but I was not worthy. Thus I am hereby fulfilling my promise and sending a letter to you in Uman. Your honor should know that, following your departure from my home, I was in a state of confusion for several days out of my great yearning and love for you. My strength literally left me, so that I was forced to exert tremendous energy and to gird my loins like a warrior in order to diligently work at my studies. For this is my portion out of all my toil. It is all through the power of our honored master, teacher and Rebbe, "the flowing spring, the source of wisdom," of holy, sainted memory, and through the merit of my father, teacher and rav, his holy student, of blessed memory, may their merit protect us. So may God continue to be with me from now on and forever that I may strive diligently for my eternal goal as I should, and give myself life with all the good that is in me. May I spend my life in Torah, prayer and good deeds in accordance with all our holy pathways and may I know and believe at all times that God is good to all.

Your journey here was indeed successful and it bore fruit as well. For as a result of the journey our dear friend, Reb Meir, may his light shine, has awakened. He has girded his loins like a warrior and taken his life in his hands to go to Uman to be counted among our holy gathering which is congregating there for this coming holy Rosh HaShanah, and to bask in the shade of "the flowing spring, the source of wisdom," of holy, sainted memory, who resides there — may his merit protect us. May God be with him and give him a successful and safe journey. May he merit to reach his goal according to all that he has in his heart, and to return home alive and well to continue his Torah studies, prayer and good deeds with greater energy and wondrous vitality as he desires. You should know, my friend, that during the time you were here, your love for the Land made a great impression on people. For a number of days after your departure, whenever I walked through town, I heard words of blessing spoken about you with great love from a number of people and I was very pleased indeed. So may God grant you success all your days.

Beyond this I have nothing new to report, especially since you will hear everything from our aforementioned friend. What is more, my mind is a little unclear, since I have not received a letter from my sons, may they live, for a long time. They wrote me a letter on Tuesday, Tazria, and since that letter I have not received a word from them. Everything that has taken place there this entire summer is concealed from me. While I am certainly disconcerted over the tightness of my livelihood and I am waiting to receive some sum through them — at least the sum that they themselves are to give me — this does not amount to one thousandth of what I am suffering over the delay in their letter which would inform me of their well-being. But, of course, it is all from God. So may God have compassion on me and put wisdom into my heart to remove from myself distractions such as these so that I can engage in the service of God with relish and clarity of mind.

I am confident in your love for me that, when you meet them, God willing, in Uman, you will speak with them lovingly about keeping in touch with me as we discussed and you will work with them for my benefit in all areas as you promised. May God Who is good give you success in accordance with His will. I ask you emphatically to make mention of me for good in your prayers whenever you are at the Rebbe's holy gravesite and especially on this coming Erev Rosh HaShanah. For my part, I will be binding myself, life, spirit and soul, to our holy gathering. May my portion be with them. You can also rest assured that I constantly mention you for the good in my prayers at all the holy sites. May God hear our prayers that we may enjoy good all our days for the eternal goal in This World and the Next forever. With this I will close and say goodbye.

The words of your friend whose love for you is boundless, sending love and and asking you to pray for him.

Yitzchak

Send greetings for me to all our comrades, may they live, from Tcherin, in particular to our friend, the distinguished, honored and venerable — may his fine and holy name be praised — Reb Nachman, may his light shine; and to our illustrious friend — may his fine name be praised — Reb Yaakov, may his light shine. My love for them is bound upon my soul. From the time they left me I have been absolutely unable to forget them. I am praying for them constantly. May God favor them with good from now on and forever. Send special greetings for me to our precious friend, "the holy fruit," the learned and honored man-of-standing, Reb Avraham Dov Ber, may his light shine. My love for him is bound upon my soul and I mention him constantly in my prayers.

16

With thanks to God, Tuesday, Tavo, 5629, the holy city of Zefat, may it be rebuilt and established speedily in our times. Amen, selah.

From the depths of my heart I call forth greetings to my precious sons whom I love as my own heart and soul, the learned and distinguished Reb David Zvi, may his light shine, and the learned and distinguished Reb Yechiel Michel, may his light shine. May they, their wives and their children, may they live, receive blessing from the Dwelling Place

of Blessings for all good, spiritual and physical. In particular, may they
be written and sealed for a good year, until they merit to live the good
life which is truly called living *and to enjoy good all their days from*
now on and forever. Amen. May it be His will.

My sons. Just yesterday I received the great salvation with
which God favored me and I merited to receive two precious
letters from you — one from Tuesday, Pinchas, together with
40 silver rubles, and the second, from Friday of that same week
along with 50 silver rubles. Blessed is He Who has kept us alive
and sustained us to this time. What can I say? What can I say?
It was certainly from God that I suffered so much anguish, the
likes of which I have never experienced. Yesterday, before I
merited to receive the letters and after I learned of the courier's
arrival, I do not know how I restrained myself. I would have
frightened anyone who saw me. Blessed is He Who gives
strength to the weary.

But, my dear sons, you committed a great error in this
matter. Did I forbid you to send a letter without money, which
is the reason you refrained from writing a letter from Parashat
Tazria until Parashat Pinchas, a period of twelve weeks? I asked
you to write me every month, even if only a line or two! I spoke
about this at length in my letter from Parashat Mishpatim and
I received your response that you would certainly do this. Now
what kind of excuse is this that it is because of the merchants?
This explains why you did not send the money, since it is
sometimes necessary to refrain from sending the money and to
wait in order to accomplish more for my benefit. But, thank
God, there is plenty of paper and ink; and even if you are very

busy, you can just write a few words of greetings so as carry out my wish. In short, what's done is done, and I certainly forgive you with all good will. For I believe that it had to be this way in order to draw my heart closer [to God]. But from now on, I implore you, do not put me through this! What is more, by doing this you will be fulfilling the commandment to honor your father and with a small act you will be able to merit long life. Why not do this, especially since my life depends on it? Therefore, be quick to benefit both me and yourselves.

Of course I realize that it does not *have* to be this way with me and I am certainly seeking a way to remove such distractions from myself. I have already cried many tears over this. God knows what is in my heart. But still, my sons, may you live, *you* must do what you can. It will be obvious to an intelligent person that, when my mind is calm, my devotions are of a much higher caliber. May God Who is good finish with me and bring me to my eternal goal. Amen. May it be His will.

How very delighted I was by the lovely words you wrote me saying that my words entered your hearts. You literally gave life to my soul! This is my whole aim. This is another reason that it is fitting for our letters to pass regularly, i.e. so that our discussions should not be interrupted. You should know that, praise God, I was in Miron last week and I stayed there for three full days, from late on Monday until Thursday night. There I found a little solace for my soul, when I poured out my heart several times on the holy *tzion* of the tzaddik, the holy Tanna, Rabbi Shimon Bar Yochai, of holy, sainted memory. Once during my stay I said the prayer which is meant to be recited there (*Likutey Tefilot* II, 47). How can I describe for you, my sons, may you live, the way my heart opened up when I said this prayer? Had I come into the world only for this, it would have been enough! I also merited to be in the cave of the holy Tanna, Hillel the Prince, and I prayed the afternoon prayer there. My heart opened up beyond all measure, and I really could not leave the cave due to the tremendous cleaving to God that I experienced there. It is all through the power of the tzaddik, foundation of the world, "the flowing spring, the source of wisdom," of holy, sainted memory, who bequeathed us blessing through his holy student, my honored master, father, teacher and rav, of blessed memory, may his merit protect us. For it is through this that my heart was opened... [section of letter missing].

I have much to say and I long to let you taste the lovely holiness of this Holy Land. But "a mountain stands between us." What is more, the job of answering each person in accordance with his request weighs very heavily upon me right now, as it is a tremendous effort for me. Thus you are receiving here a number of letters and notes which you should read first, and then you will understand how to give each one to the appropriate person. In the course of doing so you will also see a number of fine words. May God fortify your hearts to work diligently at the path of life.

I already wrote you that you can inspire yourselves with the fact that you are involved in supporting me here. You must literally consider it to be an important religious devotion; for father and son are like one person. Until I came here, *I* was the one supporting others. My sole intent was always that I should merit to see you engaging in Torah, prayer and good deeds and, with God's help, this is how it was for many years, as you know. Now, in my old age, you must be the ones to carry the burden and I, with God's help, will be free to engage in spiritual work. How good and pleasant it is that you merited to see me planted, with God's help, in our holy place, in the Holy Land! My precious sons! You can rejoice over this all your lives! This will be a *tikkun*, rectification, for all your activities! I merited, with God's help, that for practically all my life I worked for the benefit of our holy projects, to publish the contents of our treasuries [i.e. Rebbe Nachman's works].

I too received a great deal of encouragement from my honored master, father, teacher and rav, of blessed memory, in this area and he encouraged me to be happy over this. He told me explicitly that this was a complete rectification for me as far as my business activities were concerned. You, my sons, may you live, can also inspire yourselves in the same way for your good. I have a great deal more to say about this, but there will be other opportunities. May God be with us so that we may now fulfill "Rejoice, Zevulun, in your going out, and, Yissakhar, in your tents!" God willing, many years from now the same relationship will exist between you and your children, may they live for many good years to come. I hope to God that as a result of this mitzvah you will also merit now to grab true good for your eternal goal. For one mitzvah leads to another.

Read my letter to Reb Nachman HaLevi [Reb Nachman Tulchiner] and you will find a few nice things there. You also withheld sending his letter to me for a month! What this means I cannot understand. I therefore ask you again not to act in this manner in the future. I assume that you read my letter from Reb Nachman and he also writes that he has decided to inspire me with one of his letters every month. From this you can infer how many thousands of times more it is true that *you* should be doing as I wish as far as our relationship is concerned. I have said enough for the wise to understand. But of course it was all from God that I should be tormented in this way; may it be sufficient. I hereby forgive you for the past and, as for the future, I ask you to favor me with a response to this [letter] and to inspire me frequently with your letters.

Concerning the *lulavim*, I already sent you five of them through my friend and relative, Reb Lipa, may his light shine. If you only need two, only take two. I also sent through Reb Abele ten *hadasim* with three leaves at each point up and down [as required for the mitzvah of taking the *lulav*]. Presumably you have received them safely.

Beyond this, what more can I tell you? I am presently yearning to hear the good news of your being for the holy Rosh HaShanah in Uman among our holy gathering. Let me know about how holy Rosh HaShanah proceeded in Uman, about your safe arrival back to your homes and about your rejoicing. You will tell me this and it will give me joy and inspiration.

> I hereby bless you with all my heart that you should
> have all good and that I should hear joyful news
> from you from now on and forever, as both you and
> I, your father, wish. Praying for your good,
>
> *Yitzchak*

You should forward the enclosed letter to Reb Ozer from Odessa at once and try to have it result in some kind of salvation for his father, Reb Yaakov David, may his light shine. You cannot imagine the terrible poverty he is in, God spare us. May God take pity on him. If it is possible for this meritorious act to be performed through your agency, it will be counted as a great mitzvah to your credit. He may not be at home though, and in that case you should just retain the letter in your possession until he comes. Do not give it to anyone else though — just to him and him alone — and take pains that he should respond positively.

Warm greetings to all our friends, may they live, and in particular to those who frequent our study hall. Call each one by name and bless them for me that they should be written and sealed for a good year. May you all merit to experience the joy of the coming, holy Festival and may you celebrate and rejoice together with a great, infinite love!

Greetings to all our comrades, may they live, and to all our neighbors, may they live; in particular to my young distinguished friend, Reb Yaakov, may his light shine. I also placed a note for him at the holy gravesite of the tzaddik, the holy Tanna, Rabbi Shimon Bar Yochai. My love for him is engraved upon my heart and I mention him for good.

17

With thanks to God, Thursday, Noach, 5630, here in the holy city of Zefat — may it be rebuilt and established speedily in our days. Amen, selah.

To my dear sons whom I love as myself — to the learned and distinguished Reb David Zvi, may he live, and to the learned and distinguished Reb Michel, may he live. Greetings, abundant salvation and all good to them, to their wives and to their children that they may enjoy good in the spiritual and the physical all their days from now on, forever and for all eternity. Amen. May it be His will.

My sons, may you live. Give praise and thanksgiving to the Supernal God Who abundantly bestowed His kindness upon me and left me alive for you. For you should know that before Rosh HaShanah on the second day of Selichot I took to my sick-bed, God spare us, and I did not leave it until last Shabbat Bereishit. I have still not recovered completely. I can only sit briefly at the table and walk a little back and forth in the house. I am still eating like an infant and every day brings different waves [of discomfort], but with God's help the measure of good is greater.

How can I describe to you the severity of the illness I had? From start to finish I was afflicted, God spare us, with excruciating pain, but from the outset until the Fast of Gedaliah, there was sometimes a little relief. All the same though, there were nights when I screamed from my bitter pain, God spare us, and I ran from one corner of the house to the other screaming in my pain, "*Gevalt!* I am being tortured!" By day however God gave me some relief. Nonetheless, I could not get out of bed or eat anything, I just drank enormous quantities of water. From the Fast of Gedaliah, though, until the Fast of Yom Kippur the dreadful, bitter pain steadily escalated, God spare us, and I fell in a stupor with my tongue cleaving to my palate. I could not speak because of the excruciating pain, God spare us, and all the experts here had given up on me. But I, praise God, was completely lucid and clear-headed and I had a deep understanding that this was not the case. I was only afraid that I might not have the strength to endure such pain.

As far back as I can remember, I have never seen anyone as sick as this, God spare us, wracked with dreadful pain the way I was. In my thoughts from my tortured heart I cried out to God, since it was impossible for me to speak, and I asked that He have mercy on me and take away the bitter pain, God spare us. The locus of the illness was in my stomach, with my head, hands, heart and legs free of pain. But my stomach was aflame like a burning fire and from there the dreadful pains shot out to my loins and kidneys. Salvation came through the saying of Psalms. For on the day of the Thirteen Attributes of Mercy [Selichot recited two days before Yom Kippur] I gave instructions to our friend Reb Nachman Rivatzker. He showed kindness to me which I would not believe had I not seen it myself. He did not go home at all except at mealtimes and he stood by me all day and all night attending me in every way. Even on the night of *Kol Nidrei* he stayed with me overnight right up to the first day of Sukkot when, thank God, I was back in this world. May God be with him and may he merit all the true good that he wishes for himself.

As far as I am concerned there is no doubt that this mitzvah will be at the head of his escort [when he goes to the Next World]. I instructed him then mustering all my strength, "Take twenty *thaler* from my wife and gather a quorum of my friends.

Distribute the money to poor people and have the quorum recite Psalms at the holy site of the grave of the ARI, of holy, sainted memory. So my friends assembled, more than a quorum, and they went there. With burning hot tears they poured forth their hearts like water in prayer. For they indeed felt enormous pity for me. It appears that at that point the salvation began, only it was so gradual as to be imperceptible to anyone. I did not know what was happening with me either, until on Yom Kippur I began to think that things might be improving. Then, with God's help, before dawn the day after Yom Kippur the salvation arrived. At once I called my friend, Reb Nachman, may he live, from the place where he was lying and I also called my wife, may she live, and I told them the good news. May God Who is good save me completely. Amen. May it be His will.

As you can imagine I have a great deal to write, but I cannot elaborate any further because of my exhaustion. Even this that I did write took all my strength and I did it only out of my love for you. For although, praise God, my hands are fine, my stomach does not allow me to sit in one place for a long time. May God take pity on me and quickly give me a complete recovery. Right now things are progressing little by little. My only hope is in God through the merit of the great Eshel, of holy, sainted memory [Rebbe Nachman], and of his holy student, of sainted memory [Reb Noson], that He will quickly grant me a complete recovery and put strength into all my 248 organs and my 365 sinews for many good years to come. God willing, when He gives me back my proper strength, I will write you at length as my heart wishes.

With this I will close and say goodbye. The words
of one writing in great exhaustion and waiting for
complete salvation soon, until I soon merit to report
to you all good about me.

Yitzchak

Copy this letter over and send it to Uman to our dear friend,
Reb Nachman, may he live, along with the enclosed note.

My wife, may she live, sends loving greetings. You can
understand for yourselves the pitiful state she was in
[throughout my illness]. God heard her weeping, and now she
is attending to my every need day and night. May God grant
her long life amidst good and pleasantness. In this respect too
I see God's kindness to me. Just as His abundant compassion
has helped me thus far, so may He always give me good. Amen.
May it be His will.

Letters written by Reb Nachman from Tulchin,
the leading disciple of Reb Noson

1

[This letter was written by Reb Nachman of Tulchin, of blessed memory, to Reb Michel, grandson of Reb Noson, of blessed memory].
With thanks to God, Thursday, Naso, 5630, Uman.

Life, peace and all good to my friend whom I love as myself, the distinguished, illustrious and beneficent Reb Michel, may his light never be extinguished, selah, along with all his family, may they live for many good years to come. Amen. May it be His will.

I already responded to your honored person that, thank God, I received all your letters, as well as your generous contribution. Now, as for news from "under the sun," news which is vanity of vanities flowing forth and emanating from "jealousy, lust and desire for honor" — this kind of news I haven't. For this "news" is really just the same old foolishness which has caused us all, both collectively and as individuals, so much distress. May the Merciful One save us from now on.

There is plenty of news, though, from "above the sun," from the holy Torah and its *chidushim* [novellae] which the greatest tzaddikim have innovated and developed! For we have not yet merited to see and to hear the wondrous new teachings in the Chumash on its simplest level, such as in the commentary of Rashi, of blessed memory, nor the wondrous expositions contained in the Midrash Rabbah, the Holy Zohar and so on, and particularly in the Rebbe's holy books and those of his student [Reb Noson], of holy, sainted memory. May we merit to study them constantly, to see and to hear the renewal which happens in them every day, and to give life to our souls with them every moment all the time! Amen. May it be His will.

Today I studied the holy teaching (*Likutey Moharan* I, 123), "The root and the foundation upon which everything depends is to bind oneself to the tzaddik of the generation and to accept everything that he says whether it is seemingly insignificant or important...." And we already acknowledge the principle that our master, teacher and Rebbe, of holy, sainted memory, is presently the tzaddik of the generation. There is much to be explained about this. May God allow us to speak about this face to face and may we likewise merit to fulfill all the Rebbe's living and enduring words, simple and great alike. For it is to this that the verse in Proverbs refers (4:23), "Guard your heart... with the utmost care, for from it comes forth life."

The Rebbe already stated (*Rabbi Nachman's Wisdom*, pp.323ff, #185) that the rectification of our souls in This World and the Next World..., right up to the end, depends on everything he instructs us to do, even a minor thing. So may we merit to fulfill them; especially those things which are easy and pleasant to do; to study a few paragraphs of the *Shulchan Arukh* every day; to say a few chapters of Psalms and to lift up our eyes and our hearts to God at all times. And even if we can only speak a few words [such as], "Master of the World, have pity on me!" — this is also very precious. In particular we should fulfill the Rebbe's statement (*Likutey Moharan* II, 24), "It is a great mitzvah always to be joyful!" So may we merit to have new vitality in our hearts every hour of every day, "to learn, to teach, to keep, to do and to fulfill his words in joy and love and to believe in them with great faith, as both you and I, your fond friend, wish.

> With best wishes to your learned person, praying for you and yearning to see you, along with your dear brother, for sufficient time to speak about all this and more, until the holy spirit of the holy words enters our hearts [leading us] to fulfill and to practice [them]. Amen. May it be His will.
>
> *Nachman HaLevi*

Greetings to all our friends, and especially to your dear brother. All my words written above, with God's help, were intended for all of you, especially for your brother, may he live, along with all your family, may they live for many good years to come. Amen. May it be His will.

2

With thanks to God, Wednesday, Beshalach, 5632, Uman.

To my friend whom I love as myself, the illustrious, distinguished and prominent Reb Yechezkel Heshel, may his light shine. May he grow ever more successful for both his material and spiritual good. Amen. May it be His will.

Enclosed here is a letter to your dear brother-in-law, the prominent Reb Raphael, my friend, may his light shine. The letter reached me before last Shabbat, but there was no-one trustworthy traveling with whom to send it. So you should receive it now and deliver it to him. I will not go on at length.

May God allow us to go on at length with songs and praises [to Him], all of which are included in the holy song (Exodus 15:1), "I will sing to God for He is exceedingly great!" "God is great!" He has done, He is doing and He will do miracles and wonders with us, both materially and spiritually. He will never abandon or forsake any one of us, each one at his own particular station — this one in his wealth...[etc.], each and every person, whatever his situation.

But my brother and friend, you must know that each person must inevitably experience a little bitterness, as is explained at length in the Rebbe's lovely words on the amazing teaching about why "the commandment of Shabbat was given in Mara" (*Likutey Moharan I, 27*). It appears in this week's parashah that I mentioned above. The Rebbe, with his holy spirit, explains there that this hints at the fact that a person must inevitably suffer a little bitterness (*mar* in Hebrew means "bitter"). For just as it is known that all physical cures are clothed in bitter-tasting medicines, so similarly Shabbat Peace, which is the cure for all things, was commanded in Mara to hint at this point. Look there at what is taught on the verse, "For the sake of peace I have great bitterness" when Hezekiah praised God. Look there carefully and give pleasure to your soul.

My brother, my friend! I will address your honored person in Yiddish: Fortify yourself, my brother! Delve deeply into the Rebbe's words, into his lessons, his stories, the expositions of his holy student, our teacher, Reb Noson, of blessed memory, and into the Prayers! (*Likutey Tefilot*, translated as *The Fiftieth Gate*). Lift up your voice in the lovely Psalms, songs, praises and cries contained in the

Prayers! Then you will truly live. For outside of this there is no life at all. Look carefully with the wisdom and understanding that God gave you and you will see clearly the truth of these words. So may God help you and may you merit to warm your heart with the holy fire which is rooted within the heart of every Jew and to instill the fire of this holiness into all that I mentioned above. Then you will enjoy good.

There is more to say about this, but it is impossible for me to continue. I would like you to visit me once in a while. Perhaps God will allow us to discuss between us some of the words which are rooted in us from the source of our vitality, [the Rebbe,] of blessed memory, upon whom depends our vitality in This World and the Next. Send greetings for me to your father-in-law, who is more precious than gold, to all his children, may they live, and to my friend and relative, the illustrious young man, Reb Noson, the nephew of Reb Yekutiel, may his light shine. Speak a great deal with him about there being no good goal except to fulfill all of the above. And even so, may God also grant you great wealth; because "Those who seek God will lack nothing good." So may it be with us that we will merit to be true seekers of God and that we will lack nothing good materially or spiritually. Amen. May it be His will, as both you and I, your sincere well-wisher, desire.

Nachman HaLevi

3

With thanks to God, Wednesday, Behar, 5632, Uman.

To my friend whom I love as myself, the illustrious, distinguished and beneficent, the prominent Reb Yechezkel Heshel, may his light never be extinguished, selah. Peace, abundant salvation, success and all good. Amen. May it be His will.

My brother and friend. I heard what happened to you in connection with the fire that took place in your community. May God replace what you have lost. It is for this reason that I am coming now [with this letter] to bless and to strengthen you. Fortify your heart determinedly and put your hope in God that He will replace your losses many times over! Remember if you will, my friend, that statement of our Sages, of blessed memory, that "it is decreed on Rosh HaShanah how much a person will lose and how much he will gain during the coming year" (*Bava Batra* 10). It could be (and may God help that it should be so) that the gains will be many thousands of times greater [than the losses]. But still a person must inevitably lose *some* amount of money, as the aforementioned statement implies. If he is worthy, then he "loses" it by giving it to charity. May God give you success from now on in all your endeavors and may all your buying and selling be with great success. May God allow us to glean from this hints by which to draw close to Him and His Torah. For time and time again we see with our own eyes that everything is in God's hands — "the soul is His, the body is His and the money is His." It is in our power neither to make money nor to escape loss except by God's help.

Therefore, my brother and friend, let us begin now to fulfill the Rebbe's directive to set fixed times for Torah study and prayer. Fulfill his exhortation to cast yourself upon God each and every day and to set aside money for charity. Then you will succeed and grow wise in This World and the Next. And even while you are still in This World you will enjoy a good and pleasant life. For it is a fundamental principle that the world is full of bitterness on every side and there is nothing to temper it except the Torah. This holds true in two ways. First, through Torah study the suffering is tempered and reduced (see *Garden of the Souls*). Second, when a person is engaged in Torah study and cleaves and binds himself to its letters and words amidst the sweetness of its holy wisdom, he then experiences a feeling of life and vitality which also continues for some time afterward.

My brother and friend! I have been enticing you towards good for some time now and encouraging you to engage in Torah study and charity. Please, wake up! Constantly rouse yourself anew! Kindle the fire of yearning that is deep in your good heart and rouse yourself anew to Torah, to charity and to the holy pathway on which our Rebbe, of holy, sainted memory, shows us so that we may vitalize ourselves with the little good which we merit to grab, and then to yearn to grab more; to constantly make a new start with all our heart, with our our soul and with all our might and to fulfill the statement of our Sages, of blessed memory, on the verse "[You shall love the Lord, Your God,]...with all your *might*" that "whatever *measure* [good or bad] that He deals out to you, *thank* Him *very, very* much" (the Hebrew word for "might" can also be construed as "measure" and "thank" and "very"; see *Berakhot* 54a). May you indeed merit this, as your own good heart yearns deep down and as I, your true friend, bless you. Looking forward to your material and spiritual success. Amen. May it His will.

Nachman Chazan HaLevi

Send greetings and blessing to your dear father-in-law. I am waiting expectantly for your safe arrival here in the coming days, especially since I have received information from Reb Abele that you wish to be here for Lag b'Omer. Also send greetings to all Yitzchak's children, may they live. My brothers and friends! Let us constantly take it to heart anew that out of all the bitterness which every single one of us experiences, body, soul and financial, nothing will remain of us except the little good that we grab from This World. As the Mishnah states (*Avot* 6:9), "Neither silver, nor gold nor precious stones and pearls accompany a person when he dies; but only Torah and good deeds." So may we prevail to accumulate much Torah and good deeds and to bring ourselves to joy and encourage ourselves only with. Then God will give us success in the physical realm too, as you wish. Amen. May it be His will.

4

With thanks to God, Wednesday, Ekev, 5632, Uman.

To my friend whom I love heart and soul, the illustrious, distinguished, beneficent and prominent Heshel, may his light shine; peace and abundant salvation, along with the rest of his family, may they live for many good years to come. Amen. May it be His will.

Would you please be so kind to deliver the enclosed letters here to your dear, excellent father-in-law. I need say no more to a trustworthy messenger such as yourself.

My brother and friend! The holy days of Elul are approaching for life and for peace in the material and the spiritual. May God allow us to fulfill, "Take *DeVaRiM*, with you and return to God — do not read *DeVaRiM*, objects, but rather read *DeBuRiM*, words." That is to say, take up *holy* words, study much Torah, especially the Torah's mystical teachings — the holy *Tikkunim* [the *Tikkuney Zohar*] and *Likutey Moharan* — and say many Psalms and prayers. Hold onto them, my brother and friend! Study them over and over; grow old and gray with them. For through them you will be saved both materially and spiritually to be written and sealed for a good, sweet life.

Please remember as well, my brother and friend, to send me your generous contribution from what you committed to donate from the profits, etc. Be strong, my son, in all of the above and to fortify yourself to recite and study the *Tikkunim* and the *Likutey Moharan* and to give charity. Then, happy and fortunate are you indeed! May you see in yourself the fulfillment of "Happy are you — in This World, and fortunate are you — in the Next World." Amen. May it be His will.

The words of your true friend enticing you towards good, besseching you to awaken again and again that lovely good which is hidden there in your heart. So may you merit to bring it from potential to actual, as the Rebbe, of blessed memory, said, "with the mouth and with the heart." "With the mouth" means to be diligent and consistent in Torah study and in saying prayers and petitions, as discussed above; and "with the heart" means to have your hand open to our poor comrades and in particular to support the study hall which is called in the Rebbe's name. For your honored person knows that, with the money you give me for the expenses here, you are not just favoring me, but rather you are favoring our entire group. May the merit of the greater community stand you in good stead to bring success to your endeavors both physical and spiritual, as you and I, your true friend, both wish.

Nachman HaLevi

Abundant peace from the Master of Peace to the honored young man, the learned, distinguished and prominent Reb Noson, may his light shine.

My few brief words on the other side of this page were also intended for you. Take pity on yourself, my brother and friend! Praise to the Living God, He favored us with fine, beautiful attributes — a sweet heart, a sweet voice and clear, lovely speech. Have compassion on yourself and give honor to God; recite and study the *Tikkunim*, the Rebbe's books and sing Psalms and prayers with a lovely voice. Then you will attain a good, sweet life in the material and the spiritual. For God's sake, do not let your mind and your thoughts budge! Just be here on Rosh HaShanah to be counted among our comrades who bind themselves to the light of the Rebbe's soul. Then you will enjoy good. Believe first, and then you will see with your eyes. If the barriers are very strong — well, even better. For the desire and yearning to return to God gain intensity primarily through the breaking of barriers. So really be strong and God will finish well for you. "A person who comes to purify himself is helped." Be strong and God will save you! Amen. May it be His will.

Nachman HaLevi

5

With thanks to God, Monday, the 18th of Adar, 5633, Uman.

Life and peace to all our true friends who take shelter in the clear shade of faith, the light of lights, our master, teacher and Rebbe, of blessed memory, who dwell in the Holy Land; and at their head, my precious friend, the outstanding, illustrious and distinguished Reb Meir, may his light shine. May his light never be extinguished. Amen. Peace and all good to you and to all our brothers, the Children of Israel, who dwell in the Holy Land. May God abundantly bestow upon the Holy Land dew and rain for blessing, life and plenty for all our brothers, the Children of Israel who reside there. Amen. May it be His will. Amen. May it be His will.

There is no news to tell you. You already heard that, thank God, last Rosh HaShanah was peaceful and quiet. As for the new things that God brings about as He constantly renews the work of creation every day — these are deeply hidden from us. Occasionally, though, we experience a glimmer of understanding in our hearts so that we feel anew the amazing, new teachings which, with God's help, remain for us a blessing from the Rebbe's light.

After Purim we read Parashat Parah [which discusses the red heifer]. It starts out as a *PuR*, a lot — for "Purim takes its name from the lots [which Haman cast]." Subsequently, though, it becomes *PaRah*, the heifer, all of which is a preparation for Pesach. "His lips are roses dripping myrrh..." and in the Holy Torah the letters *PURIM* are hinted at in the verse which speaks about Pesach (see *Likutey Moharan* II, 74). The tune and the hints which the holy, awesome eyes and hands of the Rebbe's holy student, my teacher and rav, Reb Noson, of holy, sainted memory, showed us [when he taught this lesson] — these too are impossible to describe even face to face, let alone in writing. This is especially applicable to what the Rebbe began to say afterwards in a loud, strong voice [from the end of that lesson], "Initially all beginnings were from Pesach. Therefore all the commandments are a remembrance of the Exodus from Egypt. And now...." he drew out the words "And now..." melodiously for several moments and then he fell silent.

What can we say? What can we say? *Ashreinu*! Happy are we that our ears merited to hear all this! In particular the way that our teacher, Reb Noson, revealed to us just how exalted was the glimmer of understanding that he had of all this in his pure heart and how it was connected to many other matters. For immediately after giving this lesson, the Rebbe revealed explicitly the *tikkun* of the Ten Psalms and, with a great promise before trustworthy witnesses, he declared to all generations that he would forever come to the aid of anyone who came to his holy, awesome grave [gave a *perutah* to charity and recited these Ten Psalms] (see *Rabbi Nachman's Tikkun*). Right after that, filled with a consummately exalted fear and awe, the Rebbe then told the story of the Seven Beggars (*Rabbi Nachman's Stories* #13); and immediately, right after Pesach, he traveled to Uman.

As my teacher and rav, Reb Noson, spoke about all this he revealed hints that it was [actually] all one and that it was all bound up with in the phrase "And now..." and with the holy way that he melodiously drew out these words. *And now* it is necessary to reveal the Ten Psalms explicitly and to make the aforementioned promise. *And now* it is necessary to tell the aforementioned story and to conclude it with the words "...and I heal her." *And now* it is necessary to travel to Uman and to establish there the place of his holiness for all generations. It is good to thank God that we merited to know about all this and to have in our hearts a small glimmer of understanding like a person peeking through a lattice.

It is impossible to express all this in writing, but out of the enormous love for the truth which is rooted in our hearts from our youth I could not restrain myself from taking up my pen and devoting some of my time to at least record in writing something about this. For the mere mention of all this enlivens and restores our weak and tired souls. May we just merit to see each other face to face again in this lifetime and to speak about all this in person. But the bottom line is, *Ashreinu! Ashreinu!* Happy are we! Happy are you that you dwell in the shade of the Holy Land and presumably yearn to roll in the dust of the holy, awesome *tzion* of the Rebbe where he dug down and found the root of the holiness of the Land of Israel, as is hinted in his holy books (*Likutey Moharan II*, 109). [Rebbe Nachman teaches in that Lesson that the graves of the tzaddikim have the sanctity of the Holy Land.] And happy are we that we merit here to roll in the dust of the holy, awesome *tzion* where the Rebbe dug down and found the root of the holiness of the Land of Israel, and we yearn to roll in the dust of the holy soil, of the Holy Land. So may God increase our desire so that we will yearn with an intense longing, until God finishes for us for good. Amen. May it be His will.

> Your true friend, Nachman, son of my master, father, teacher and rav, Avraham HaLevi, of blessed memory.

Greetings to my blood-relation and true friend, Reb Yitzchak, whom they call Reb Itzele from Tulchin. I received word today that he already merited to realize his desire and to go to the Holy Land. It is good to thank God. I received the note from Odessa and I read it quite closely. *Ashrekha*! Happy are you that you merited to have the good words bound so very tightly to your heart! May you inspire your soul with them all the days of your life. As I heard from the mouth of my holy teacher and rav, Reb Noson, of holy, sainted memory, "Just *Azamra! Azamra! Azamra!* Just [go with the teaching] 'I will sing to God with the little that I have left!'" until we, together with all our brothers, the Children of Israel, merit to truly ascend to this. It is impossible to continue any longer. May you inspire yourself with all this all the days of your life for many good years to come. Amen, selah. Amen. So may it be His will.

I also showed the note to our friends and they all received great pleasure from it. It is good to thank God. My friend and relative. I received a letter of greeting from your dear son, may he live, and I sent him some words of response. I hope to God that they will inspire him. Greetings to our friend, the venerable Reb Chaim Krasinstein from Breslov with a great love! Happy are you that you returned to the Holy Land! Heed my words, my friend! I encouraged your honor to fulfill in your settling in the Land of Israel what is written in *Pirkei Avot* about the study of the holy Torah — namely, "Study it over and over. Grow old and gray with it and never leave it." So may you indeed carry this out. If you still have any ruble or gold coin outside of the Land, for God's sake, draw it into the Holy Land; and give instructions that not a single *perutah* be taken outside the Land. Or maybe just a little for a mitzvah. Then when your time comes in your ripe, old age after many good years, your flesh, your bones and the toil of your hands will all whither away in the holiness of the Holy Land and the poor people of the Land of Israel will eat [from] it. However they are, they are holy, sanctified with the holiness of the Holy Land. May you indeed merit this. Amen. May it be His will.

Your friend, with best wishes as always and with greetings to all our friends in the Holy Land. I just do not have the time or the energy to list each one individually, but please consider it as if I had.

6

With thanks to God, Tuesday, Ekev, 5633, Uman.

To my beloved friend and dear in-law, the distinguished, beneficent and prominent Reb Yechezkel Heshel, may the light of his success grow brighter and brighter. Peace and abundant salvation to him and his family, and mazal tov on the birth of his new daughter, may she live. May they all live on for many good years to come in perfect health in all their 248 organs and 365 limbs. Amen. May it be His will.

I received your lovely, letter last week, along with your generous donation. You really uplifted me with your contribution and with your fine, correct words which you wrote in your letter, both of which clearly show that faith and trust are indeed rooted deeply in your good heart. This is the foundation of our Judaism and the foundation of the entire Torah and all the commandments, as our Sages said (*Makot* 24a), "Habakkuk came and based them all upon one [thing] — 'the tzaddik will live by his faith'."

So, my brother and friend, really fortify your good heart in correct faith and trust that He will never, ever abandon you in either the physical or the spiritual realms. And if a person sometimes experiences some darkness or misfortune, in body, soul or money — he must never become discouraged or lose heart. Rather, he must believe in what is clearly written in the verse (Lamentations 3:32), "If He brings on grief, He subsequently shows mercy in accordance with His abundant compassion." "God's kindnesses never run out; His compassion never ceases" (*Ibid.* 3:22), To the contrary, His kindnesses are renewed every morning, as Rashi comments on the verse, "They are new every morning, great is Your faithfulness." So fortify yourself determinedly every hour of every day in this faith and this trust and constantly prevail to grab Torah and prayer!

And know, my friend, that if you can pour out your heart before God — this is certainly an excellent thing, whether it be with Psalms, Prayers or *hitbodedut*, as our master, teacher and Rebbe, of holy, sainted memory, taught us. But if the heart is stopped up and we have no words to say, as our forebears cried,

"We have no mouth with which to speak..." — then the main thing is to lift up our eyes to Heaven. For God cherishes this beyond all calculation, as is explained in the words of our Prophets and Sages.

Time does not allow me to elaborate. As our teacher and rav, Reb Noson, of sainted memory, discussed at such length on the verse (Psalms 25:14), "The secret of God is with those who fear Him...": He revealed to them [i.e. to His Prophets and Sages] the enormity of His compassion and kindness. Therefore, [the Psalm continues,] "My eyes are always to God, for He will remove my feet from the net" in the physical and the spiritual, in body, soul and money. So may God help and protect you and all your family, may they live for many good years to come. May you and all your family, may they live, enjoy a good, sweet year starting now, as the glow of the days of Elul grows brighter. So may we merit to receive them with love and with a desire to appease and to placate God Who is appeased by prayers and placated by supplications. May we fulfill "our eyes are lifted to You," until He favors and blesses us and all our brothers, the Children of Israel, with a good, sweet year in body, soul and money, as both you and I, your true friend, wish. Mentioning you in my prayers all the time, blessing you for a good year and asking that you be in touch,

Nachman HaLevi Chazan

I ask you to convey greetings for me to my relative, the young man, Reb Noson, the son of R. Yekutiel, may his light shine. I do not have time to write much at the moment. For the

time being, my good friend, you should send me the kind
donation which you owe me from Chanukah-time. I am extremely pressured right now with expenses, as I am engaging
in... [missing]...etc; so I ask that you assist me with a doubly large
donation. As a result may you be blessed by God with a good,
sweet year, starting now. Amen. May it be His will.

Your genuine friend,

Nachman HaLevi

in memory of

Rabbi Zvi Aryeh Benzion Rosenfeld

who devoted his life
to disseminating the teachings of

Rebbe Nachman of Breslov

by

Meyer and Roxanne Assoulin